D0466809

# Indebted

# Indebted

*How* FAMILIES MAKE
COLLEGE WORK *at* ANY COST

...

## CAITLIN ZALOOM

PRINCETON UNIVERSITY PRESS
PRINCETON AND OXFORD

Requests for permission to reproduce material from this work
should be sent to permissions@press.princeton.edu

Published by Princeton University Press
41 William Street, Princeton, New Jersey 08540
6 Oxford Street, Woodstock, Oxfordshire OX20 1TR

press.princeton.edu

Library of Congress Control Number 2019931718
ISBN 978-0-691-16431-1

British Library Cataloging-in-Publication Data is available

Editorial: Fred Appel and Jenny Tan
Production Editorial: Jill Harris
Text Design: Leslie Flis
Production: Erin Suydam
Publicity: James Schneider and Kathryn Stevens
Copyeditor: Jennifer McClain

Jacket images: Shutterstock and iStock

This book has been composed in Arno Pro with Futura Display

Printed on acid-free paper. ∞

Printed in the United States of America

10  9  8  7  6  5  4  3  2

**33614081670282**

# Contents

■ ■ ■

# Acknowledgments

...

My first debt is to the families who opened up their lives for this book. From their mundane challenges in making ends meet to their tenderest hopes for the future, our discussions required sensitive, thoughtful, and sometimes difficult reflections. I am honored and grateful that they chose to share their stories.

*Indebted* took several years to research and write and, along the way, colleagues and friends have inspired and sustained me. The brilliance of three women—Jessica Blatt, Liza Featherstone, and Kim Phillips-Fein—provided momentum from the first idea to the final word. Their incisive observations and always necessary humor were vital to the project. Essential conversations came in many different guises too, some in formal seminar settings, some over lunch, and some by timely accident. Kathryn Edin and Andrew Cherlin offered advice and encouragement at a critical stage. Harvey Molotch and Dana Polan were the model readers every author wishes for.

Charley Ballard, Laura Bear, Dominic Boyer, Finn Brunton, Lily Chumley, Arianne Chernock, Charlie Eaton, Matthew Engelke, Nancy Fraser, Sophie Gonick, Linda Gordon, Jane Guyer, Keith Hart, Andrew Lakoff, Shamus Khan, Margaret Levi, Sharon Marcus, Jennifer Morgan, Terry MacDonald, Federico Neiburg, Julia Ott, Mary Patillo, Mary Poovey, Allison Pugh, Liz Roberts, Natasha Schüll, Lisa Servon, Rachel Sherman, Ellie Shermer, Brenda Stevenson, Erica Robles-Anderson,

Tom Sugrue, Fred Turner, and Matt Wray all helped me understand the questions of debt and family life more deeply.

Thinking and working has always required great companions and there could be no better than Daniela Bleichmar, Brooke Blower, Bruce Buchanan, Miles Corak, Debi Cornwall, Cybelle Fox, Wendy Edelberg, Bob Frank, Tom Frank, Batja Gomes de Mesquita, Terry Maroney, Liz Maynes-Aminzade, Doug McAdam, Kelley McKinney, Rowan Ricardo Phillips, Ben Platt, Eyal Press, Anne Rademacher, Imani Radney, Megan Stephan, and Natasha Warikoo. Their intelligence and wit have helped me see a wider world.

Lively debate is one of the chief privileges and pleasures of academic life, and I am grateful to audiences at Brandeis, the Center for Advanced Study in the Behavioral Sciences at Stanford, Columbia, CUNY, Johns Hopkins, London School of Economics, the New School, Princeton, the Russell Sage Foundation, Stanford, the University of Chicago, the University of Pennsylvania, Universidade Federal do Rio de Janeiro, the University of Southern California, and Washington University in St. Louis for pushing me to think on my feet. Every confab improved the book, as did engaging with the detailed commentary of the one anonymous reviewer for Princeton University Press.

I have been graced with a set of outstanding collaborators who have worked as research assistants on this project. Max Besbris, Daniel Cueto, Max Cohen, Margaret Czerwienski, Alexandra Friedus, Keshan Garib, Caitlin Petre, and Katie Winograd were each essential to the research and writing.

From the beginning, Brettne Bloom's conviction helped me see the potential in this project; I am thankful to have an agent whose smarts match her savvy. I was lucky to have Fred Appel's editorial acumen behind the book's development. His insight and enthusiasm kept me at the keyboard. Emily Loose's structuring prowess and pointed questions helped strengthen my arguments. More recently, Meagan Levinson has brought her discerning eye to the book and the crack team at Princeton University Press—Matt Rohal, Jill Harris, and Dimitri Karetnikov—as well as copyeditor Jennifer McClain winged *Indebted* into printed existence.

I couldn't have written *Indebted* without the time to dive into the research and then the space to reflect and to write. The generous institutional support of the Russell Sage Foundation, the Center for Advanced Study in the Behavioral Sciences at Stanford, and the Paduano Faculty Fellowship in Business Ethics at NYU's Stern School enabled these scholarly essentials. Their extraordinary resources have complemented the ongoing support I am fortunate to receive from the staffs of NYU's Department of Social & Cultural Analysis, Business & Society Program, and Institute for Public Knowledge. They have kept me working efficiently, and laughing to boot.

The heart of this book lies in the life I have built with Eric Klinenberg, whose abundant mind and lavish enthusiasm make each day we spend together dear. His devotion to our family is a true, immeasurable gift; it is also an inheritance. My own mother, Carolyn Grey, and my husband's parents—Rona Talcott and Ed Klinenberg, as well as their spouses, Owen Deutsch and Anne McCune—have built relationships strong enough to sustain us all.

My best insights come from loving Lila and Cyrus Klinenberg and caring about their futures. They make each day a pleasure, and every tomorrow sweet. *Indebted* is dedicated to them.

# Indebted

CHAPTER 1

# Introduction

**...**

College—where to go and how to pay for it—is a central concern of contemporary middle-class families, because higher education shapes young people's future possibilities. For my parents' generation, who came of age in the 1950s and 1960s, a college education delivered economic security and reason to feel confident about the future. Middle-class people believed that their lives would be full of opportunities and that their children's lives would be too. This is no longer the case. Today being middle class means being indebted. It means feeling insecure and uncertain about the future, and wrestling with the looming cost of college and the debt it will require. It means being dependent on finance—and, crucially, on family—in ways that analysts of class, culture, and economy have not fully registered.

This book is based on a unique research study: more than 160 in-depth interviews with parents and students who are taking on debt to pay for higher education. The conversations broach topics—family history, job security, debt, aspirations, anxiety, and hope—that are rarely discussed outside the domestic sphere. These conversations showed me that the process of dreaming about, planning around, and paying for college leads parents and children to assess and remake their responsibilities to each other. The bonds they establish and renew through this shared experience are intimate and personal. But family obligations are also, by necessity, mediated by the pressures of debt and promises of investment that parents and children use in an attempt to fulfill them. *Indebted* argues that the problem of paying for college today involves such profound moral, emotional, and economic commitments that it has, in fact, redefined the experience of being middle class.

This means that the public issue most often labeled "student debt" is far more encompassing than our conventional framing implies, and touches more parts of our lives than we usually consider. Middle-class families begin to face the problem of paying for college well before young adults sign their loan commitments. For parents, the worries often begin in the first days of a child's life, if not sooner. Why? Because a college degree seems today to be the surest way to unlock the promises that the United States has made to the middle class.[1] Parents across the country wonder how they can best position their children for success in college. That means attending good schools from the very beginning, which means living in a good school district, which often means paying a high mortgage for housing. Even before their children apply to college, parents must spend enormous sums to prepare their offspring for higher education. And for a simple reason: Parents believe their children are worth the price.

In recent decades, the meaning of college has changed too. A four-year degree used to be something few needed to achieve; it is now essential for a foothold in the middle class. At the same time, the cost of college has spiked, levying a financial burden on families. This is why college and the debt it requires have become hot-button issues. Media headlines warn "Student Debt Is Crushing Millennials," ask "Will Student Debt Sink the US Economy?" and declare "The Student Debt Bubble Is About to Pop," all because the nature of our contemporary, financial economy has changed middle-class life.[2] But despite widespread awareness of the problem, the terms of the debate about what it means for families to be so indebted are too narrow.

Most commentators either decry the large quantity of student debt young adults carry or defend the American college finance system. Typically, critical accounts focus on how government policies, universities, and the financial industry have placed an undue burden on students and families. They draw on good evidence that the American system is causing considerable hardship for many families, and genuine distress for some. They also argue that debt loads are constraining the life choices of young adults after graduation—in some cases imperiling their financial security and that of their parents as well. And they often focus on for-profit universities and loan servicing companies that have exploited students and their families, generating massive revenues while offering a dubious quality of education and engaging in abusive practices.

I share these criticisms, and in this book I show how the system for financing higher education sets traps for students and their parents. I also identify the hardships that student debt so often inflicts. But this book is more than an argument against the system. At its core, it is about the largely unexplored ways that the financial economy has shaped the inner dynamics of American middle-class family life by forcing parents to confront the problem of paying for college.

Why do I focus on middle-class families? Because they are especially squeezed by the rising cost of college, and that has subjected them to a distinctive set of conflicting pressures. Middle-class families occupy a special place in the financial economy, because they have no choice but to use debt and investment in the attempt to achieve their aspirations. Sending young adults to college carries a unique significance for the middle class too, because striving to help children achieve a better life has long been one of the values and practices that makes a family middle class.

Countless definitions of the middle class circulate in the social sciences and popular culture, and reams of studies have shown that the great majority of American families consider themselves middle class. Here, however, I introduce a conception of middle-class life that is symptomatic of this economic moment. I define the middle class by their capacity to pay for college. I consider families to be middle class if the parents make too much money or have too much wealth for their children to qualify for major federal higher education grants, and if they earn too little or possess insufficient wealth to pay full fare at most colleges.

My emphasis is on how this imperative to secure financing has introduced a set of moral tensions into their lives—tensions between the sacred responsibilities that parents feel toward their children and the cultural expectations of fiscal prudence that financial advisers, lenders, and policy makers prescribe. On the one hand, parents are deeply committed to providing opportunities for their children to flourish, to pursue their dreams and fully develop their potential. College education is crucial to that project. On the other hand, both parents and young adults want to make good decisions about long-term economic security—their own as well as each others'. In the United States, these are moral imperatives as well as economic ones, and families voice the importance of both. The high cost of college, however, means that for middle-class families, figuring out how to honor both duties requires a challenging juggling act and causes a good deal of stress and conflict. In some cases, it leads to crisis.

Nearly every middle-class American family is wrestling with this problem. Yet most parents and students view their struggle to finance higher education as a personal and private problem, one that they must solve on their own. Few families connect their experience with those of their neighbors or fellow citizens around the country. That's because family finances and the stresses caused by them are not generally considered topics to discuss openly and honestly outside of (or, often, even inside of) the home. The secret, unspoken nature of family financial situations means that we know little about how families cope with the strains, how and why they make the difficult decisions about their finances, and how they navigate the moral conflicts they face.

As middle-class families use investment and debt to fund college education, they encounter the financial system's particular moral vision. Financial assessments and the terms of loans instruct families in how they should conduct their lives. That vision conflicts in a number of ways with families' realities as well as with their deeply held values. Because the financial system wields power over middle-class families—they need the money, after all—these models of ideal behavior have teeth. Compliant families reap benefits; those who resist or don't fit pay a price. The system's moral imperatives are also characterized by internal contradictions, rendering even the most amenable families baffled at times. Too often it serves up blame rather than assistance and winds up injuring those it is supposed to help.

I launched an extensive study to learn about the hidden costs of student finance and to examine the lives of middle-class families who face the problem of paying for college. The project, which I describe in the pages that follow, led me to three main arguments about how financing education is influencing middle-class American family life. The first is that families' lives are now organized in critical ways around the problem of paying for college. The second is that the system has introduced difficult moral conflicts for parents as they seek to honor what they see as their highest parental duty: providing their children with the opportunities that will allow them to fulfill their potential and pursue wide-open futures. The third is that middle-class families are being encouraged, if not required, to engage in what I call *social speculation*. By this I mean that the costs of college are now so high that both parents and students are forced to, in effect, place bets on whether or not they will be able to pay without jeopardizing their financial security and whether a college degree will, in fact, pay off.

Spending on college is speculative because parents cannot know for sure whether it will allow their children to pursue the open futures they want for them. Life is full of uncertainty. What sorts of opportunities will be available and whether students will be able to earn a comfortable living by pursuing their dreams are great unknowns. But parents and children must put money down—today—on the promise of the future. They draw down savings, invest, and take out debt based on hopeful visions that may or may not come to be, often for reasons beyond their control. Understanding how and why parents and their children place this bet requires not only answering the usual questions of public policy and economics but also recognizing the powerful cultural forces influencing family behavior.

## What It Means to Be Middle Class

Parents and children engage in social speculation in large part because, in the contemporary American economy, getting a four-year college degree is the sine qua non of obtaining a middle-class life. Despite parents' and children's anxieties about the costs, for most middle-class children getting a college degree is a given, a necessity for remaining in the middle class or perhaps even reaching a higher economic station. This belief in the value of a college degree is backed up by economists' data. So the commitment to college is in part economically pragmatic, a well-founded calculation—but only partly, because college has always been about more than the hope of achieving economic security.

Pursuing a college education fulfills crucial cultural mandates that being middle class requires. It demonstrates that family members subscribe to fundamental values that define middle-class life, especially committing to the next generation's future. Middle-class parents believe that one of their principal responsibilities is to help their children become independent. Raising children who can take care of themselves and make decisions about their own well-being secures a family's middle-class identity as much as it preserves the parents' standard of living.

The historian Paula Fass has shown that American families have long subscribed to "the desirability and possibility of making children independent of their parents and giving them the tools to become so."[3] While parents might have little control over the world their children will launch into as they begin their adult lives, what they can do is prepare their children to handle—and, ideally, thrive in—whatever that future brings. This means cultivating children's talents and moral capacities. Most importantly, it means developing their ability to adapt to the uncertainties they will face. Today, more than ever, higher education is essential for this project.

Paradoxically, families are also willing to pay high costs and take on debt because middle-class ethics demand that they be autonomous. Families should be independent, free from relying on government assistance or support from kin and friends. The high cost of college today means that middle-class parents and children must, in fact, rely on financial support from others. But the norms of middle-class culture mean that these others should be parts of the financial system: government, banks, and schools. Finance seems to preserve families' ability to decide the best path for young adults' education. Together, in private—because it's culturally proscribed to discuss financial matters like income and wealth with friends and even with most relatives—the family selects where students should attend college and how much they're willing to pay. This is crucial to what many parents described to me as their paramount duty to their children—providing them with the means to pursue an "open future."

The concept of an open future is crucial for understanding why middle-class families invest so much in education. By "open future," I mean one in which young adults are free to make themselves into the people they want to be. Fass shows that this is another long-standing cultural ideal, tracing it back to the American Revolution and its rejection of the norm that social position, and therefore one's lot in life, must be inherited. American children wouldn't be bound by that tradition; they would create a new world, casting aside the strictures of social hierarchy and reshaping society and the political system, governing both in accordance with the revolutionary vision. Children would be able to leave behind their social stations, overcome whatever educational and economic limits their family's history might impose. This freedom to exercise their full potential would be the foundation of an empowered democratic citizenry. For centuries, assuring that children are prepared for this pursuit has been the sacred role of American parents. Although many Americans did not then—and do not now—have the resources to assure this opportunity for their children, the parents I interviewed in my study revealed that the belief in their responsibility to provide it, and their desire to meet that obligation, remains strong.

Education holds a special place in this American ethic of opportunity not only because it is the most powerful means by which children can invent themselves and build their open futures. Higher education also provides a forum for rising generations to coalesce around new ideas and develop novel ways of being together. In colleges and universities, young adults define and redefine their values and views, sometimes affirming and sometimes breaking from those of their elders. This is how, and where, young middle-class adults build a vision for tomorrow. The philosopher John Dewey argued that this is a key reason schools are a linchpin of democracy. They can facilitate interaction with people across cultural and economic lines that so often divide us, challenging those with different beliefs and traditions to engage with each other, cultivating citizens who are able to keep learning and change their minds. All of this, Dewey insisted, is vital to a healthy democracy, because a democratic society must evolve as cultural, economic, and political circumstances change, and that requires a well-educated citizenry.

American policy makers have long agreed with this premise. Over time the government came to support broad access to higher education with public programs, providing grants to students and funding to colleges and universities that kept tuition reasonable. Of course, there have always been deep inequalities in the US education system, with low-income students, and particularly students of color, subjected to restricted access to universities, a problem that is still significant today. But the ideal vision remains a powerful goal.

Today, although Americans by and large continue to believe in, and demand, public resources to help students attend universities, college support for middle-class families comes largely in the form of loans. This transformation in the national project of funding college education occurred over several decades and involved deep changes of political morality that are written in financial terms.

# How Finance Entered Middle-Class Life

For decades, American families have taken on debt and have also assumed the financial risk of investment. Today, however, gaining access to higher education usually involves an engagement with the world of finance so significant that it has redefined what it means to be middle class.

In earlier decades, social scientists described the middle class largely as a function of occupation. Sociologist C. Wright Mills solidified this understanding in his mid-twentieth-century classic, *White Collar: The American Middle Classes.*[4] For both Mills and his contemporary, William H. Whyte, who penned *The Organization Man*, not only did the nature of jobs and their level of pay determine whether someone was middle class, so did adherence to a social ethic that an individual's career and life goals should be in harmony with the goals of the organizations that paid them.[5] Finance was always a part of the story, however.

White-collar workers also sought suburban housing and the mortgages they required. The process of financing home purchases through mortgages was the first step that brought millions of American families much more deeply into the financial system. Americans took on debt for home ownership willingly, because they were motivated to provide better lives and greater opportunities for their children. Mortgages allowed young parents to move to suburbs, where they could send their children to good schools.

The federal government and private lenders encouraged and subsidized these choices, enrolling the American middle class in a larger national project.[6] As the Cold War got going, the government subsidized real estate development for the white middle class as a foundation of strengthening US democracy and fighting communism. To this purpose, the federal government built infrastructure for transit and energy in rural regions, setting them up to be new residential areas. It partnered with private banks to encourage more families to purchase homes and guaranteed their loans. Home ownership became a bedrock of middle-class wealth, and of achieving financial security, when these new homeowners either paid off their mortgage or sold their home for an increase over its purchase price.

In the classic, twentieth-century American mobility story, purchasing a home became a primary means of securing financial independence. Racial preference for whites and exclusion of African Americans and others from government home ownership programs meant that finance as a means of mobility was also a driver of inequality. For those included, however, home ownership enabled two prized cultural aspirations. High-quality suburban schools offered good educations for children, and a well-tended home filled with the bounty of postwar consumer goods improved the social standing of the family while promising financial security for retirement.

The middle class took another significant step into the world of finance with the passage of the Higher Education Act of 1965, its reauthorization in 1972, and the Middle Income Student Assistance Act of 1978, which, together, established and expanded the federal loan program. At the time, the government did not want to be in the business of directly offering education loans, so it created incentives for banks to make them, and it supported college students to borrow from private lenders by backing the loans, as it had done with home mortgages.[7]

The 1980s brought the next giant step, this time into the sphere of investment, with the proliferation of tax-advantaged 401(k) and 403(b) accounts. Corporations, which were questioning their commitments to workers, began phasing out "defined benefit" pensions and replacing them with opportunities for workers to invest in "defined contribution" plans, backed by the federal government with tax incentives, or, in many cases, not offering any retirement support at all. The US public program for retirement, Social Security, was too limited to underwrite a middle-class lifestyle in retirement, and without a private pension, a retirement investment account became essential.[8]

The 1980s also saw the federal government revising its understanding of its responsibilities to the public, a shift in political morality that gave support to a rising commitment to fiscal austerity. One clear target was student aid. President Reagan's budget director, David Stockman, summed up the politics justifying this sea change in 1981: "I do not accept the notion that the federal government has an obligation to fund generous grants to anybody that wants to go to college. If people want to go to college bad enough, then there is opportunity and responsibility on their part to finance their way through the best way they can."[9]

State legislatures enacted a similar set of policy cuts. Across the country, state governments chipped away at appropriations for public universities and colleges, which have continued to the present day. These cuts have imperiled the budgets of public universities. In response, universities both raised tuition bills for in-state students and began to court out-of-state and out-of-country students and charge them considerably higher tuition and fees, often on par with those of private universities and colleges. Meanwhile, the costs of private universities and colleges also rose.

To enable qualified students whose families couldn't afford the higher prices to attend, both public and private colleges and universities began to operate with a "high-tuition, high-aid" model, charging elevated sticker prices for more affluent families while funneling a portion of those dollars to support admitted low-income students. This arrangement put parents with middling incomes in a particularly tight bind. Their earnings had been stagnating since the 1970s, while their jobs had become less secure. In addition, home values had fluctuated more than in the past, making calculations about their finances less certain.[10] Most didn't have the discretionary income to foot the higher college bills. Outside financing would have to fill the gap.[11]

During the 1990s, banks and the federal government came to agree that debt was the way students should fund college education. They started vigorously promoting student loans and made them available regardless of need—some offered directly through the government, others through private lenders. Students from middle-class families took advantage of the opportunities, and borrowing soared.[12]

Meanwhile, costs continued to rise. Why is hotly debated. Some argue that the key reason stems from colleges competing for highly qualified and wealthy students by spending more on expensive amenities, like elaborate athletic facilities and lavish dormitories, to attract them. Others point out that colleges and universities have greatly expanded their high-salaried, administrative staffs. Another widely circulated theory proffers the idea that the availability of aid funds may have led colleges to increase costs. Whatever the explanation, costs increased especially steeply in the years after 2000. According to the College Board, a nonprofit dedicated to expanding access to higher education, the cost of tuition and fees for in-state students at public universities has risen more than threefold since 1987, with private college costs rising far more.[13]

The 2008 financial crisis led to a dramatic change in lending. In 2010, with banks largely withdrawing from offering student loans, President Obama and Congress took over student borrowing. Federal loan programs were placed almost entirely under the government's wing at the Department of Education, though the job of collecting payments was awarded to nine private loan servicers (including Navient, once a part of the federally linked Sallie Mae), which take a healthy profit in the process.

In 2018, student debt made the federal government the largest consumer lender in the United States.[14] Approximately forty-four million Americans, including both parents and students, carry federally sponsored loans for higher education that total almost $1.5 trillion. For perspective, Bank of America held about $200 billion in consumer loans; JPMorgan Chase held about $100 billion.[15] The federal government extended $101 billion in education debt in 2018 alone. Even so, federal loans often do not provide enough to pay the entire college bill, and an elaborate system of funding has emerged, with states, private lenders, and schools offering a convoluted and often confusing range of options.

Many middle-class families must engage in a difficult boot-strapping process, with both parents and students taking out loans, students contributing funds from either work-study jobs or off-campus employment, and parents often tapping into their savings and home equity. College funding has become a complex challenge that would have been inconceivable in the 1980s and 1990s, when the parents of today's college students were themselves in school.

## The Student Finance Complex

To cobble together the various forms of financing available, middle-class families must now make their way through a thicket of financial policies and programs that link government, banks, and universities together into what I call "the student finance complex." The federal government is the gateway. The

Department of Education collects information on household earnings and assets from families to assess their need. It then informs families of an amount they will be required to pay, called the *Expected Family Contribution*, and determines their access to federal aid.

Financial aid from states and colleges also depends on the information collected by the federal government. Colleges and universities take charge of assembling students' financial packages, combining the offers of federal and state funds with their own support in a package assembled individually for each family. College aid officers serve as the human face of the student finance complex, whom students and family members can turn to for advice when their packages fall short, when they need certification for parent loans, and when the federal government fingers them for "verification," the euphemism for a student aid audit.

The complex also includes private investment firms, which have collaborated with the federal and state governments to offer savings and investment vehicles with tax incentives intended to help parents build up their college funds. The minute newborns receive their Social Security numbers, for example, parents can open educational investment accounts, known by their tax-code moniker as 529s. Mutual fund giants like TIAA-CREF, Fidelity, T. Rowe Price, and Schwab manage their deposits.

The student finance complex is even more labyrinthine than this, including a vigorous market in the secondary sale of loans. Private banks repackage loans and sell them to investors as student loan asset-backed securities (SLABS). Silicon Valley gets into the action too, with companies like SoFi refinancing the loans of high-earning graduates and securitizing them. Such trading operates among banks and largely out of public sight, however, and most families do not get involved in these more esoteric parts of the leviathan.

The need to invest and borrow funds for college has led to a vexing paradox for families, the consequences of which we explore in depth: the pathway to open futures is available only if families are willing to become financially dependent and to conform to the requirements of the student finance complex. They must provide information about their private lives on its terms. This dependence and scrutiny clashes with the middle-class standard of autonomy.

What's more, the student finance complex undermines the independence of young adults, tying the generations together for years after children leave home. For one thing, aid is largely determined on the basis of parents' financial situations. Students are not expected to have saved enough on their own, so it is parents who pay the required family contribution. Parents also often take on debts and responsibilities that tie them to their children's lives long after graduation, effectively extending the period of children's dependence on their parents. Many parents are paying down college debts long into a child's adulthood, longer still when they've helped more than one child go to college or helped out with the loans carried in a young adult's name.

## Moral Mandates

Financing college might seem like a purely economic matter, but even the most apparently simple economic activities are shaped by cultural values, practices, and commitments. The funding system's components, however—the 529 account, the Free Application for Federal Student Aid, the Expected Family Contribution, the Parent PLUS Loan Program, the Direct Loan Program—reference primarily the exchange of money and obligation to pay. Their explicit message is that they have a purely economic function. But, as a social scientist, I have learned to look for the cultural mandates embedded in such economic vehicles.

When it comes to the terms for college funding, families are subjected to moral instruction, not only about how they should conduct their finances but about how they should live their lives. These moral imperatives are largely obscured by the bureaucratic appearance of the forms families must fill out and the "strictly business" directions for opening investment accounts and borrowing money; but families feel the pressure of financial morality, especially when the mandates conflict with their own values.

The most foundational moral instruction of the student finance complex lies in the requirement that children obtain a college degree in the first place, one reinforced by the fact that the federal government has structured a vast financial system to support it. The Department of Education, alongside the financial advice industry, presents sending children to college as an obligation for responsible, aspiring families, one that has personal benefits but also fulfills an obligation of middle-class citizens. Young adults prepare themselves to contribute by attending college.

Another moral mandate is that the nuclear family, in which two parents in a first marriage live with their children and support them solely from their own labors, is the gold standard. The financial aid families receive is awarded after an assessment based on this idealized and outdated model of the family. Families that conform to the model have an easier time securing federal loans and grants from states, colleges, and universities. The financial aid forms instruct applicants on which members should be included as family, leaving out grandparents, cousins, and chosen kin whom millions of American families consider central to their family unit and who are integral to their webs of support.

The forms also promote clear views about how families should conduct their financial lives and even their personal communications about them. Applying for aid is much easier for married parents who keep their books completely open to each other, which not all couples do. It's also less complicated for families in which parents are willing to be completely transparent about their finances with their children. The financial aid form is done in the child's name, but the information required to fill it in is rarely known by children, and many parents fill it out.

That parents take charge of the college finances is in keeping with another of the system's moral mandates: one generation should help fund the college education of the next; parents hold a moral obligation to pay. Following from this, the complex instructs parents that they must accept a trade-off, spending less on their present family needs and wants in order to put away savings for college. Middle-class parents and their maturing children cannot have it all. On top of accepting constraints on spending, parents must do their duty to put adequate money into investments for their retirement to ensure that they do not become a burden to their children, their communities, or the state. The government reinforces this message by offering tax benefits for retirement investing, instructing parents that they should succeed in balancing their own accounts.

If families' funds are tight, it is still their responsibility to manage their household budgets with a careful eye and tight fist. If they can't come up with the funds for college by being fiscally prudent and investing, then they must be willing to take on costly debt, and they must therefore also accept whatever future constraints on their spending and life choices the cost of repayment imposes.

The emphasis on taking out loans sends yet another message: parents and students should not find the costs of loans to be a burden because, for judicious people, finance is really just a mechanism for making time work for you. Loans allow for tomorrow's income to be useful today. Here the implication is that a college degree increases the odds that students will find steady, well-compensated work that allows them to repay their loans. It's their responsibility to get those jobs, and the standard terms reinforce that mandate by requiring them to begin repaying what they've borrowed a mere six months after graduation.

This emphasis on jobs contains yet another moral premise: that the value of higher education is primarily financial rather than about open futures. Students should choose courses of study and careers for their potential income, not kidding themselves about following a passion or commitment that has little prospect of earning them a good salary, and not taking time for personal exploration, such as by taking "frivolous" courses in the arts or liberal studies. As for parents, in addition to getting and staying married, the morally tinged assumption of the student finance complex is that they will have no problem paying back their loans if they manage their careers well, no matter how the conditions of their fields might evolve.

As for 529 accounts and other investment vehicles, finance bridges the gap of time in the opposite direction, allowing present resources to be so much more useful when money is needed later. In theory, families can calculate what they need to invest in securities markets today so that the money will grow adequately by the time college bills are due. The risk involved, the system implies, is minimal.

The force of these moral mandates is amplified by a cast of policy experts, pundits, and advisers. Online, in television programs, in popular columns, and in thinly veiled advertisements, experts tell families how they should run their households and plan for their futures. Their advice is couched as if it's based only on economic common sense. They endorse thinking of funding college as a purely financial matter, advising that college costs be kept at an appropriate level to allow for discerning household management, both in the present and the future. For example, the common wisdom they promote is that parents should think about their own retirements before their children's prospects. If parents' jobs haven't paid enough to save adequately or to support the debt needed to pay for their dream college, then parents should curtail their spending for their children's education and their children should go to a less expensive school. Or their children should take on more of the burden to pay. This advice fails to acknowledge the depth of parents' commitment to nurturing their children's talents and opening opportunities to them.[16]

This is the heart of the moral conflict that the student finance complex levies on middle-class families. Yet even as they are caught in those very conflicts, families rarely speak openly about them.

## Talking to Families

As a professor at one of the world's most expensive institutions, New York University, I knew that debt was a great concern of students. But in class, when the subject came up, my students would never say exactly how much they owed, whether or how much their parents paid, or if the costs stressed their family lives. Public discussions of student finance also seemed constrained to the price of tuition alone. That was despite the fact that during the 2016 presidential contest, the popularity of Bernie Sanders's tuition-free college platform pressed Hillary Clinton into making college affordability part of her agenda.

I knew the challenges of paying for college that my students and their parents faced were part of a tectonic economic shift. The mention of finance evokes an exotic world of high-flying global bankers and traders directing torrents of money and siphoning off massive profits. This is the breed of finance I first wrote about, after I'd studied the dealing floors of global futures markets in Chicago and London. From that vantage point, I came to understand that the finance sector had taken on greatly increased significance both for the US and globally since the 1970s.

Finance, as countless books and articles have demonstrated, has come to define our economy, and since the 2008 crisis, it has become painfully clear that what happens at the summit of this esoteric world touches all of us. I became interested in how finance was reaching into private lives, applying pressures that shape intimate family relationships, those that we imagine to be protected from the demands of the marketplace. If we want to make sense of how the financial economy has shaped social relations, even our most sacred and cherished ties, examining middle-class families as they scramble to plan and pay for college is an excellent place to start.

As an economic anthropologist, I was well versed in the problems of gaining access to closely held financial information. I knew that the only way to learn about the complexities of families' experiences was to speak with young adults and their parents in private, but that wouldn't be easy. American families generally don't talk openly about their wealth, their investments, or their debt. Sex, politics, religion—Americans are far more likely to discuss these sensitive topics with friends, neighbors, and relatives than they are to share information about how much money they make, save, and owe. Talking about financial matters is taboo. I have long believed, however, that bringing private discussions about money into public view is one of my essential tasks. The first challenge I faced was figuring out how to hear them myself.

For the interview study, I started close to home, interviewing NYU students who carried loans. I then reached out to their parents. Because NYU is a rarefied case—a private university with very high tuition and the high cost of living in New York City as well—I expanded the study to reach across the country with a group of interviews in Michigan, which has an especially strong tradition of public higher education. A team of research assistants helped me find students and parents who were willing to open up about their families' finances (no small achievement!), to discuss their histories and the challenges they faced paying for college. Together we conducted interviews in which students and parents shared closely held details about their financial lives. I offered them anonymity so that their privacy would be protected and they would be more likely to be open and honest. The eighty interviews that gave me the most insight paired separate conversations, one with a student and one with that student's parent; an additional eighty interviews, with either a parent or a student, helped me deepen my understanding of the patterns I saw in my core interviews. (Please see the Methodological Appendix for a more detailed description of the research design and interview process.)

Trained to do long-term, ethnographic fieldwork, I made a point of getting to know a smaller set of families much better. Readers will encounter some of these families across the book's chapters: Bruce, Peggy, and their boys, Tom and Aidan, from suburban Michigan; the Gates family from Columbus, Ohio, via Mississippi; Kimberly and her mother, June, from suburban Philadelphia. I visited these families at home and kept in touch with them over long periods of time. I traveled with them on occasion and visited their alma maters with them so we could experience the schools together. Each discussion and experience with these families guided what I asked and how I listened to all the interviewees.

Across the chapters, I have written the family stories as parents and students told them to me. They are, after all, the authorities in their own relationships, feelings, and experiences. It was heeding these stories that led me to my argument that families' deeply held values clash with the moral mandates of the student finance complex. Honoring these stories also led me to offer details from our discussions not directly related to the particular issues I was focused on. In writing this way, my aim is to open a classic ethnographic invitation to readers: to perceive each family's contingent and unique situation, and to let the text illuminate how the student finance complex intersects with and patterns these circumstances (and where it doesn't). By providing richer material, I encourage readers to pinpoint novel elements in the families' stories and to draw conclusions beyond my own.

I continued the study by examining work from across the social sciences to understand the broader trends that families face more deeply. Research in economics and policy studies in particular was important in another way too. These powerful disciplines do not simply illuminate the nature of the college payment problem; they actually intervene in the processes of financing, helping shape the design of aid and investment programs and providing rationales for the advice of popular experts. They are an explicit part of the college finance landscape that families face. In addition, middle-class families read about this research in the news, and they feel its effects as it shapes the financial tools they use.

My perspective on student debt is most informed by the anthropological tradition that attuned me to how the accumulation of debt—and speculation for the purposes of future gains—shapes people's understandings of their responsibilities and exerts control over the course of their lives. This is not a novel insight. In the early twentieth century, Bronislaw Malinowski observed the exchange of valuable ornaments by Trobriand Islanders and found that the debt taken on when someone received an ornament established powerful ties between those who gave and those who received.[17] Debts, as the French anthropologist Marcel Mauss also showed, obligated the givers to continue the exchange, creating bonds across time and establishing the possibility of the relationship extending into the future.[18] Debts also granted the giver leverage over the receiver; debtors are subject to the demands of those who lend and those who determine the rules. In other words, debt is a tool of social power.[19]

## The Paradox of "Priceless" Independence

Middle-class people feel the pull of that power; they talked about the pressure to comply with the moral mandates of the student finance complex. But they feel that weight as only one side of a profound moral conflict between either following financial morality or fulfilling their higher duties as parents and students. This conflict has made the question of what to pay for and how to pay for it a subject of intense debate among them. The conflict also requires deep moral reflection. Families have to decide what *they* think they should do; whether they're going to uphold the principles of financial restraint or to honor their obligations to their children's independence. This question carries a compelling irony. Rather than convincing them to limit their expectations, the morality of finance leads them to place even greater significance on assuring their children's open futures. In fact, by urging economic restraint, the student finance complex elevates the sacred character of the middle-class family.[20] Because the values of independence, autonomy, and open futures are so important, both parents and young adults are willing to pay great sums and take on burdensome debts. It's prudent to save, but the pursuit of independence is priceless.

This paradox is a novel extension of what the sociologist Viviana Zelizer found when she studied the evolving value of children across the late nineteenth and early twentieth centuries. Before then, children worked in factories and on farms from a young age, contributing to household incomes. Progressive Era social movements promoted a new idea: that childhood should be sacred, economically valueless but emotionally priceless. "Sacralization" inspired child labor laws, which nullified their contributions as workers. At the same time, children's elevation above economic value generated new ways of accounting financially for their new sentimental worth. Companies began selling life insurance for parents to honor and protect their children, and courts began to award astronomical damages in cases of children's wrongful deaths.[21] Exalting sacred family principles, Zelizer argued, became very expensive. The same is true today, as middle-class families devote their resources to celebrate young adults' open futures.

Loans and their ready availability encourage families to think imaginatively about these futures. Every scenario in which they all benefit from sober financial restraint is matched with another in which young adults thrive and have little trouble paying back their loans. In many of my interviews, parents joked about their financial predicament by saying that they might win the lottery. Others, coming slightly more down to earth, imagined their young children winning athletic scholarships. This is speculative thinking. Families can envision themselves on the winning end of probability, able to overcome later financial constraints. The student finance complex cautions parents and students to exercise financial restraint while opening the floodgates of debt.

In delaying the reckoning, the structure of college financing encourages social speculation.

## From Social Reproduction to Social Speculation

My concept of social speculation builds on a term introduced by feminist economics scholars in the 1970s and 1980s, who focused attention on the importance of families to capitalism. The family, they pointed out, was organized to raise children to become the industrial workers that the economy needed. Families (and specifically the adult women who ran the home) played a vital economic role in maintaining households and caring for the young, work that was uncompensated by the firms that reaped its benefits. As the political theorist Nancy Fraser has pointed out, the entire economic system "free rides" on the care and provisioning that families supply and "accords them no monetized value."[22] Family, this tradition of research has shown, performs the work of "social reproduction," turning out workers much like assembly lines produce products, but for no pay.

Today middle-class families provide an economic boon in a new way—through their speculation in funding college. The commitment of parents and young adults to upholding their middle-class values has become an economic lever. In the financial economy, the bonds of love that tie parents and young adults operate as what the anthropologist and historian Karl

Polanyi once called a "fictitious commodity," something that can be bought and sold that was not produced for the market, like land or human ingenuity. The financial system monetizes the power of those bonds with its instruments for social speculation; it promotes the morality of fiscal restraint to families even as it banks on their risk taking.

## Inside This Book

The book takes readers through the student finance complex in the same order that families encounter it. Each chapter highlights a component of the system, one financial tool, and examines a central conflict it introduces into families' lives. Chapter 2 begins with the first instruments of the student finance complex that call out to parents: the 529 plans. I show how these tax-advantaged accounts, which instruct parents to start investing for college when kids are small, rest on the assumption of a moral obligation to plan in a way that most families are not prepared to carry out.

The next chapter picks up with the application for student aid in the months before young adults commit to a specific school. Filing the Free Application for Federal Student Aid—the FAFSA form, as it's colloquially known—is the gateway to college for middle-class Americans. This process reveals the power of the federal government's moral vision, particularly how it sanctions and enforces a model of family that doesn't reflect the lived realities of most who use it.

I take the next step alongside families who have applied for aid by examining the Expected Family Contribution (EFC), which is the amount, based on official calculations, that the federal government deems families are able to pay. The moral designation of "need" structures this calculation, but rarely corresponds to families' own sense of their responsibilities and capabilities. The EFC is then passed on to universities, which use it to guide their own aid calculations, directing exactly how much families will have to pay toward their children's education. The EFC complicates family life because it binds parents and children together in financial obligations at the same moment that young adults are supposed to be gaining autonomy.

The final two chapters examine different kinds of federal loans that middle-class families rely on for higher education. Families who can't pay their required contributions in cash are given another option, taking out parent PLUS loans. For reasons related to their unique history of being denied access to wealth and income, African Americans use these loans more than other parents. This chapter examines the impact of historical racial inequalities on how African Americans face the problem of paying for college today.

The final chapter examines direct loans, the most common form of credit that the federal government extends to middle-class young adults. The terms of these loans undercut young adults' open, autonomous pursuit of their futures because they must be paid off in the first, most vulnerable decade of graduates' lives. Direct loans push students to pursue lucrative work even if it doesn't fulfill their true ambitions.

Threaded throughout the book are comparisons between the moral mandates directed at the middle class and those more explicit and often more punitive assistance programs aimed at lower-income Americans. Although middle-class families get spared some of the worst condescension and poor treatment that lower-income Americans face, assistance through finance inflicts other kinds of damage. For instance, assistance through finance tends to impose on families a sense of personal responsibility for the indebted condition that the system mandates. When things go badly, it also generates feelings of failure and shame.

These problems have long been hidden from public view. Why? Because assistance through finance operates privately, and families do not discuss what they owe and how they borrow any more than they share how much they earn. This system for paying for college supports middle-class claims to autonomy and maintains the illusion of independence that has long been vital to American culture. After all, middle-class families apply for aid from their kitchen tables and keep their dependence a matter of their own personal business. Breaking the collective silence around debt would require admitting to the fragile nature of their finances, imperiling the very middle-class identity that they are trying to shore up by sending their children to college in the first place.

But this silence comes at a steep price. The prevailing norm of middle-class privacy has prevented families from understanding that others have been wrestling with debt in many of the same ways and for many of the same reasons that they have. This makes the struggle all the more stressful and isolating. The collective refusal to speak openly about money has also impoverished our vocabulary for describing the trade-offs and dilemmas that the financial system imposes on families, and undermined our capacity to understand how being indebted shapes family life.

My goal in this book is to bring these private moral conflicts out in the open, and to provide the lexicon we need to understand how the student finance complex affects us. My hope is to spark an open, honest, and public debate about how to support middle-class families and the rising generation in ways that live up to our highest ideals.

# CHAPTER 2

# Best-Laid Plans

...

When I recently opened the home page of the website for the New York State 529 college savings program, I was greeted by a series of snapshots chronicling a young girl growing up. In the first, she appears to be seven years old, tooth buds peeking out from her wide smile. In the next, a look of happy surprise lights up her fourth grader's face. Last, she appears as a self-composed teenager, hair brushed back, smiling confidently, ready for her next step toward independence. At the same time that the photos celebrate her successful coming of age, they congratulate her unseen parents. They have followed the prescriptions of responsible parenthood the student finance complex promotes, setting aside money for their child's college education and watching it grow as she has. They've paved her way to an open future.

Scroll down a bit further on the page and another child appears: a toddler in a swing seat gazing happily out at the viewer (figure 2.1). An accompanying message addresses parents explicitly, extolling the rewards they can secure by wisely investing in an account: "You can look this happy too. Enroll in the *Direct Plan* to be eligible for a New York State tax deduction of up to $10,000."

Responsibly investing in their children's futures, the message highlights, will not only set their children up for success but will pay off in the present. Taking advantage of the 529 tax breaks will give current family finances a boost, even as they set aside income to put into the account, making their investment not only

You can look this happy too

Enroll in the *Direct Plan* to be eligible for a New York State tax deduction of up to $10,000.*
We thought that would make you smile.

FIGURE 2.1. From the New York 528 College Savings Program website.

conscientious but also fiscally prudent. In addition, parents will reap an emotional reward. Those who avail themselves of the financial planning opportunities provided by the government and financial services industry, the images imply, have a right to be proud and pleased with themselves.

Government-sponsored college investment programs, like the 529 option, are more than the simple tools of personal finance they appear to be. They embody ideals of parental responsibility and promote the virtue of being good managers of family finances. These financial mechanisms are tools of moral instruction. They are also material manifestations of an economic creed that presents investment as eminently logical and market vehicles like the 529 as providing the means to balance the prudence and risk-taking that good financial planning requires. To follow the script of the 529, parents should begin depositing money soon after their child is born. Spreading their outlays over many years requires, in this narrative, a small sacrifice in the moment but promises great rewards in the future when the family will realize the profits of stock market increases and face reduced stress on their finances once it's college time.

In effect, the student finance complex is telling two parallel stories about middle-class family life that parents should bank on. The first focuses on children's futures. It's a simple and idealized story of their life course: children are born, they grow, they go to school, and, if parents have prepared them well, when children turn eighteen, they go to college. Though looking to the future, this story's instructions concern how parents should act today. They must literally invest in this narrative of their children's development, which leads to the second story. Parents should hand over income to financial services companies, who will assure their money grows in a way that will support their children's futures. Together these stories direct parents that they must embrace a central virtue of the student finance complex's moral code—they must plan.

Planning is treated as a purely practical matter, a simple problem of math: tallying income, assessing future costs, adjusting spending to free up funds, and placing the savings in a well-crafted financial investment that will grow reliably. In truth, for most families, planning requires just as much conjuring as calculating. The financial planning scenario promoted by the 529 website—and the student finance complex more broadly—portrays an ideal trajectory that few American families can expect their lives to follow. It's a morality tale that fails to take into account the realities of family life and the precarious security of middle-class Americans. It also presents financial investment as safe and predictable, downplaying the risks.

The scenario is built on a set of fictional premises that deny core uncertainties of middle-class life. Where the student finance complex portrays a clear and defined trajectory for all, only those in the upper echelons of wealth can actually rely on the idealized scenario. The fact that only a tiny fraction of American families—3 percent—invest in a 529 or related type of account reflects this fact. According to a survey by the Government Accountability Office, even among parents who said college saving was a priority, fewer than 10 percent held these accounts. Those who do put considerable money into the various tax-advantaged accounts are quite wealthy, with assets on average twenty-five times the median of all American families.[1] These findings highlight the first misleading premise of the planning story: that planning leads to financial stability. In truth, it's the other way around—planning requires stability in a family's fortunes, a stability in both family life and their finances that is uncommon for middle-class families today.

Another dubious assertion regards the ability to predict the future. The promise of planning is that if a family puts the right amount into a 529 or similar account at the right time, the growth of those funds will be sufficient to cover the portion of college expenses parents must contribute. This assumes predictable rates of growth, both in the costs of college and in securities markets. Neither has proved to be steady enough to count on.

Parents could not have anticipated how college costs have skyrocketed since the birth of today's college students. Since the late 1990s and early 2000s, when today's college-age children were born, costs have risen at a rate of increase that no parent could have predicted. For a child born in 2000, a 529 investment of $50 per month would amount to about $10,000 in college savings, if it tracked the Dow Jones Index. This would cover a single year of average in-state college tuition without room and board.

The Institute for Research on Higher Education at the University of Pennsylvania has found that, even since 2008, college has grown less affordable for low- and middle-income students. Student financial aid does not cover as much as it once did, and families' incomes are already taken up with everyday expenses, leaving little to invest for college.[2] All these trends undermine predictability, and so do trends in the economics of American family life.

Over the last several decades, employers have abandoned their commitment to long-term jobs for their workers. This means that many middle-class people now depend on income from free-lance work that waxes and wanes.[3] Others face volatile wages even within the same job, which makes household incomes rise and fall unpredictably, as Jonathan Morduch and Rachel Schneider have documented in the US Financial Diaries Project.[4] In middle-class households, income can vary as much as 30 percent from month to month.[5] Add to that the fact that Americans marry, divorce, and remarry at high rates—much higher, in fact, than Western Europeans—with 17 percent of Americans marrying two or more times.[6] The solutions that we now offer for stabilizing a family's financial future—investing in securities—are also uncertain. Few families can foresee how their lives will unfold, in terms of either the stability of their relationships or their finances. Even if parents follow the planning script closely, supporting their children's higher education often requires much more of them than the script acknowledges. Finance now enjoys a central place in government policies, but the inevitable instabilities in family life undermine planning as a political tool for providing security.

What, then, do college investment programs accomplish? One answer is that they promote an official definition of family life that's sanctioned by the student finance complex and given the weight of its resources. Anthropologist Jane Guyer calls this kind of official sanctioning "formalization."[7] Programs like 529s encourage parents to understand their love for their children in the program's terms; investing for their college future is an expression of how much they care. In addition to drawing the program's benefits, parents must think in the program's time frame, making that commitment right from their children's birth. They should organize their expectations of themselves and their children around preparing for college. The programs officially establish family obligations—many of which parents already subscribe to—and give parents a way to express them through buying into investment. The 529 and similar programs enjoin families' compliance with a moral vision of responsibility to family and financial accountability as a single compelling story.

That story leaves out, though, the conflicting obligations parents carry in caring for their children as well as the complex sources of family stability. To begin exploring how the realities of middle-class family life challenge parents, and how they belie the planning tale, consider the case of a family who has done everything planning advocates promote.

Laura Nowicki shared her family's experience of funding college by beginning with her own story. As she drove to her home from her nursing job at a Detroit area hospital, she recalled the process of selecting a college for herself, and how much less financially taxing getting her degree was. She always knew that she wanted to be a nurse and, fortunately, although not many public universities in Michigan offered nursing programs in the 1980s, she did have two good choices. One was Northern Michigan University, not far from her hometown in the Upper Peninsula, the finger of Michigan that cuts across Lake Superior and touches Canadian territory. But she longed to spread her wings and experience life away from her "tiny" hometown. Oakland University, another public Michigan institution, offered her a small scholarship, and that made the difference. She headed south to the Detroit area.

During her years in college, Laura took out about $10,000 in student loans. She remembers vividly the pinch to her spending money from the $100.51 a month she paid in the years following her graduation. Her parents had contributed toward her education from her dad's teacher's salary too, although not much. It wasn't until recently that she talked with her mom about her parents' financial situation back then. They kept the family's focus on their daughter's college choices, not on the money it would take to send her there. As Laura was preparing to send her own sons to college, her mom reported that those years had been "tight and scary," although they didn't let Laura or her two brothers know it at the time.

Now that Laura and her husband of twenty-five years, Chris, are supporting their sons' college educations—Sam at Western Michigan University and Mark at Grand Valley State University—she is amazed that her own education was such a bargain. She describes herself as "kind of crazy" about the finances for her boys' college expenses. "The price of college is such a huge burden on the family," she told us, one they've been carrying and planning for since their kids were small.

Laura and Chris, who works as a care manager at the same hospital, pay for the "excess," costs not covered by their sons' federal loans. Their older son takes out $7,500 a year and their younger son borrows $5,500. The additional cost their parents cover varies year to year (the fluctuation is due to machinations of the system I explore later). Helping pay is important to Laura. In part, she wants to make working toward a higher education "easier" on her boys. "I don't want my kids to be so in debt," she told us. She is clearly committed to preparing them for an open future. She also believes that, by contributing, she and Chris are sending a strong message to the boys that college is essential. She had gotten this message from her own parents. It was never an option for her *not* to go to college. Unlike when she attended, however, she feels the commitment to help pay is now a central part of that message. Their contribution encourages her boys, she believes, by saying, in effect, "We're backing this and we're going to be there with you." It conveys that higher education is an integral aspect of the type of family they are.

Chris and Laura have also sent a strong message of responsibility to their sons. They're required not only to take out loans but also to apply their talents and get good grades. "I don't want to hand it to them on a silver platter," Laura says. "So I expect them to work, I expect them to take out a student loan, and I expect them to see, okay, this is your contribution, this is my contribution." Laura informs Sam and Mark about every penny involved, unlike her parents and many of the parents we interviewed, who, as we explore later, hide the financial strains of their children's college education from them. Laura reported that for each son, "I make spreadsheets [showing] how much his tuition is per hour, how many credit hours he's taken, how much his room and board is, how much every book cost."

Every summer Sam and Mark settle into jobs. Sam, who wants to be a doctor, has worked at the hospital as a safety attendant and as a laboratory assistant. Mark has changed oil and flat tires at a family-owned collision shop and worked in a health insurance office, which he hopes will smooth his path toward a job in health finance. The boys live at home and save their earnings. During the school year, Laura wants her sons to focus on what she considers to be the most important work: studying. "I expect good grades," Laura says, "because I'm paying for some of this. I mean, if you're up there partying, the money won't be there for you." She and her husband would pull back their financial support at that point. But they haven't had to. Their boys have both dedicated themselves to their studies and seem poised to move toward their chosen futures in medicine and accounting.

As for their share, Laura and Chris have cobbled together various sources. Laura has taken on an extra shift at the intensive care unit, where she's been on staff for more than thirty years. When the boys were young, she worked part-time; nursing gave her the flexibility both to make money and to devote time to raising her boys. Now she works more. Her regular schedule is five twelve-hour shifts per every two-week pay period. With the additional shift, she is working seventy-two hours per period. In addition, they draw on a Michigan Education Savings Program (MESP), a 529 account they opened when their boys were in elementary school. Most months they diverted about $100 into each of the boys' accounts, which grew to about $20,000. Each year they draw down about $5,000 per student, which covers about a fifth of each boy's costs.

Laura's parents also opened a 529 for the boys when they were young. They always prioritized education and made it their goal to support their children and grandchildren in their studies. Laura's father worked a second job to earn the funds. When Laura was in high school he opened an A&W franchise, a seasonal business that he could run when school was closed. Laura and her brothers worked there every summer pulling root beer floats. The A&W sat on land that grew more valuable over the years. When Laura's father finally sold the property, he had enough to put away for his grandsons to each have $20,000 when they enrolled in college. This support was a godsend. Laura told us, "I've been truly blessed."

Even so, the money from the 529s doesn't cover all the costs. In addition to the funds they take out from the 529s, Laura and Chris also send each of their sons $400 a month to supplement their savings from their summer jobs and make sure they can cover their rent, electricity, heat, and food bills and still have some "fun money" left over. They send the money and the boys are free to decide how to spend it, reflecting the value Laura and Chris place on their sons' increasing autonomy. "The boys know we work hard," she told us, "and they have always spent the money responsibly."

Laura stresses that paying for college now requires "a whole family to make it happen," highlighting that in their case this includes three generations. Their ability to pay has also involved the security of a steady marriage, their solid jobs, and good health. As we'll see through the stories of a number of other families, if circumstances had been different in any of those areas, their ability to support their sons' college education might have been dramatically curtailed.

The Nowicki family also benefits from their home state's particularly strong options in public universities, among the best in the country. But the state's support for higher education has receded significantly in recent years as it has become a leader of the pack in shifting the costs of college to students and their families. The Great Recession of 2008 intensified a national trend that began as early as the 1960s.

The nonpartisan Center on Budget and Policy Priorities reports that forty-four states spent less per student in 2017 than they did in 2008. The Michigan schools have addressed this loss with fund-raising and by recruiting wealthy out-of-state and foreign students who pay private school prices. These students displace some of Michigan's own young people, however, restricting the options of middle-class and lower-income Michigan residents. The result is that paying for college requires much more of middle-class families than it did even ten years ago at the same time that the number of university spots for Michigan residents has shrunk.[8]

The Nowickis also chose to work in fields—education and health care—that have remained strong sources of employment. Many of Michigan's middle-class families that relied on jobs at Ford, GM, or Chrysler or in industries that supplied the "big three" auto makers were faced with financial instability when Michigan's car industry cratered in the 1990s, taking the state's economy with it. The stability of the Nowickis' jobs and of their family life has allowed Laura and Chris to follow the planning model promoted by the student finance complex. Planning relies on these unacknowledged conditions.

The student finance complex and its morality has become the silent background for the Nowickis' life. It gives structure to the basic tasks of parenting, sorting good parenting and grandparenting from bad, and setting Laura and Chris's expectations of their boys as emerging adults. The student finance complex also shapes what Laura and Chris expect from their sons' public universities; it determines what assistance will look like for middle-class families like the Nowickis.

Preparing for kids' college education by cobbling together finances—some debt here, investment funds there—all coordinated with their sons' universities is simply how the system works, Laura accepts. She even expressed her appreciation in terms of the student finance complex. "The college does help you," she reported. "Like if you call the financial aid office, they will say 'this is how much it's going to cost.' Western has been so helpful. . . . Every time you call them they call you right back. [They don't] give you money, but help you through the process."

The Nowickis might seem to exemplify the wisdom of financial planning and to provide real-life evidence for its moral imperative. But behind their experience lies a powerful critique of investment and family as sources of middle-class support. Even with both parents and grandparents contributing, their 529 accounts fund only a fraction of their college costs. Instead, their family's stability across generations and its good fortune, rather than planning itself, have been their financial foundation. For many families, these conditions are elusive. Common challenges can undermine even the best-laid plans.

## Unpredictable Futures

Patricia Walsh was a teacher in the Florida public school system when she first noticed the advertisements for the state's prepaid college tuition plan. As in all of the eleven states that offer prepaid tuition, in Florida parents can pay for any of the state's public colleges and universities in advance of their children's enrollment, and at current prices. Payment can be made all up front or, more commonly, by having the state draw month-to-month from a bank account. This arrangement is attractive because tuition costs have increased so relentlessly.

Patricia knew that her teacher's salary would preclude her children from getting the free ride for college that she had benefited from. She grew up in New Jersey, born to Irish Catholic parents who were, she recalls, "really poor," but also smart and ambitious. Realizing their aspirations, Patricia won entrance to Rutgers, New Jersey's top public university, and as a result of her parents' low income, she didn't have to pay tuition.

Once she got to college, she found that she didn't know what sort of work she wanted to do after graduation, but that was OK. She was "idealistic" about learning, she says, and majored in English, feeling free to take the liberal arts classes that interested her. After graduation, she had no career plan, and after starting out in office work, she moved on to a lower-management position for a railroad. Before long, she quit and moved to Florida, where she worked in restaurants and cleaned houses. She'd always considered getting into teaching, though, and eventually thought, "Well, you know, maybe I should go and give this whole education thing a shake." Soon after she had her own grade-school classroom, she met and married her children's father, and over the next several years gave birth to Maya and Zachary.

As a grade school teacher and young mother, Patricia's ears were primed to pick up on promotions of the program, but she recalls the ads were so constant that "you couldn't *not* hear about it." Patricia signed right up, and she says her investment helped motivate her to stick with her teaching job for many years. She found her work stressful, relating, "The toll it takes on your body and your mind and your emotions is grueling." She was also unhappy that her job took her away from her children for so many hours, leaving them with only scraps of time together at the end of her taxing days. But she felt her work had paid off because, after five years of contributions, tuition for Maya and Zachary was secured.

Maya grew up to be a stellar student, earning accolades from her high school teachers that helped her win scholarships to cover much of her college expenses. Between Patricia's prepaid tuition plan and Maya's award money and jobs, her college was easily paid for. A contributing factor, Patricia mentioned proudly, was that Maya understood "how to stretch a penny."

The family fortunes took a wrenching turn a year and a half before Maya graduated, however, when Zachary was a senior in high school. Their father walked out on the family and has sent them no financial assistance since. Though Maya was emotionally devastated, she was well on her way to independence and she persisted with college. By contrast, the abandonment profoundly disrupted Patricia and Zachary's lives.

Patricia was suddenly left without the financial security she had counted on. The couple owned two properties and, without telling her, her husband had taken out two lines of credit on them. He used the money for "his 'travel and entertainment,'" she reported, laughing sardonically. Once he was gone she wanted to sell the houses, but the recession still had the Florida real estate market in its clutches. Meanwhile, her ex-husband had accumulated debts that totaled nearly $400,000. When she was finally able to find a buyer for one home, she made little profit, which had to be put toward paying off his debts. She was also forced to empty her retirement account to pay them off.

For a time, despite the upheaval, Zachary's life proceeded according to her plan. He moved north to Gainesville and enrolled in community college classes there, also getting a job. Patricia worries that she shouldn't have let him go away to school, but "things here were so ugly with the long separation and divorce that, at the same time, I was really grateful that he wasn't here. I knew that he wanted to get as far away as he could."

Separated and without employment, Patricia looked for work for six months, and then, suddenly, "God blessed me with three jobs," she recalls, "and I had a brief spell for a couple of years where I was making more money than I had ever made before." This allowed her to send Zachary money for college fees and rent, and of course his tuition was already paid for. But Zachary's trajectory began to veer off plan.

"He had a way of getting fired," Patricia said, losing his first job and then a second. His college career also stalled. Patricia commented that his professors praised his intelligence and engagement, but still he didn't do the course work to get good grades. Eventually, he stopped signing up for classes, and, five years after starting, he sits several courses short of an associate's degree. Today he's managed to find new work and is supporting himself, except for his car insurance, which Patricia is happy to cover.

As Patricia looks back, she chides herself for not seeing warning signs. Zachary was always an inconsistent student, and his father's abandonment only made it worse, she realizes. She had always believed in her son's future. Her investment in his tuition was an expression of her faith in him.

In my conversations with families, middle-class parents often discussed the importance of having faith in positive outcomes for their children in college and expressing that faith to them. Parents are not simply engaging in wishful thinking; their expressions of faith are well advised. For one thing, their belief is in line with what they have witnessed in their own families and among their neighbors. They've seen what the broad statistical picture shows: children will most likely graduate from college if their parents have. And, having earned a degree, those young adults will likely earn a middle-class income.[9]

Faith matters. Parental expectations carry children forward, sociologist Stephen Vaisey has shown; they are central to students' achievement.[10] Psychological studies also reveal that positive parental expectations boost students' own aspirations even when parents themselves haven't done well in school or gone far in their careers.[11] Student achievement can, in turn, lift parental expectations of their children, creating a virtuous cycle that supports students' success.[12] Parents' aspirations can even make up for teachers' dismissive attitudes toward students.[13]

The middle-class faith in children is, therefore, a cultural value with clear effects. This devotion is also essential to affirming parents' middle-class belonging and establishing the same for their children. In other words, parental faith is not a matter of statistical evidence, supportive as that may be. Patricia's investment in her children's tuition was much more than a matter of rational actuarial accounting. Her son might have been a capricious student, but her responsibility, Patricia understood, was to believe in her child. Having faith in his college-going future and acting on it was key to Patricia being a middle-class parent and Zachary being a middle-class child and becoming a middle-class adult.[14]

The class-making power of faith in a child's educational success is easiest to see by envisioning its opposite. Patricia had the challenge of mothering a smart but mercurial boy who didn't always live up to his own talents. She could have told him, "Zachary, you're not meant for college; you probably won't graduate, so it's not worth the cost for me to send you." And in parent conferences, she could have delivered that assessment to his teachers: "Zachary doesn't show promise as a student. Sure, he's smart. But let's be realistic about his chances."

College investment programs like the 529 and prepaid tuition are premised in part on this same notion that parents should believe; that they should hold children's potential as sacred.[15] They seem to be supporting parents' aspirations, but they also require calculations that go against their faith in their children.

Putting money into these vehicles requires parents to accept that the logic of investment applies to their parenting; they should assess their child's potential like accountants. The unexpressed, and contradictory, implication of offering investment opportunities to parents is that they should ask, Just how likely is my child to graduate from college? Does it make sense to take the risk of devoting my savings to that possibility?

Although they understand the logic of investment, parents see calculating the odds of their children's success as undermining their paramount value of nurturing their potential. Patricia invested not out of rational calculation but out of love.

In the vise of this moral conflict, Patricia chose to act on her parental instincts, as most parents in my study did. Patricia expressed the tension by looking back conditionally. "If I'd had a crystal ball," she lamented, "I wouldn't have gotten in the program for Zachary." By following the advice of the prepaid tuition plan promotions, Patricia has ended up with an investment that

## COLLEGE?
## DEFINITELY!
AN ASPIRATIONAL COLLEGE SAVINGS BLOG

# Busting the Top 7 Myths About
# Prepaid Plans

FIGURE 2.2. From the Florida Prepaid website.

she can't fully recoup and has forgone the earnings she would have made if she had invested the money differently.

As in other states, the Florida prepaid plan penalizes families whose lives do not adhere to its model. The plan stipulates that it will likely refund only the principal invested if a child doesn't end up attending college, or, as in Zachary's case, uses only a fraction of the money in the account and if the family doesn't have another child in college to whose tuition the funds can be directed. In that event, Florida takes the earnings from parents' investments. In Patricia's case, that amounts to growth over almost two decades. And, in fact, she can also be charged a fee to close out Zachary's plan.

The plan's website addresses this possibility, but only sidelong (figure 2.2). Tucked away in "Busting the Top 7 Myths About Prepaid Plans" explanation, in the middle of the page, myth number 5 worries, "I'll lose all of my prepaid plan savings if my child doesn't go to college." The response offers a weak caution: "You won't lose everything, but if your child decides not to go to college and you can't pass it on to a sibling, most prepaid plans will only refund the principal. In some cases, you may be charged a cancellation fee." It makes no mention of the potential lost investment income.[16] What's more, next in the list of myths, is the advice that parents can double down on investing, telling them they needn't worry that purchasing a prepaid plan precludes them from also investing in a 529 plan; they can do both. This advice implies hearty approval of any parents who would be so shrewd as to want to do so. Financial risks remain unacknowledged, as do most families' limited household funds that prohibit them from investing in the first place. This is not for a lack of planning, but because they are tending to their children's potential in the present.

## Planning versus Provision

In addition to looking the other way about the vicissitudes of life and of investing, the planning precept fails to acknowledge its central conflict: parents also feel the need to spend adequately on their children in the present in order to settle them among their peers and to prepare them for the future. The presumption of the student finance complex that parents should discipline themselves to invest for college does not take into account the intense parenting pressures that middle-class families face in the moment.

Experts that marry the study of psychology and economics have characterized this present focus as either irrational or due to lack of understanding. Behavioral economists have shown in laboratory experiments that their study subjects consistently value the present much more than the future, giving it far less weight than they should by economists' standards of rationality.[17] They call this feature of human psychology *hyperbolic discounting*.

To counter this failing, people should educate themselves about their human defects, other behavioral economists suggest. With self-reflection, they will be able to appreciate the wisdom of using "commitment devices," like 529s or 401(k) investment plans. These mechanisms bind savers to their "good" decisions in the present by penalizing them if they withdraw funds. Some experts have also advised that policies should "nudge" people to contribute through the design of the programs. For instance, Richard Thaler and Cass Sunstein convinced the federal government to change the default option for enrolling in retirement savings and investment plans. When employees take on a job in a firm with a 401(k) benefit, they are automatically enrolled in the plan and, if they prefer *not* to invest their money, they have to make the conscious decision to opt out.[18]

The behavioral economics finding that people often act against their long-term interest dovetails with the argument that failure to invest in 529s is a result of poor education: Americans don't save or invest for college because they are financially illiterate. They don't comprehend the long-term effects of spending in the present or realize how much good financial investment can do for them. Financial literacy scholars do not make claims to financial failing rooted in universal human psychology. Instead, they acknowledge that financial literacy is distributed unevenly. The economist Annamaria Lusardi has shown that women, people of color, youth, and low-income Americans score low on financial literacy tests, with more than half misunderstanding basic concepts like compound interest, inflation, and risk diversification.[19] Writing in the *Atlantic*, sociologist Marianne Cooper emphasizes that the poster child for financial literacy is a white man with college-educated parents who held investments themselves.[20] For critics like Cooper, relying on financial literacy to fix the problems of the system only ends up blaming those denied access to money and power in the first place. For advocates of financial literacy, like Lusardi, education can and should close that gap.

Although both explanations—failings of psychology and of education—are illuminating, they go only so far. A broader analysis of the student finance complex and the consumer economy is necessary to understand the reasons most middle-class families aren't investing in college accounts. The American middle class once saved for the future enthusiastically. In 1975 the personal savings rate in the United States hit a peak of almost 14 percent. Today it hovers at 2.5 percent.[21] Putting that dramatic change down to either basic psychology or financial illiteracy ignores the vast economic changes the middle class has faced. Parents in my study were not unaware of the wisdom of saving and investing. On the contrary, they often discussed how helpful it would have been if they'd put away more for college expenses and spoke of their regret that they had not. The interviews revealed that many parents had not saved more largely because they felt they could not both invest in and provide for their children's current needs at the same time.

A planning precept fails to address the fact that providing a middle-class life for children has become increasingly expensive while, at the same time, middle-class incomes have stagnated. The middle class simply takes home a smaller share of the country's wealth than they did in prior decades.[22] In addition, starting in the 1990s, many middle-class parents took on large mortgage debts and were left underwater when the 2008 crisis hit. This tight financial squeeze has presented them with another vexing moral conflict: good parenting requires that they both spend considerably in the present and save responsibly for the future, and in this conflict between planning and provisioning, provisioning has won out.

Financial morality would direct critics to argue that these families ought to have enough funds to invest and that their current spending on their children is excessive, perhaps even labeling it as materialistic. My interviews revealed a quite different story, however. Again and again parents explained that their desire, and sense of responsibility, to prepare their children for open futures required them to stretch their finances in the present. They explained that they had spent on houses that taxed their budgets in order to assure their children attended high-quality schools. They spent on sports lessons and equipment and music classes to offer their children the opportunity to discover talents and to develop discipline. They purchased vacations to give the family time out from their daily routines and the stresses of work, school, and social life. In their days away, they believed, family relationships deepened and grew stronger—a value on its own, but also a resource children and parents could draw on in an uncertain future. They also spent on stylish clothes and birthday parties and toys, goods that might seem to be more difficult to justify in the trade-off between present and future priorities, though their motivations are again more compelling than such moral admonition allows.

In her book *Longing and Belonging*, sociologist Alison Pugh gives readers access to school playground chatter and to revealing discussions with parents that illuminate the nature of children's desires for things and their parents' willingness to buy them. She shows that parents' and children's purchases are guided by an "economy of dignity," in which video games, sneakers, dolls, sports and music classes, and trips all represent tokens that afford esteem. For Pugh, these tokens establish children's social existence and are a bid for membership among their peers. Goods and experiences enable children to vie for status, an unavoidable part of claiming a place. Importantly, Pugh found that this was true across classes, from the upper-class Oakland neighborhood to the middle-class and low-income ones where she conducted research.[23] In a consumer economy that ties social status to owning goods, parents spend on these tokens for their children in order for the family to belong.

Many parents in my own interviews described feeling trapped in a moral dilemma: whether to provide their children with the life they believed would allow them to flourish or to deprive them of aspects of that in order to save more. Some have jeopardized their own financial futures in their effort to manage this conflict, and many more carried this fear. Far from a lack of responsibility, what I heard from parents was self-accusation for not managing to do both, even within the limitations of their resources.

A middle manager at McDonald's corporate headquarters living in the Chicago suburbs, Dennis had two children in college and another who was a recent graduate when we spoke. His own father, who worked for a utility company in Ohio, had told him that he had no choice but to go to an in-state school. Dennis was adamant that he wouldn't place the same restriction on his children; they would go where they wanted and, together, they would make the financing work. This decision lay at the center of Dennis's middle-class aspirations, which came to life in other ways too. As things turned out, two of his children chose to go to Illinois state schools anyway (one was in community college), while the other went to Xavier University, a private Jesuit school in Ohio.

Dennis and his wife, Debbie, are struggling with credit card debt, accumulated as they sought to provide a comfortable life.

They were initially both teachers, but when she became pregnant, Debbie quit her job and Dennis began working in corporate middle management where he's spent his career since. They enrolled the kids in private Catholic school, moved from a townhouse into a large suburban home so the children could each have a bedroom of their own, and took the family on vacations, traveling by car to destinations like the Grand Canyon.

Dennis now regrets some of their spending. He reported, "If I look back on our marriage, we've made impulse-type decisions; not very well thought out." He blamed himself, for example, for his decision to buy a new Chevrolet minivan. "I look back on it now and I think, Well, why didn't I buy a used one? Did I need a new one, you know? . . . We're not very good planners financially."

Karen, an emergency room nurse married to a hotel cook living in the Detroit suburbs, expressed similar doubts. "I just kind of look back and wish I was a little tighter on the reins with some money. I wish I would have started a separate [college] account." Her son's community college tuition hasn't been a struggle, but paying for her daughter to attend Michigan's Ferris State University has required loans for both herself and her daughter. She shouldn't have bought her children all the things she did, she told us, but she had worked full-time from when the children were young, and she gave them things she could buy to "overcompensate" for the lost time with them.

When her daughter was young, Karen "went the extra mile on My Little Pony," and when her son wanted hockey cards, "he got hockey cards. Did they really need them? No." As her kids grew, they cycled through different sports that Karen and her husband fully supported. Stephanie took dance and skating lessons and competed on a gymnastics team, which meant purchasing "all her different costumes." Her son played hockey and swam; at least, she said, bathing suits were less expensive than pads and protective gear. "We spent a small fortune on [their sports]. But they were good kids and they did well. And they weren't in trouble." Karen expresses the conflict between understanding the sense of saving and the desire to provide for children as they grow. If she had it to do over again, she told us, "I probably would have saved a little bit more. But I don't regret spending the money I did on the kids."

Even Laura Nowicki, who has followed the planning template, rebukes herself for not putting more away. Discussing the $50 a month she and her husband put into each of their children's 529 accounts since grade school, she said "We probably should have put double that," adding, "I didn't realize how important [it was]. We should have cut back on our other frills and put more into that. . . . But you don't think like that when you're growing your children and you don't realize how fast eighteen years goes by."

Rather than viewing middle-class parents as simply irrational and uninformed, or berating them for being irresponsible, understanding their choices requires appreciating the dilemmas they confront. It is the admonition itself that should be closely questioned, as scholars have when people of color and lower-income Americans have suffered reproach for a supposed failure to plan. This moralizing has long fed social bias, even though research has pointed out again and again that lower-income people aspire to more secure lives and strategize conscientiously about their futures.

In the mid-1960s, then assistant labor secretary Daniel Patrick Moynihan introduced the world to a new concept: "the culture of poverty." Although anthropologist Oscar Lewis coined the term, Moynihan's report, "The Negro Family: The Case for National Action," brought the phrase to national prominence. Moynihan's report blamed African Americans, in particular mothers, for an insufficient commitment to future success for themselves and their children, a deficit that trapped black Americans in ghettos and in dependence on government aid. Lower-income African Americans lacked, Moynihan asserted, exactly the cultural attributes that middle-class African Americans had mastered. Lauding the upper half, Moynihan noted that these wealthier African Americans made plans and showed the self-control to execute them. He highlighted, for example, that middle-class African Americans had fewer children than their white counterparts, "indicating a desire to conserve the advances they have made and to ensure that their children do as well or better."[24] Lower-income people needed to learn these lessons, Moynihan lectured.

Countering this view with nuanced and thoughtful analysis, anthropologist Carol Stack's *All Our Kin* described her ethnographic research with African American families in a Midwestern urban neighborhood she called "the Flats." She documented how residents there strategically built and maintained "networks of exchange" among households to help cover current needs and also hopefully secure future assistance.[25] Since then, every decade has seen another powerful study countering the moral accusation that lower-income parents do not plan. In fact, anthropologists and sociologists have found that these parents give detailed attention to both their economic situations and their children's futures. The challenges of pulling together enough to get by in the present, however, means that saving and investing in conventional terms don't make much sense. Even when they have some extra funds, lower-income Americans do not necessarily turn to the banks and investment houses that cater to wealthier Americans.[26] Instead they often place their trust in family members and close friends who can help them in the future, giving gifts of favors and money that these relations will return when they are needed.

In the 1990s, the moral charge against low-income Americans focused, again, on African American women. They should be required to work in order to receive aid, critics complained; such a condition would teach them to be "independent," to earn and to value work enough to save and invest. Writing in a 1994 essay, political theorist Nancy Fraser and historian Linda Gordon observed, " 'Dependency' is the single most crucial term in the current US debate about welfare reform," and noted that the word is replete with both moral and psychological connotations. The term also drew a powerful distinction. Even when both middle- and lower-income people relied on government programs, they argued, those rebuffed as "dependent" were relegated to a low status and the programs they relied on—"welfare," or Aid to Families with Dependent Children (AFDC)— carried suspicion and more punishing terms.[27] Others who relied on government old-age insurance, Social Security, were not burdened with stigma. Their honor as members of the middle class was protected, even as they accepted the aid.[28] As anthropologist Elizabeth F. S. Roberts has argued, misrecognizing dependence and disparaging assistance come most often from the upper echelons of the United States in which wealth and income support the illusion of autonomy and give a distorted view of the punishing realities of life in lower-income communities.[29]

Spurred by the same moral accusations that Fraser and Gordon identified, sociologist Katherine Edin and anthropologist Laura Lein set out to investigate how maligned single mothers were actually making ends meet. Edin and Lein asked hundreds of parents—mostly African American and Latina, some who relied on the welfare program and some not—to keep detailed records of their income and expenditures, and interviewed them about their priorities. Edin and Lein found that these single mothers had access to work only in the most insecure and lowest-paid parts of the service sector. Mary Ann Moore, a single African American mother of four whom Edin and Lein profile in their opening pages, was working for $8 an hour at a soup kitchen job that she'd held for a calendar year and that paid her more than any other she'd had or could have gotten with her education and skills. Such security had been elusive in her work life. She had held two dozen different jobs since she'd graduated from high school fifteen years before and had relied on AFDC in between. Other women that Edin and Lein spoke with worked in child care, as nurses' aides, and as low-level secretaries, and all faced the uncertainty that Moore described.

The jobs the single mothers could get produced a horrible irony too; they were actually often a source of insecurity for families. The women frequently faced daunting and expensive commutes, rent increases in their public housing, and day care expenses when they went to work. Their low-level positions also meant that they could not take days off and were forced to jeopardize their jobs just to stay home to care for sick children. Many had to rely on relations and boyfriends, and to take on extra jobs over and above full-time schedules. Even double work in the formal sector cost a lot in travel and taxes, however, and informal jobs, like working off the books in a restaurant, paid well under minimum wage. As a last resort, these mothers would sell whatever goods they could, legally or illegally.

These women had to focus on immediate survival; planning was simply not a realistic possibility, even for such modest goals as secretarial school, which some of the women believed might provide a secure and steady existence. Edin and Lein found that "good mothering" and worry about their children's futures were the central concerns in these parents' lives, and that the uncertainty and insecurity they faced meant they directed their energy to getting by in the present.[30]

Writing about a lower-income Chicago neighborhood in the early 2000s, sociologist Sudhir Venkatesh documented similar circumstances, showing that residents, especially women, "provide for the simplest things: food, clothing, and shelter for their families . . . muddl[ing] along by pooling resources, bartering for goods, and developing intricate schemes to exchange services."[31] Cautioning against scolding residents that they should be focused more on building a better future, Venkatesh wrote, "In thinking about the future, one should not import too quickly a middle-class perspective in which the experience of time is colored by all manner of planning, including saving and investing, prioritizing rationally, acquiring full information for decision making, and proceeding methodically without fear of impoverishment or physical danger on the horizon."[32] He points out that those he spoke with divided the future into two distinct time frames, one very near and one very far away, with little in between. Even while they faced their day-to-day struggles, they also dreamed of distant goals, like home ownership.

The careful documentation of these scholars has demonstrated that lower-income Americans do organize their lives with the future in mind, but not in ways that people from more privileged economic stations or the policy establishment generally choose to recognize. Under the conditions of instability that Stack, Lein and Edin, and Venkatesh have documented, planning simply does not make sense. The financial challenges and uncertainties that have become hallmarks of middle-class family life are subject to a similar blindness and will not dissolve under moral opprobrium any more for middle-class families than for lower-income ones.

Even when family seems to offer resources to secure both the present and the future, uncertainty remains the rule. Consider one more story of a family that seemed to have enough financial resources to be able to focus on provisioning children. Kerry Lynn Bailey and David Goldstein placed family at the center of their sense of security. They were fortunate that Kerry Lynn's parents contributed significantly to their finances, in keeping with the long-standing American tradition for one generation to support the next. Their reliance on family, however, left them vulnerable.

Kerry Lynn's father, Bob, had grown up in rural Arkansas and had never graduated from high school, but he had nonetheless become a pilot for a major airline, making the most of his military service to enter the lucrative and glamorous career that flying used to be. Still, for Bob and his wife (who stayed home with the kids), higher education for their children was always a priority. They drew on Bob's generous paycheck to pay for college for Kerry Lynn and her younger brother. Kerry Lynn was the first in her family to earn a college degree, attending a Texas state school.

Kerry Lynn met her husband, David, at a college interfaith student retreat. They were both religious—she was Christian and he was Jewish—but both understood their faith to be more about living according to spiritual values than following strict religious precepts. In deciding to marry, they saw an opportunity to create a family life that blended their faiths in a way that worked for them. Their educations would be a resource for creating their new experimental family. In his interview, their son, Caleb, described his parents as the "new educated," a distinctive class with a different, but similarly lofty upward trajectory from the "new moneyed." At parties and at the dinner table, talk focused on big questions of faith and politics, and the couple committed themselves to designing their lives according to carefully considered ideas and values.

Kerry Lynn and David quickly had Caleb and then his sister, Rachel. Kerry Lynn began her training to become a pastoral counselor when the kids were young, and David started to work on a divinity degree. The couple wanted to make sure the kids understood their dedication to their respective faiths and education alike. As the children grew out of toddler stage, the parents decided to raise them to be Jewish, but also with knowledge of their mother's Christianity and respect for their differences. They joined a synagogue that would welcome their mixed-faith family. Not being able to rely fully on a single set of traditions, they would need to devote themselves to making their own customs and creating a new kind of family.

Neither Kerry Lynn nor David would make much money in their chosen professions, and her parents wanted to help them live the life they wanted. Bob bought a house in the Houston suburbs where the new family lived and where they did not have to pay rent. Every year he transferred some of the equity in their home to the new couple. Kerry Lynn's mother, Linda, gave them help too, taking care of the kids when Kerry Lynn was first at school and then at work. Kerry Lynn and David took the money that they saved on rent and child care and put it toward a private Quaker school for their children's elementary years. Kerry Lynn was saving a small amount in her retirement plan, but they were mostly spending to live by their values.

When the kids were entering high school, the couple decided to work with a professional financial planner to help them plan for their children's future college enrollment and their own retirements. Their planner would need to understand their family's goals—that they were not only concerned with financial security but with doing work that supported their communities and spending the money they felt was required to raise their children within their beliefs, like for their children's Quaker school. Although Kerry Lynn and David found a planner that they believed understood this, over time they found her to be "very, very conservative" financially. She pushed them to keep watch on their spending and save more. Kerry Lynn described that her planner was constantly delivering bad news about the future, asking them to change their spending and saving in line with coming expenses, like college and retirement. Kerry Lynn and David did not want to value the future more than the present, however. They saw their spending as connected to their family experiment; the school and their yearly sailing trips both fed a focus on faith and family they wanted to cultivate with their children.

The couple largely ignored the planner's advice. They remained focused on their priorities and counted on Bob's unwavering commitment, which he showed again by putting $5,000 for each of his grandchildren into college savings accounts. It was reassuring to have those funds, even though they would cover only a portion of the costs. But Kerry Lynn and her husband gave the most thought to the substance of what college could offer their children. They wanted Caleb and Rachel to focus on how they—like their parents—could use their educations to develop themselves and contribute to the well-being of others.

When it came time for Caleb to apply for college, he was in good shape academically. He had won an award for being a top scholar-athlete in the region, which included a stipend of $1,000 for college expenses. He wanted to attend a private liberal arts college, which would provide a new environment and real challenge for him. His parents worried about the cost but kept their focus on whether the colleges he'd applied to were a social and intellectual match for their son. Caleb was admitted to a selective private college in the Northeast, and between loans, their own resources, and Bob's college funds, they were able to come up with enough money for him to attend. Kerry Lynn and David saw their paying for Caleb's liberal arts education as a gift to their child who had always been so dedicated to both his sports and his studies. Kerry Lynn described their dynamic around choosing college. Caleb "was never pushing for what he had to have. I mean it wasn't coming from a place of entitlement on his part." His parents' decision to commit to the expensive private school "was coming from a place of 'we want to give this to you.'"

The family took out Caleb's full complement of federal loans across his college years, a total of about $30,000. His parents committed to paying them when their son graduated, even though they were in his name. Kerry Lynn and David also contributed from the family income, and Caleb pitched in with earnings from jobs awarded to him by the federal work-study program, making sandwiches at a campus deli, assisting students with their software problems in a computer lab, and working as a resident adviser. His grandfather's money provided a vital bridge, and together the family made it work.

At the same time Caleb was distinguishing himself on the baseball field and in the classroom, Rachel began to veer off the path her parents had imagined. Kerry Lynn paused heavily as it came time to speak about her daughter's story. As if to start the interview over, she asked how much I really wanted to know. "These are really complicated issues that go into so many layers of expectations, plans, and how plans get dashed," she reported.

When Rachel was in high school—during Caleb's first year in college—she became addicted to drugs, and getting her the help she needed became Kerry Lynn and David's constant concern. When they were finally able to enroll her at a residential treatment center, the cost also strained their finances. "Every bit of money that Rachel could have had for education went towards drug treatment programs," Kerry Lynn told us. The expense was so high that she and David took out an equity line of credit on their house. Kelly Lynn also took money out of her retirement account. They were glad that they didn't yet have to pay off Caleb's loans too, which wouldn't be due until six months after he graduated.

"Life teaches you some really profound things when addiction comes into the picture," Kelly Lynn told us. "What addiction takes away from you as a parent is your hope for what your children's future will be. You don't get to have that anymore." Today Rachel is working as a waitress in another state. Kerry Lynn is happy simply that they are speaking and that her daughter is sober and has kept her job. "Addiction eats expectations for lunch every day," she commented. The stress of Rachel's addiction also drove a wedge between Kerry Lynn and her husband. The worry, disappointment, and fear for their daughter consumed their marriage. Today Kerry Lynn and David are divorced.

Another cloud has also cast a shadow over Kerry Lynn's future. During Caleb's first year of college, her father was diagnosed with Alzheimer's disease. He can no longer contribute to her finances, and any inheritance she might have counted on now goes toward paying for his 24-hour care. With Rachel's treatment having consumed most of the nest egg Bob had built for her, Kerry Lynn's own financial future is now insecure, and she is struggling to keep up with current expenses. She must continue to make payments on the home equity loan she and David took out, and is only paying off the interest, so the amount she owes won't decrease.

"For me," she told us, "money is ineffable at the same time that it's also very concrete." She has learned how quickly money counted on can vanish. Planning requires a vision of the future, and Kerry Lynn had one. She had faith that between her parents' support and her small but steady income, she and her kids would be secure enough. Instead she now faces her own compromised future. As she approaches her later-middle-age years, divorced and trying to regain her footing, Kerry Lynn told us she takes life "one step at a time," as she's learned from Rachel's group therapy sessions. The future no longer plays a significant role for her. Instead she controls what she can, focusing on her actions in the present even while she knows that she won't be able to absorb any more shocks like she's had with Rachel and her father. As for many parents in my study, faith is a sustaining force in Kerry Lynn's life as she confronts the uncertainty of her future.

Kerry Lynn has learned a vital truth about planning that the reductive, moral narrative of the student finance complex can't accommodate. "Life changes a lot. It isn't always what you think it's going to be," she says. "The future is uncertain; pretending that it is not defies both logic and God's nature."

The moral mandate to plan distributes virtue to those who possess stability—particularly those with wealth—and denies it to those who don't. Programs like 529s also distribute financial benefits upward. Monetary rewards flow along the same lines as virtue. Recall that the vast majority of those who do save in these accounts are far wealthier than most Americans, with assets on average twenty-five times the median of those who do not participate, and far higher incomes.[33] This fact is well known to the federal government and has been for some time. In fact, the Obama administration tried to abolish the 529 program in 2015 but relented under pressure from wealthy parents and from bipartisan representatives like Democrat Nancy Pelosi and then

Speaker Republican John Boehner, who demanded that the president withdraw his proposal "for the sake of middle-class families."[34] More recently, the Trump administration has expanded the 529 program, making invested funds available to pay for private school as well as college, while still touting the program as helpful for middle-class struggles.

The federal government devotes significant resources to these plans. In 2014, college accounts that carried federal tax advantages represented almost $2 billion in forgone Treasury revenue, a number that grows year by year as the assets in these accounts increase in value.[35] And they have been rising rapidly, as the stock market has boomed since 2008. Although these accounts drain government coffers, they provide a windfall to financial firms. According to the College Savings Plans Network, a group associated with state treasurers, assets invested in these plans rose to almost $250 billion in 2015, from which they collect handsome fees.[36]

## Economic Fact and Fiction

Fiction is an unusual word to use in relation to savings and investment, which more often are characterized as rooted in reasoned analysis of data. But anthropologists and sociologists who have studied the finance sector have shown that economists, financial analysts, derivatives traders, hedge fund managers, and even central bankers develop scenarios of the future and create models of financial decision-making that are premised on imagination. Investors and traders anticipate the future by creating fictional expectations of market activities that guide where they place their bets.[37] Central bankers also carefully craft stories about the future of economic conditions and activities to guide consumer behavior and that of businesses, governments, and investors. They set expectations about how markets will influence economic decision-making from producing cars to trading stocks, buying food, and saving. Their influence coordinates expectations, organizing the market they seem simply to describe, anthropologist Douglas Holmes argues.[38] In this perspective, economic choices are based as much on imaginative projection as on hard facts and solid reasoning.[39]

The line between economic fact and fiction has never been a clear one. Social historian and literary scholar Mary Poovey revealed in her book *Genres of the Credit Economy* that seminal economic thinkers, such as Adam Smith, deployed imaginative scenarios in establishing their theories. Smith, for example, used allegorical tales to support his analysis.[40] Thorstein Veblen placed aspirations for social ascendance at the center of his theory of the American economy. "Conspicuous consumption"—and all the manufacturing, buying, and selling it requires—relies on imaginations of upper-class tastes as those lower on the class ladder attempt to emulate those atop the social hierarchy. Another eminent economist of the twentieth century explicitly promoted the role of inventive future-thinking in a healthy economy. John Maynard Keynes elicits the vision of patriotic housewives, husbands, and nations, encouraging them all "to see schemes of greatness and magnificence" and to design and carry them out.[41]

Narratives help investors and traders, housewives and husbands look forward enough to decide how to act in the present. So even while the student finance complex describes the logic of investment as incontrovertible—that the facts show that risk lies only in *not* following the program—it is really telling its own story. The one sure fact about the future is that knowledge of it can only ever be a matter of fiction. Although those who fail to plan are subject to accusations that they indulge in whims and that they defend themselves only with short-sighted and self-serving justifications, those who promote the idealized planning narrative commit their own folly and serve their own largely unacknowledged interests. In her book *Pound Foolish,* financial pundit Helaine Olen rued the fictitious nature of her advice and the harm it may have done. Looking back at her years as a personal finance columnist for the *Los Angeles Times,* she concluded that her column gave readers a dangerous "illusion of control."[42]

Promoters of planning have promulgated a narrative that foresight and responsibility can secure the future. This morality tale obscures the conflicts middle-class and lower-income families actually face and obstructs the vision necessary to acknowledge the need for assistance and to design it well. It also endorses a political imagination that sees college within the too-narrow confines of the nuclear family and its future.

# CHAPTER 3

# The Model Family

...

Sorting papers into piles on the kitchen table, Bruce Kaminsky sits down before his laptop. Welcome late-winter sunlight streams through the bare trees of his suburban Michigan yard and floods the little kitchen nook he sits in. Come May's warmer glow, his wife, Peggy, will gather her graduating seniors on the porch just outside. They will toast their hard work and their alma mater, the state university where Peggy teaches. Peggy and Bruce's oldest son, Tom, is himself heading into his last year of college, and Bruce settles in to get on with the family business of applying for Tom's student aid.

Winter marks a ritual time for college students and their families. Before students can enroll each year, they must arrive at a financial agreement with both the federal government and a college or university. Filling out the Free Application for Federal Student Aid—the FAFSA, as it's commonly called—is the first step. As the entry point for obtaining financial assistance, the form ushers all young adults and their families into the federal aid wing of the student finance complex. The Department of Education processes twenty million of these forms every year.[1]

Bruce clicks his way into the FAFSA website. With another son, Aidan, in his junior year of high school, the cost of college weighs heavily on Bruce's mind. This is his fourth go-round with the FAFSA, and he launches into filling it in like a professional. Bruce has agreed to walk me through the process with him. "It's not so complicated," he claims, but it sure looks that way to me.

Intended to assemble an accurate picture of family finances, the FAFSA appears much like any other tedious form to fill in, though perhaps longer than most, made up of 105 fields comprising a seven-section spreadsheet. It starts by asking about the student: citizenship status, marital status, state of residence, gender, selective service registration (if male, since only men are subject to military draft), drug conviction record, education completed, savings, and income as reported to the IRS. The next section asks for information about the student's parents. Here the requests become more complicated for applicants to address. The form is written as though students are filling it in—though parents often do—and it acknowledges that some of the information asked for may be difficult for them to provide and that the effort to obtain it may strain family relationships, such as when parents do not cooperate easily or are divorced. A twelve-question section of frequently asked questions details some of the challenges students may face gathering the correct information. For those with still more problems, the FAQ section provides a number to call at the Department of Education: 1-800-4FED-AID.

The process of obtaining information can be tricky and unsettling. Consider, for instance, that even when students do not live with two parents, they must nonetheless provide the Social Security numbers of both, as well as report their income. These requests can be very hard to make, especially for students whose parents are difficult, absent, or unavailable. The information required gets much more detailed too. It includes the levels of education of both parents, their savings, their national service statuses, and any payments they receive from other government programs, such as food aid or disability assistance. If parents are divorced and with split custody, the student applicant must indicate which parent pays more than half of their overall parental financial support.

Other requests the form makes seem straightforward in theory; however, when applicants begin to answer, difficult questions arise. In order to fill out the form, applicants can be forced to distort their own family's contours and resources, such as how many people are living in their household. Many households have fluid boundaries, and the mix of household members departs from the depiction that the form allows applicants to portray. The form determines that household members must be limited to the student applicant, the parents living with them, other children under the age of twenty-four at home, and other children of the student applicant's parents who receive more than half their support from them, even if they don't live in the home. This potentially leaves out family members and responsibilities to others the family honors, such as to grandparents.

Even determining who is a parent can be a problem (figure 3.1). The FAFSA's definition of parents does not track neatly with the realities of many families. People who provide parental care may include grandparents, foster parents, legal guardians, widowed stepparents, aunts, uncles, and siblings. Yet the only parents that count for the FAFSA are biological and adoptive parents, and they must be included no matter whether or not the relationship stands solid or where the parents reside.

The questions the FAFSA leaves out are just as important as the makeup of the ones it requires families to answer. Other aspects of an applicant's family life and their resources are not offered space on the form. It does not ask, for example, about financial support a family extends to relatives or friends who fall outside the narrow legal definition of dependence. They might

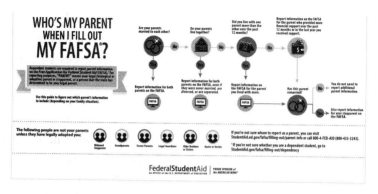

FIGURE 3.1. With this flowchart, the Department of Education acknowledges the trouble its definition of parents may cause for applicants.

send money to support a cousin's physical therapy, or to help out an unemployed aunt, or support an applicant's grandparent. None of this is registered as a legitimate responsibility that government might take into account for the purpose of determining how much aid a family needs. The FAFSA also fails to ask about many other types of expenses that drain household coffers. Credit card and other kinds of debt, transportation bills, and medical costs cannot be reported. Instead the Department of Education applies a standard formula that allows a generic cost of living.

The FAFSA also blinds itself to the wealth middle-class families build up through the accumulation of equity in the value of homes and in their tax-advantaged retirement accounts. This unstated benefit to families who have built these assets affords a rarely discussed privilege.[2] These families' financial resources may be considerably more robust than the FAFSA image of their ability to pay for college conveys. At the same time, other families may have fewer resources available; their expenses are hidden from the Department of Education's view.

The FAFSA's assessment of resources requires defining a vision of where families begin and end, what their legitimate responsibilities are, and selecting which resources will be counted. Although the form gives the appearance of meticulous measurement, its apparent exactitude leads to flawed portrayals. Even with all the details it requests, the form fragments complicated and rich histories and relationships into informational bits. When that data is reassembled into an image of a family and its finances, it is often one that family members don't recognize.[3] In short, the process of assessing need imposes a definition of family that distorts the resources and responsibilities of families' lives as they actually live them.

This inaccuracy is inevitable. Forms like the FAFSA reduce more complicated realities by their nature. Bureaucracy's work depends on such simplifications and standardizing grids. They are essential to modern governments, as political scientist and anthropologist James Scott has pointed out, because they render households "legible" to central administrative agencies.[4] But such forms are always more than data collection devices; they mandate moral strictures about how families should conduct their lives that will enable citizens to fit themselves into their cells.

Embedded in the FAFSA's questions—both the ones asked and the ones left out—lies a set of implicit judgments about how families have lived, how they've managed their household finances, and how they should behave if they want to benefit from government largesse. The directives begin by limiting the scope of the family: nuclear families are the ideal. They continue by defining responsibility in ways that enforce the boundaries of the nuclear family: parents should limit their support to themselves and their children. The form also carries messages about how couples should conduct their relations: they should share financial power and responsibilities between them, closely monitor their saving and spending, and communicate openly, even after divorce.

The FAFSA directs nuclear families to share responsibility for major middle-class milestones, especially paying for college education and securing retirement for parents. The form highlights, implicitly, that home ownership plays a central role in making good on both the sanctioned form of family life and its goals. Owning a home ties nuclear families together across generations. Homes not only create a space where parents and children can live together; they are assets that facilitate both parents' and children's success along the nuclear family's authorized path. First, a house represents an investment in children's education— since parents buy homes for the school district as much as for shelter. Strong local schools pave the way to college. The equity families can build in homes is also an educational resource because they can draw on it when it's time for their children to enroll. Home equity can also support parents' later-life financial security, supplementing their Social Security income with profits from a sale. The FAFSA advises students and parents that ownership of a home, by a nuclear family, is the ideal.[5]

The FAFSA's final instruction is that managing the family's financial information is a private matter, one that couples and their kids should manage at their own kitchen tables. The online form is designed to support families to file for aid discreetly, without needing to ask for assistance that would bring outsiders into the self-contained sphere of the family. If students and their parents successfully supply answers to the form's requests, they can receive government support for college education without intrusion by government agents or visits to government offices.

The FAFSA represents what I think of as a "moral technology," a device that delivers and enforces cultural and economic mandates. As a moral technology, the FAFSA form turns abstract ideas about how families should live into an instrument that families must apply to their lives. The FAFSA is an example of a particular type of moral technology, however; a material document that mediates between governments and citizens. Even when such a technology is inscribed in pixels on a screen, it's a "graphic artifact," to use anthropologist Matthew Hull's term. The moral strictures of these technologies are not spelled out explicitly, and they derive much of their power from the fact that their mandates remain unstated. Agencies, like those of the federal government, present these forms as transparent; they seem to simply request important content, not to carry it. This "graphic ideology" drapes moral power in bureaucratic garb, concealing it in plain sight under an appearance of technical neutrality and disinterest.[6]

The interviewees in my study did not generally perceive the FAFSA form as a powerful conveyor of moral instruction, and they expressed no resistance to its requirements. Students and parents who conformed to its moral mandates understood the form to be a necessary, if tedious, part of the aid process. Those who struggled with it felt they had no choice; they had to force their family into meeting its requirements or forgo aid. In short, although the FAFSA is written in the wan hand of the accountant, it rings with the moral voice of the preacher.

The model family life endorsed in the FAFSA—one that is neat and nuclear, with boundaries that end at the threshold of the home and with two parents who share financial planning responsibilities, freely and regularly communicating about expenses and working together to build savings—was only ever an ideal. It was promoted by the government, schools, and industry. It was always a chimera, but now even the fantasy has become badly outmoded.

## The Middle-Class Model

This idealized model of family life is so ingrained in American culture that, for those whose lives don't chafe against its strictures, it can be difficult to see. Such terms for family life have not always prevailed, however, and their history reveals their moral construction. In the early twentieth century, new principles for middle-class family conduct reshaped the prevailing ethics about family life and economics, establishing the model brought to life in the FAFSA.

At the end of the nineteenth century, husbands' wages lay mostly in their own control. Men were given their pay at the workplace, and they could keep the money for themselves, spending what they liked and offering their wives only what they chose. Reformers concerned that men were flouting their family responsibilities, heading for saloons with their earnings rather than home to their wives and children, agitated for a new norm. Whether or not husbands drinking away their wages was as pervasive a problem as the reformers asserted, the prevailing custom did not give wives grounds to demand information about the family finances or control over spending.

A burgeoning middle class positioned itself as the steward of a new kind of family and a new way of managing the household economy. Rejecting the custom of sole male economic control, middle-class families increasingly accepted a new proposition: that they should create a more "modern" way to live. In particular, husbands and wives should work together to elevate the family's social and economic standing. The new model family should organize itself around planning for the future. Defining their aspirations together, couples should carefully define long-term goals, organizing their finances to meet them. Education held a central place in this vision because earning a college degree would open the door to better-paying and higher-status jobs, facilitating the family's social rise. These characteristics of middle-class family life would distinguish them from those below their station, both economically and socially, advocates averred.[7]

The new scientific field of home economics promoted this novel family life by creating a new American concept: the household budget. In magazine columns and college classrooms, these experts taught that husbands and wives should, together, record their spending and saving with care in a small book so that they could reach their goals. Monitoring the family budget inculcated power-sharing between spouses. It also helped institutionalize aspiration as a core middle-class value, creating a material testament to a couple's commitment to the financial management that achieving aspirations required.

Today many middle-class families take for granted that finances and family goals should be developed together, not only between spouses but even, selectively, with children. Parents might teach children about financial planning, for example, by instructing them about how to open a savings account once they are making some money from an after-school job. The FAFSA form reinforces this standard of family conduct, encoding family power-sharing as the precondition for aid.

Power-sharing, particularly between spouses, is part of the FAFSA's code of model conduct. Married parents are expected to share their financial information freely and truthfully and work together to achieve their vision of the future. The underlying message is that communication and financial truth-telling between married partners are critical to establishing a family on a middle-class trajectory, both to achieve middle-class benchmarks and, increasingly, to create the conditions that will support a lasting marriage itself. Many married interviewees described power-sharing around finances as central to their unions. Many of those in divorced families highlighted that open communication between exes bolstered their prospects of getting aid.

Families who are able to comply with this standard of communication can request aid on favorable terms without reflecting much on the process. But for many families, this is simply not feasible, and the demand to share information can hamper applications. As young adults attempt to fulfill the FAFSA's requirements, they can be put in the painful position of mediating between warring exes or trying to crowbar financial information from parents who are reluctant to give it. In addition to pressuring families to conduct their lives in ways that are unrealistic and might also be undesirable, imposing the need to ask for sensitive information from an uncooperative or absent parent can also ignite trouble within families.

Take the case of Emma Lutz, a student at NYU who was forced to try to pry information from her noncooperative mother, a process that went on for months during the school year and through her final exam period. The Department of Education had selected her FAFSA form for "verification." Every year, approximately one-third of FAFSA forms are selected by a risk model. The Department of Education keeps the calculations under wraps, but it states that it looks for inconsistencies across data points in family reports. Suspect filers are then asked to send in proof of the information provided.[8] Emma told us that she always forgets the word *verification* when she thinks about the months of struggle this process required. Instead the dreaded word *audit* comes to mind. "It felt like an audit," she related, "because it was just prying into all of our lives."

When Emma asked her mother for the financial documentation needed to corroborate the financial information she had provided, her mother stonewalled her. That was surprising because, when she was selecting a college, both of her parents had been very detailed in figuring out what they could pay. That was despite the fact that, at the time, they were barely on speaking terms. They had divorced when she was thirteen, and her father had left Southern California to chase work with his new wife. But when it came time for college, the exes sat down with their daughter. "We spent a long time with whiteboards," Emma described. Her mom "wrote out the dollar signs and broke it down by month." Their calculations yielded amounts that each parent would contribute for the year. Emma was impressed. "It was a very pragmatic breakdown of expenses: what I was projected to get in scholarships and what I would take out in loans." She signed the documents and enrolled in the private East Coast university.

It was during her freshman year that the Department of Education told her she would have to verify her FAFSA information with documentation and Emma turned to her mother for help. Her mother had always resisted the expectations of authorities, but she'd been a consistent and stable source of support for Emma and her refusal seemed out of character. It turned out that Emma's mother was in financial trouble, battling with the lender that had provided her mortgage. She didn't want to provide her financial documentation because she feared the disclosure would compromise her situation with the bank. Emma was forced to negotiate between the university, which was acting as the verification agent for the Department of Education, and her mother.

Meanwhile, Emma found it difficult to understand exactly what documentation would satisfy the Department of Education's demands. Although she did manage eventually to complete the verification, the struggle's stress took its toll. She became distracted and anxious, feeling undermined by her mother, unsupported by her school, and threatened by the federal government. The FAFSA's demands for particular family conduct created a spiral of vulnerability: a precarious financial situation at home generated peril for Emma's schooling.

The ideal of a nuclear middle-class family can end up punishing even families that comport with the nuclear ideal. They too can end up in challenging situations that the FAFSA's assistance doesn't account for. To see how even these families can be trapped by the model's strictures, let's return to Bruce Kaminsky and his application process, and take a closer look at the story of his family and their experience.

## A Model Family

As I sit quietly beside Bruce, he pulls out a W-2 form that lists his wife's salary and enters it into one of the FAFSA fields. He then enters his own from memory. Unlike for Emma's family and others, the form's questions do not cause much trouble for Bruce. He and Peggy have conducted their life together very much in accordance with the moral mandates the FASFA embodies. Bruce can answer its questions easily, and in the terms of the FAFSA's cells their family situation looks neat. But they have a history of financial uncertainty and their future looks taxed, despite conforming to the form's expectations and being much better off than most American middle-class families. The form conceals these aspects of their lives.

"We're lucky, of course," Bruce says to me as he continues filling out the FAFSA. As a social scientist who teaches at one of Michigan's state universities, he knows the basic statistics of the middle-class squeeze. He knows, for instance, that the median household income in the United States has barely budged since before the Great Recession, hovering at around $57,000, and that

Michigan's median stands lower, at around $53,000 per household.[9] Bruce and Peggy's combined income is well above this level. They are both professors (Peggy is also a social scientist) with full-time secure jobs. Their level of educational attainment also sets them apart. Only about one-third of US citizens have received a bachelor's degree and 2 percent hold PhDs, which both Bruce and Peggy have earned.

Their vision for their children's education also distinguishes the family from most others in the US. Although they are encouraging each of their sons to follow his own path, they raised the boys with the assumption that they would attend college and graduate with a degree. This expectation was so unquestioned that Bruce and Peggy spoke about it with their sons only indirectly, asking questions to help the boys define their particular interests and laying out the options for which schools might best cultivate their talents.

The length and strength of their marriage also sets Bruce and Peggy apart. The two met during their college years, on an airplane returning to school in Boston from visiting their families in western Pennsylvania. They married in their early twenties and have been together ever since, which is no longer the norm for American families. Although well-educated and well-off Americans are more likely to stay in an original marriage, for most middle-class and working-class Americans, divorce and remarriage—what sociologist and demographer Andrew Cherlin calls the "marriage-go-round"—are quite common.[10]

Yet even with so many positives in their corner, and even though they have been conscientious about their finances, Bruce and Peggy find themselves short on savings for retirement, and they'll be working past age sixty-five to make up the difference. Their story of later-in-life success highlights how the FAFSA's family model delineates more than a particular nuclear shape and corresponding set of behaviors. The model also assumes a particular trajectory through middle-class life, with work, children, college, and retirement lined up neatly along a defined path. The rewards of middle-class life depend on milestones coming together just so, on a timeline few today can count on but that continues to affect the assistance families receive from the student finance complex.

The puzzle pieces of Bruce and Peggy's family story did not always fit together as neatly as the contours of their current family situation might imply. As they built their careers and raised their sons, they faced unpredictable twists and turns, navigating not along a clear path but amid the economic uncertainties that have come to mark middle-class life.

Bruce is the primary financial manager of the family, a role he enjoys. That's in part because he and Peggy have always tended to their finances conscientiously and they've seen eye to eye about their goals and how to spend their money to achieve them. For many years, though, they had to spend most of their income simply to make ends meet, and they could put away little in savings. Their first son, Tom, was born in 1993, not long after they finished graduate school, and his younger brother, Aidan, was born a few years later.

Bruce and Peggy were keenly aware that they would need to plan carefully to secure themselves financially and solidify their place in the middle class, especially to provide their children with the education that would allow them to do as well, or perhaps even rise higher in the pecking order. Though they were both close to their parents, they would not be able to turn to them for financial assistance. Both grew up near Pittsburgh, and in Peggy's family, most of the men worked in the steel mills, even after her grandfather died in an accident on the shop floor. Her father was an exception. He studied welding, and when he returned from the Philippines, where he was stationed in World War II, he got a job repairing switchboards for AT&T and became a union steward. The work paid well, and the family moved to a suburb.

When Peggy first met Bruce's parents, she was sure she was marrying up. The first time she brought her dad to meet them (her mom had died during her senior year in high school), Bruce's mother opened the door wearing a tennis outfit. They paid another woman to clean their house. Peggy's family ate out only on Mother's Day; Bruce and his parents went to restaurants all the time. What Peggy couldn't see was their mounting debt and the shrinking profit statements at the furniture store they owned, where Bruce worked as a teenager. Starting in the 1970s, larger retailers—Levitz and other discount houses—came to the area and their business dissolved little by little. They eventually declared bankruptcy. In their tight-knit town, Bruce's dad was able to find work as a salesman for others. As he aged, neuropathy in his legs inhibited his ability to meet with customers, yet he continued to work until the day he died.

As Bruce and Peggy embarked on their own life together, they expected to be able to save up enough to pay for half of their sons' tuition, room, and board. The assumption was reasonable, given what seemed to be their career prospects and the costs of college at that time. Both had recently completed their degrees at one of the country's most respected universities. They knew that finding faculty positions was not going to be easy, though, especially finding two in the same city. Still, they each had a PhD, and in 1993, when their first child was born, a year of undergraduate tuition and fees at a four-year public college in the US only cost around $4,500 (in 2017 dollars), or just under $11,000 including room and board.[11] The future they envisioned seemed entirely plausible. Unpredictable circumstances, however, prohibited them from saving as they had planned.

They tried for years to find permanent professorship positions in the same city, but couldn't make that happen. The first of them to get a secure job was Peggy, at a university in Michigan. The family moved there in 1997, hoping that eventually Bruce would also find a job nearby. They found a cheerful home to buy for $118,000 with a spacious backyard. The town's schools were strong and Peggy's office was just a ten-minute drive from the house. Even if Bruce had to take a job further afield than they hoped, one parent, at least, would always be close to their boys. Sure enough, after an exhaustive job search, Bruce took on a punishing four-hour commute to teach in Indiana.

To manage, Bruce had to stay over weeknights in a rental apartment, leaving Peggy to parent their two young sons alone except on weekends, when he would return to his family eager but exhausted from the drive. His rent cut substantially into the family income. They could still afford their new mortgage, but they had to stretch their budget to do what they thought was important for their financial future. The 1,300 square foot home not only provided the comfortable nest they wanted for themselves and their kids, it was a fundamental component of building the future they envisioned across the long trajectory of their lives.

Their monthly payments would allow them to build equity that would support them in their retirement years. The mortgage would not be paid off until they were seventy, but if they needed to, they could sell it and realize a good profit, they believed. That would allow them to be autonomous in their old age, not imposing their financial needs on their children, which would help their sons start their own families.[12] The house purchase would also assure that their sons went to good primary schools, preparing them to gain admission to college and start them on their own middle-class life trajectory. They believed, as many middle-class families do, that stretching the budget to buy into a neighborhood that gave access to strong schools was an investment in both their children's futures and their own.

At the same time that Bruce and Peggy were buying their home, families across the country were struggling as a result of exactly this decision. Researchers Teresa Sullivan, Elizabeth Warren (now Senator Warren), and Jay Westbrook found that, in the 1990s, the most likely group to declare bankruptcy were two-income couples whose mortgages pushed the boundaries of their incomes. A job loss or illness could quickly tip them into bankruptcy.[13] Others, including Bruce and Peggy, who lucked into good health and benefited from steady work, managed to skate along the knife-edge of this vulnerability, their fragility concealed.

Bruce and Peggy consulted the balance of equity and interest on their mortgage stub every month, and they never missed a payment, even in the difficult years. Each spring they received the federal government's reward for their diligence, their home mortgage tax deduction. This boon for middle-class families adds to the value of mortgage payments, boosting economic benefits of home ownership.

Other than their growing home equity, their expenses meant that Bruce and Peggy built up little household savings. And then Bruce's parents began to need financial support. Starting when Tom was seven, they gave hundreds of dollars a month to Bruce's parents for a period of twelve years. Bruce's father passed away in 2002, and his mother was left with few resources. When her health began failing at age ninety, Bruce and his siblings could not afford to pay for in-home care without damaging their own future security. They also couldn't afford the assisted living facilities where many of his mother's neighbors resided. Fortunately, with a few savvy financial moves, their mother qualified for nursing home care under Medicaid. They sold off her car and converted a life insurance policy to burial insurance, which Medicaid would allow her to keep. She lived until she was ninety-three.

Other expenses they felt they could not forgo cut into Bruce and Peggy's savings. One was travel costs to present their research at conferences. The state universities where they each worked covered only a fraction of these expenses, even though building their scholarly profiles was central to their jobs. They also paid for their sons to be members of a travel soccer team and for oboe lessons. Their sons' friends were involved in such activities, and they wanted to allow their children to pursue their passions for sports and music as well. They were cognizant that their college savings were not accumulating as they'd planned, but they reasoned they'd figure out how to cover the expenses later.

As their boys' college years approached, they sat down to assess their financial situation and realized they were in a bind. Their salaries had grown, as had their benefits, and they were able to hold on to more of their income after Bruce's mother passed away. Their home, though, was not proving to be the secure asset they imagined. Its value plummeted in 2008. They appreciated the painful irony: As Tom approached his college years, according to the FAFSA measures their financial picture looked strong. Aid programs wouldn't consider either their compromised retirement nest egg or the credit card debt that they'd accumulated.

They did receive one unexpected financial windfall: a modest inheritance from Peggy's father, who passed away when Tom was in high school. Peggy and Bruce had not had to contribute any financial support for her parents. Her sister had stayed near their parents, supporting them in the daily details of their lives. Her older brother had joined together with her father to buy an apartment, which they rented, and her father's share of the rental income supported him in his old age.

After her father passed away, Peggy's brother sold the apartment, the value of which had appreciated dramatically, and Peggy inherited $40,000 from her father's estate. She opened an account with the Michigan Education Savings Program and deposited half. The other half she placed in a savings account, reasoning that, although these funds were for her boys' college educations, they could also be available for rainy days. And good thing too: Two broken car transmissions and a roof replacement ate into the money substantially.

When Tom decided to attend the nearby state university, Bruce and Peggy took another close look at their financial situation. As they reported their income and assets on the FAFSA form for the first time, the details of their family histories were much on their minds. When they opened Tom's aid package, they found out that the family would need to pay $27,910. They would get $7,500 in unsubsidized loans, no scholarships or grants, and no work-study support. That left Bruce and Peggy responsible for just over $20,000 for the year.

The amount left from Peggy's inheritance had lost about 15 percent of its value since the 2008 crash, but there was still enough to pay for the family's contribution to the first year of college and then some. The problems, they could see, would come when the account was drained, which happened Tom's junior year when Aidan was also enrolling in college. For Aidan's private university, their family contribution climbed past $35,000. For Peggy, the FAFSA's financial image of their family was shocking. "That a middle-class family like ours can come up with $38,000 in a given year (with some loans) is enough to throw you into a fetal position," she related. "Somehow we have done it, but it does not mean that it is easily doable."

Bruce and Peggy are approaching sixty. They feel lucky that their teaching jobs are not physically demanding and remain secure. Both will need to keep working beyond the benchmark age for retirement. Both have also taken on work outside their full-time jobs. The extra teaching helps them make the college payments and wards off drawing more from their retirement savings than they've already had to. Securing the opportunities they want their sons to have for their futures has come at the cost of uncertainty about their own.

Bruce and Peggy have done all they could do to build secure middle-class lives. Still, even if they'd saved all they planned around the time of Tom's birth, they would have fallen short on funding their boys' college educations. That is because just before Tom was born the twin forces that have reshaped the landscape of middle-class economic life gained momentum. College costs began their steady upward climb, while at the same time policy shifted, requiring families to pay more while government contributed less to higher education. There was no way to plan for those sea changes. If any parents might have been able to foresee how high college costs would go, Peggy and Bruce were well positioned as college professors to do so. They had seen the state of Michigan fall into recession years before the national one hit, and the state cut back funding for the universities, shifting the burden to students and their families. In 2000, attending Michigan's universities cost in-state students about $6,600 in annual tuition and fees, or just under $14,000, counting room and board, in 2017 dollars.[14] By the time Tom was ready to enroll in 2011, the same universities were charging Michigan residents nearly $21,000 per year for tuition, room, and board.[15]

The moral mandates of the FAFSA, and the broader student financial complex, simply do not acknowledge the unpredictability of life in the middle class today even for families that conform to its nuclear model and financial precepts. For families that do not conform, the student finance complex can be more punishing. For still others, however, the mismatch between the outdated ideal and their situations can present unintended opportunities.

## Gaming the System

Although the FAFSA draws a precise portrait of a family's life, that profile is rarely accurate. This gap between the image and practice opens opportunities for some applicants to take advantage of the FAFSA's measurement schema and game the system. Consider one family who used a common piece of creative accounting available to families with cooperative exes. When Sarah divorced her husband, his finances were already on the rocks. "He lives on the edge of foreclosure," she reported. He has been able to keep his house, but only barely. He was never able to hold a job or even take care of a car for long despite his advanced degree and early promise. It did not surprise Sarah that he hadn't gotten on his feet since their separation. Still, she and her ex-husband have remained good friends and maintained close communication around parenting their three kids. They share custody, with the children spending equal time with each parent, even as Sarah moved into a new, permanent relationship.

In the years before the federal government recognized same-sex marriages, Sarah wed her new sweetheart in Massachusetts; their union was not recognized by their home state of Pennsylvania or by the federal government for a number of years. Sarah and her wife worried about the expense of college, and they predicted that by the time Sarah's children were of that age, their marriage would be officially sanctioned by both the state and federal government, which would qualify Sarah's wife as a stepparent. Because stepparents' incomes must be reported on the FAFSA form, and her wife's income was somewhat higher than Sarah's pay as a clinic counselor, they were concerned that they would not get substantial assistance through the FAFSA process. With the costs of college so high, and with the children's father able to contribute little, their expenses would be stretched.

As they became more familiar with the FASFA requirements, they realized that Sarah's ex-husband's poverty could prove useful. The Department of Education stipulates that the parent who files the form should be the one with whom a child resides a majority of the time. In the case of joint custody with equal time, the parent who provides more financial support shoulders the responsibility. Because Sarah and her ex-husband split custody straight down the middle, and because she contributes more to their children's support than he does, she was supposed to be the one to file. But the three parents decided to declare the father to be the children's custodial parent instead.

Sarah, and many middle-class parents like her, possesses finely honed bureaucratic skills built over years of navigating assistance systems. Her own higher education and her work as a state clinic counselor have taught her what to do and where the advantages lie. This has given Sarah a confidence few lower-income parents possess. Sarah's shrewd use of the rules turned her family's non-conformity into an economic advantage. Sarah and her coparents gamed the system to win additional aid for their three children's educations. Her family required state assistance no matter what; middle-class families like Sarah's simply cannot send their children to college without help. They count on not only the availability of state funds but also their own aptitudes for unlocking them.

In contrast to Sarah's skillful working of the system, many low- and moderate-income families feel overwhelmed by the FAFSA. In fact, the form itself can create a barrier both to applying for college and to graduating from it. In a field experiment, economist Eric Bettinger and his colleagues worked with H&R Block to assist more than 23,000 individuals seeking their tax assistance with filling out the FAFSA. Their experiment showed that the help filling out the form substantially increased the likelihood of submitting the application, enrolling the following school year, and receiving increased aid. For students applying together with their parents, the effect was particularly strong. Those who got help with the FAFSA were 40 percent more likely to complete and file the form.[16] Two years later the economists checked in with the families that the accountants had helped over the first two years of college. They expected that the students would benefit and they did. Those whose parents had received assistance with the FAFSA were significantly more likely to have completed two years of college in the three years following the experiment.[17] Designed with the implicit assumption of bureaucratic skills middle-class workers often learn, the form can be either a boon or an obstacle to college education.

## The Hidden Touch of Middle-Class Assistance

The FASFA's seeming transparency and the private nature of its process perpetuate a myth of middle-class economic independence. This myth masks just how much these families depend on government aid. The middle class is defined in part by the idea of its economic autonomy, but home ownership and retirement—key middle-class benchmarks—have always required financial supports. In fact, the middle class as we know it today was built on government subsidies both for families and for the financial industries that gave them access to homes and to security later in life. Today middle-class families require financial assistance for higher education too. As government has rolled back supports for free and low tuition, aid for college has become a particularly pressing need. After their home mortgage, higher education represents the second largest investment most American families make.[18]

Despite the government's assistance, the process of applying for federal student aid props up the notion of independence. At the moment when families must reckon with their reliance on the student finance complex, the design of the procedures affirm their self-sufficiency. Families apply for aid at arms-length from government and financial workers, logging onto the Department of Education's website through their own computers and offering up the details of their personal finances and family lives from within the privacy of their homes. The federal government has covered its interventions more fully in recent years too, through a bureaucratic design that automates a key aspect of the application for assistance. Now the Department of Education can download a family's IRS filings directly into the FAFSA form if the applicants choose that option. Such mechanisms smooth the process, creating a feeling of immediacy and ease that masks the detailed monitoring and extensive management around the exchange of data.[19]

The ability to seamlessly integrate Department of Education requests and IRS figures lends a patina of privacy to applying for college aid that is common among middle-class financial transactions. Withdrawing funds from an ATM, for instance, masks communication among accounts and between banks, all of which happens without users ever seeing or experiencing the assessment of balances and ledger transfers that result in the machine dispensing cash.[20] With the FAFSA, conflicts with private IRS data or random verification checks can interrupt this smooth flow, exposing the extent of the student finance complex's interventions into middle-class lives. Even when there are problems with a filing, however, families are afforded a degree of privacy in working out the solutions, as Emma was. Although she was dragged through a stressful and complicated process to resolve discrepancies in her family's FAFSA information, she was not publicly shamed in any way. The conditions of aid establish and maintain a critical dividing line between classes.

In contrast to the privacy afforded to "independent" middle-class student aid applicants, "dependent" lower-income citizens must often submit to obtrusive processes for obtaining aid and expose themselves to censure. Consider the way in which children are treated if the applications for the federally supported free and reduced lunch programs their parents have to file are not filled out properly, or when parents have failed to send in a 40-cent daily copay. School cafeteria workers across the country have been instructed to take these children's trays away from them at the cashier, in front of the other children in line, a practice that has been called "lunch shaming."

Sometimes the cafeteria worker then hands the child a paper bag with a sandwich and milk, which are cold comfort following such humiliation. Other children are left empty-handed and hungry.

The Department of Agriculture, the *New York Times* reported, admitted in 2017 that nearly half of all school districts practice lunch shaming.[21] More recently, several states, led by New Mexico and Pennsylvania, have outlawed lunch shaming. This is only the most recent attack on the dignity of those citizens labeled dependent and therefore unworthy of assistance, however.

Demeaning government intrusion has been the norm for federal programs for lower-income applicants. For instance, early state assistance programs imposed the "man-in-the-house" rule, subjecting recipients to scrutiny of their living arrangements and their sexual relationships. Any male presence in the home could disqualify a woman and her children from receiving aid. The Supreme Court ruled this surveillance practice unconstitutional in 1968. Yet new incursions continue to be proposed. For instance, in March of 2017, Congress opened the door to requiring applicants for unemployment insurance benefits to pee in a cup in order to verify that they are not using drugs.[22]

No such attack on a family's dignity attends applying for the core middle-class supports. In fact, the process reinforces their sense of competence, self-direction, and freedom. Applying for federal student aid is treated as a matter of pure choice. Despite the fact that middle-class families require financial assistance, no state official will sanction a family for failing to submit their forms. The exchange of information for aid appears voluntary, and the loans students and parents receive are awarded as contracts entered into at will. In contrast, the public funds offered to lower-income citizens represent poisoned gifts; the intimidating oversight with which aid is administered damages their dignity even while it may extend necessary financial support. Exclusion from these punishments elevates middle-class families to their place in the social hierarchy.[23]

Compliance is central to the awarding of aid without any apparent coercion. The FAFSA process counts on middle-class families to submit, without resistance or error, and assumes that they will train their children to adopt and maintain this compliant relationship too. Bruce, Peggy, and their son Tom are again exemplary. In the state of Michigan, where they live, getting a driver's license involved another, quite serious, commitment to obedience with government rules. When young men like Tom obtain their license, they are registered with the Selective Service System, the federal database that maintains information about young men who could be drafted into the military. In thirty-one states, Selective Service registration is also required for access to higher education benefits and to government jobs, although Michigan has not enacted such laws.[24] Bruce and Tom, who was named for the 1960s antiwar activist Tom Hayden, were reluctant about the state's requirement of registration to obtain a license, but they accepted it.

Educating children to cooperate with the government generally begins earlier than applying for college, as with getting a driver's license or with the shock of seeing the bite Social Security deductions take from a first paycheck. The FAFSA form takes this to the next level, teaching them more about how the student finance complex and the financial system beyond it requires them to reveal information about their incomes, savings, and their family lives. Learning the ropes of compliance might seem like simple common sense, but the pressure to act according to the family ideal comes along with it, even as a college education promises independence and an open future.

The myth of middle-class independence not only hides the distribution of aid, obscuring the political morality that favors these families, it also encourages families to maintain silence about the challenges they face in sending their children to college and in other matters too. Families again comply because acknowledging the need for assistance endangers their middle-class identity. Financial assistance programs that operate privately abet the mythology of middle-class independence and reinforce the silence. The hidden touch of the state also obstructs a national reckoning with the true legacies of government assistance in building and maintaining the middle class, and it is crucial to obscuring the imposition of moral mandates that press, silently but powerfully, on students and their families.

# CHAPTER 4

# Enmeshed Autonomy

...

Helping children achieve autonomy is a guiding principle for American middle-class families. Across my discussions with parents, they emphasized how college was essential to their goal of enabling young adults to take charge of their own futures. Parents also stressed the need to keep their own end of the autonomy bargain, maintaining their households separately from their adult children once they're on their own, leaving them unencumbered. These long-standing aims have come to involve an unavoidable paradox: independence must be cultivated under conditions not only of intimate connection but also of extended financial assistance. I call this situation *enmeshed autonomy*, and this chapter explores the particular tensions it generates in middle-class family life.[1]

The paradox was created by the political morality that, beginning in the 1980s, shifted primary financial responsibility for college onto the shoulders of middle-class families. The requirement to pay so much for college means that families stretch the expense over decades, from saving (or worrying about not saving) when the children are young, to paying out and taking on debt over the college years, to paying off the loans and making up the savings deficit far into the future. The US is unique among affluent democracies in the way it treats students and their parents. To appreciate the conflicts families face, it is helpful to understand how other countries enable autonomy more fully, despite American cultural commitments to the notion of individual independence.

In the US, the high cost of college and the moral mandates of the student finance complex have led to an open secret on campuses and in homes: for middle-class college students, obtaining autonomy requires extended dependence on their parents. Sometimes this dependence is easy to see, as when children return home after graduation or after they have initially launched out on their own, a phenomenon sociologist Katherine Newman has described as the "accordion family."[2]

The widespread concern over this development underscores the cultural importance of young adult autonomy. Young adults returning to live with their parents raises fears that there has been a fundamental failure somewhere, whether in their upbringing or in the broader economy, which should be able to provide them with jobs that support independent lives. Moving back in with parents might be a well-known trend, but the depth of continuing dependence and the extent to which it has changed the lives of middle-class families may be surprising: in the 1980s, more than half of young adults in their twenties were fully financially independent. Since 2010, almost 70 percent of twenty-somethings have received money from their parents.[3]

This dependence has exposed both young adults and their parents to censure. College graduates who return home or take money from their parents have been criticized for "failure to launch." Psychologists have even identified this pattern as a syndrome and have organized a therapeutic industry around it.[4] As for parents, financial planners and media advisers scold them for putting both their current and future financial security in jeopardy. The responsible way to deal with the strain on their budgets, they lecture, is to put money away and to limit their contributions to their children's college education so they pay only as much as prudent retirement goals allow. They also should not support their children after gradation; college graduates should be able to make it through their twenties on their own.

One common analogy draws on flight attendants' directions to parents traveling with children: in the event of a loss of cabin pressure, they should first strap on their own oxygen masks and only then assist their children. Parents' financial autonomy in their retirement years will prove of even greater value to their children in the long run than current assistance, this comparison suggests, but parents might have to leave their kids struggling for breath in the present. Such a simplistic and strictly financial narrative may appeal to those who believe that economic considerations should always come first and who insist, despite the evidence, that separating parents' and children's fates is possible and desirable. But in practice, it's out of sync with the role that American middle-class parents actually play in their children's budding autonomy. It also conflicts with both the mechanisms and the moral mandates of the student finance complex, which tie young adult children to their parents.

## Financial Ties That Bind

The student finance complex has fostered enmeshed autonomy by speaking with two voices. The Department of Education's Direct Loan Program instructs applicants that funding their degree is their responsibility by compelling students to take out loans in their own names. The message is unmistakable: young adults should separate their finances from those of their parents, which means launching themselves into adulthood with the engine of debt. Even when parents say they will help pay the loans, it's the student who signs on the dotted line, and it's the student who will be held accountable when the payments are due. In taking out loans, students are being told to trade dependence on their families for the "independence" of relying on finance, another paradox.

At the same time, as I've discussed, the government and universities require that middle-class parents play a leading role in the process of applying for loans and other funding, because they—not their children—are the ones who carry the family finances and know the most about them. Financial assistance is linked to a family's wealth, income, and spending; government and universities alike oblige parents to contribute funds, assigning them payments often so hefty that it binds them to their children for many years past graduation.

To determine a family's baseline financial need, the Department of Education applies a formula that encodes the values of the student finance complex but only rarely reflects parents' sense of their own financial lives. Soon after filing the FAFSA, the Expected Family Contribution (EFC) arrives as part of the Student Aid Report, but it gives no indication of how the Department of Education calculated this critical number. This determination affects parents deeply and emotionally, a clash with the bureaucratic commitment to the impersonal and mechanistic nature of the judgment. Parents are unlikely, however, to dig into the elaborate algorithm, which changes yearly and is published annually in the *Federal Register*. It comprises thirty-six pages, most of which are dedicated to walking through the weighting of factors that determine what families will pay.[5] The formula takes a portion of parents' income and sets that aside for living expenses, taking into account dependents at home and enrolled in college. It sets aside some savings and allows that amount for the parents' emergency funds. Recall that the FAFSA also privileges certain types of investments, such as homes and retirement accounts, by excluding them from calculations. The model weighs the remaining income and assets of the parents and the student, coming up with an assessment of the family's "financial strength," which is the formal name for the measure of prosperity and need.

For middle-class families, whose incomes are too high for their children to receive need-based grants but not high enough to pay for college out of pocket, the EFC can come as a shock, especially since the FAFSA often accounts only for a portion of parents' actual expenses, ruling out contributions to older family members or parents' siblings who might need aid, for instance. The gap between what parents think they can pay and what they are expected to pay can grow too, as the application process continues. Colleges and universities apply their own formulas, combining the EFC with their own assessment to craft the full aid package they will offer.[6] Colleges and universities can require more information from families and take into account a greater range of assets, including often the value of the parents' home and their retirement accounts.

The College Board, a not-for-profit organization made up of more than six thousand member educational institutions, designs the College Scholarship Service Profile (known as the CSS Profile). Used by almost four hundred colleges and universities, the application requests information about "additional income," including flexible spending accounts, which employers make available to fund family health and dependent care expenses. Under assets, it also counts the balances that the parents might have accumulated in 529 savings plans both for the student and for any siblings, and it requests details of any business ownership, including market value, debt owed, and gross receipts. Colleges then weight these assets in their calculations of need, often offering less aid than the federal government's calculation advises.

The result of all these calculations is a combined family contribution, which is then subtracted from the college's sticker price, or cost of attendance. The gap is what is considered the family's financial need. To help students and parents fill that gap, colleges and universities offer an array of aid packages. The aid offered varies widely from student to student, but all offers depend on an individual student's eligibility for federal programs, like subsidized work-study jobs on and off campus, as well as subsidized and unsubsidized loans.

After federal programs are exhausted, other judgments of family and student need also come into play. The CSS Profile provides space for students to elaborate "special circumstances" that affect their family's expenses, like a sibling who needs private education because of a learning disability, or a business that foundered in the financial crisis that began in 2008 (the examples the College Board features in its CSS Profile tutorial video). Blameless bad fortune or evaluations of special moral worth may lead colleges to reconsider the standard aid calculations and to extend accommodations and benefits. Some colleges and universities offer funds to students whom they identify as deserving in other ways, providing merit-based aid to students with strong academic records, for instance. These are scholarships that presumably reward hard work, but, in fact, colleges and universities use these awards to address other considerations that have little to do with academic performance.

Colleges are always concerned about their rankings, for instance, and some use merit aid to recruit students with high grades and test scores. These students elevate a school's overall rating, and that, in turn, makes a school more desirable for the next year's applicants. What's more, high rankings confer status on students and, by extension, their parents, helping to bring in more students from families who can afford to pay a higher proportion of costs. These students bring in a double financial benefit for colleges and universities: not only do they pay more in tuition, they cost less in financial aid.

Through "enrollment management," as it is known in the financial aid business, colleges and universities sort students to achieve an optimal balance of higher-paying students and lower-paying ones. Ideally, this process would free up aid funds for lower-income families after higher-paying students were enrolled. In fact, the opposite has happened. The expansion of merit aid has led colleges and universities to give preference in admission to students from middle-class and upper-class families whose grades and test scores reflect their class advantages and has directed scholarship funds toward attracting them. Instead of increasing resources for low-income students, merit aid curtails them. For example, in 2013, a study conducted by the New America Foundation showed that Pennsylvania State University awarded approximately $14 million per year in student scholarships and grants, but that merit aid had hijacked the budget.[7] So much Penn State money was going to students from well-off families that the lowest-income students actually paid more on average than other students higher up the economic ladder.[8]

The elaborate process of calculating need produces unintended consequences. From the vantage point of the government, colleges, and universities, the EFC and the attendant calculations are messy, demanding, and complicated. And the system can impose great strain on families. In a recent national survey of 1,600 undergraduates and their parents conducted by Sallie Mae, one-third of respondents reported that they were "frequently or constantly" anxious about educational expenses. Education costs weighed on families twice as much as either medical or housing expenses, and uncertainty about financial security in the future was the main source of worry.[9]

College aid snares middle-class parents in the moral conflict when schools assign parents a payment that stresses their finances. Parents who've followed the moral scripts for middle-class life by saving, buying a home, and accumulating other assets can feel punished for their virtue. By basing aid evaluations on family income and wealth—tying students to their parents' histories—the student finance complex feeds off families.

Colleges and universities bank on the fact that middle-class families are willing to stretch their finances if it means sending their children to schools they believe will give them the best opportunities. These institutions of higher education know that what they have to offer—the prestige, the classes, the access to peers who can remain lifelong friends and acquaintances—leads parents to feel an ethical commitment to spend whatever they can to help their children gain these advantages. Parents may object to the calculation of the contribution they should make, but if they want to send their children to their chosen school, they are on the hook for whatever that school says.

In my interviews, I found that parents do not take the decision to stretch their own finances lightly; they engage in thorough consideration and think seriously about the trade-offs. They often discuss with their children what ignites their budding passions and what they want their futures to look like, all to reach an understanding of which college options are best for the young adults. Parents ask tough questions of themselves about their moral duties regarding autonomy and the responsibilities each generation owes the other: How much can they really pay? How much should they tell their children about the pressures those expenses will put on their own financial security? Where do their responsibilities to their children begin and end? Their answers to those questions often contradict the dictates of responsibility they hear from financial advisers.

To see the situation through a parent's eyes, and to appreciate the bind that the student finance complex imposes, we must look more closely at the hidden moral directives that go into the calculation of the EFC, the moral mandates levied on parents, and the ways that parents define their own responsibilities and those of their children.

## The Political Morality of Human Capital

The legitimacy of the EFC and the process of assigning need on a case-by-case basis is rooted in a political morality established in the 1980s. The shift of the burden to pay for college onto families was premised, in particular, on the view that getting a college education develops "human capital," a technical terminology that conceals a distinct moral perspective: that college education is first and foremost a private benefit to the family. By contrast, from the mid-twentieth century up to the 1980s, the US government had prioritized higher education for twin reasons. A highly educated citizenry was deemed vital to the nation's prosperity and security; an educated workforce would boost national economic growth, which also strengthens defense. Supporting college educations for more Americans contained a loftier goal as well: it would advance the promise of equal opportunity. These broad national benefits supported the rationale for direct aid to students in the form of grants, as well as subsidies for low-interest loans and other forms of higher education support.

Since the 1980s, the argument that a college degree primarily confers private benefits has justified an analogy that underwrote the expansion of student loans. A college degree should be considered like another major family asset: the home. Advocates of this perspective accept that, like a home, a college education should be an expense borne by families. And they view the rewards of a college education as measurable—as they would be in a home—in the private value that it will deliver over decades, by way of a good job with a solid and growing income. Following this analogy, higher education aid should also carry the essential features of a mortgage. It should be paid for with private debt that spreads the onus over many years.

The morality of the human capital view does support some government assistance for families. Parents and students who do not currently have the cash should have access to government-sponsored loans that can assist them in purchasing the asset of a degree. As economist Sandy Baum highlights, the role of government is to help "solve cash flow problems" by offering loans.[10] The government should *not* be paying for students to go to college, unless that is to correct for family disadvantage (and, even then, with only limited grant funds). Young adults' educations should be reckoned with primarily in economic terms, and families should shoulder the responsibility.

This view has recently come under fire, but it has held sway among policy makers for decades. In fact, this premise of family responsibility is so ingrained in American political morality that it renders alternative approaches to student aid hard to imagine. Contrasting the roles that other countries ask parents to play in their children's college education throws into relief how the morality of human capital has contributed to enmeshed autonomy.

## State-Sponsored Autonomy

Consider Sweden. Contrary to what one might expect of the famously generous welfare state, Swedish students take on levels of college debt that are unusually high among people in the world's affluent countries. Although tuition is free at state universities there, students must pay for room, board, and other expenses, such as books, and the government offers them loans that cover those expenses. No family support is expected or required.[11] Students are considered adults and fully autonomous from their families.

The Swedish government's rationale for free tuition is based on seeing college students foremost as citizens. In the Swedish view, each person's education benefits the nation as a whole as well as the individual, the same rationale used to argue for public primary education and direct support for college in the US. The country's student loan administrator, the Board of Study Support, declares on its website that its mission is "to make it easier to study and thereby contribute to a high level of participation in education."[12] The concept is that students should not have to work for money while they're focusing on their courses. Time spent at a job to support themselves draws students away from the more essential labor of studying and developing projects and plans for both their personal and their national futures. Swedish students' loans divide the responsibility for their education between themselves and their government; students should become autonomous from their parents' financial support when they enter college. The Swedish system unhooks students from the financial condition of their families, freeing them from the weighted histories of their parents and ushering them into adulthood, alongside others of their generation.

Swedish higher education policy is premised on the notion that, for those who win admission, going to college is a social right, as education is in the younger years. The Swedish government declares all Swedes entering college to be equal, separate from the histories they carry forward from their parents. Regardless of their family background, each should start with the same possibilities as an adult. Swedish state support of higher education, the Board of Study Support continues, "is intended to level out the differences between individuals and groups in the population so as to make society fairer."

The systems for college payment in other countries offer interesting variations on the problems of family support, financial responsibility, and children's independence.[13] Germany, for instance, offers free tuition but requires families to support their young adult students' living expenses. If that represents too much to pay, as it might for low-income families, the government extends zero-interest loans to students. They are available specifically to families with incomes below 38,000 euros (about US $42,000). Only about 20 percent of German students graduate with debt. And of those who do take loans, half carry less than 4,000 euros into their adult lives, a sum that they're expected to repay according to their income.[14] Although their families must, legally, support them, students' family histories weigh lightly on their futures.

The same is true in Australia. There public higher education is less expensive than in the United States, but the repayment system is the greater difference. Parents and students don't stress about the impact of paying for college on either the young adults' futures or their own.[15] Australian graduates repay their loans based on their incomes, and they don't pay back at all until they earn the equivalent of about $33,000 per year. Then their repayments are capped at a percentage of their pay, rising to a limit of 10 percent when they cross into affluence at around $97,000.

To date, these international models have had little influence on American policies. In the US, calls for free tuition have gained prominence in recent years and have had significant success at the state level. But the proposal and New York State's free tuition program have drawn criticism from across the political spectrum. After Governor Andrew Cuomo implemented a free tuition plan at the state and city universities for residents with family incomes under $125,000, David Brooks, a conservative op-ed columnist for the *New York Times*, voiced one common objection.[16] Free tuition is regressive, Brooks argued, because it aids affluent families who don't need financial assistance, and it directs assistance dollars away from low-income students. In effect, he argues, a great deal of the tax money devoted to covering tuition costs will be going to those who don't need it. The liberal Brookings Institution has argued against free tuition on the same grounds. According to a 2016 Brookings report, eliminating tuition would deliver 24 percent more dollar value to families with incomes in the upper half than to those in the lower half of the income distribution.[17] *The Atlantic* voiced a second objection based on higher education's private benefit. Students will earn more based on their college educations, so they should pay.[18]

Critics of free tuition at public colleges and universities in the US also point to other problems. Arguing against free tuition based on free market principles, they claim it would give unfair advantage to those institutions over private schools in competing for students. Private colleges join the chorus in making this case. The narrowness of the debate hides as much as it illuminates. A better system does not necessarily require free tuition; it requires only that aid conditions support an open future for young adults and don't place an undue burden on parents. The student aid systems in Sweden, Germany, and Australia enable students to move into their adult lives without their parents providing much, if any, support to them; the US system links students to their families for well into their adult lives, drawing down parents' resources at the very same time that they nudge their children toward autonomy.

The financial stress of college on American middle-class and lower-income families is hardly inevitable. It results from a prevailing political morality that establishes a specific way to treat students and their families, and a specific strategy for distributing the burden of responsibility. In the halls of think tanks and the back rooms of legislatures, the student debt problem is presented as an economic problem in need of a technical solution. But looking at other nations' programs for supporting students shows that the American system is based on culturally distinctive, and largely unspoken, arguments about the relationship between students, families, society, and the state that deserve critical attention.

## Generational Responsibilities

In my interviews, parents described an ideal division of generational responsibilities linked to a broad middle-class cultural imperative: parents should support themselves free from assistance from others, and they should support the freedom of the next generation by funding their children's education. Young adults, if they reach middle-class status, will be expected to do the same. Still, parents accepted their obligation to provide financial support for their children as long as these monies assisted their children in pursuing their independence. The costs of college were paramount in this commitment.

Both parents and students were exquisitely attuned to the issue of dependence that paying for college often entails, and neither parents nor children wanted to contribute to the other's insecurity in ways that might lead parents to require financial help in later life or that would undermine children's burgeoning autonomy. Relying too much on each other as adults would fray the boundaries between households and blur the desired autonomy of the generations. The fact that they have to pay for college, and often pay more than they feel they can bear, makes both parents and children anxious about the limits of their independence. The financial ties of enmeshed autonomy do not allow a clean separation.

Parents and children both used the language of burdening to explain the pressures they felt living within enmeshed autonomy. Whenever parents or young adults described a fear about "being a burden," it pointed to a clear set of culturally laden anxieties about threatening the independence of others. The feeling came up often. One-third of my interviewees used the concept of being a burden when they discussed the financial relationships between generations; many others expressed the same apprehensions in other language.

In the leading dictionary definitions of the word, *burden* is described as a load on the body, but the characterization quickly moves from physical to moral weight. A burden is likened to a duty, although not all responsibilities are laden with the word's crushing affect. A burden is an obligation carried on the back and in the spirit. It is a responsibility, or a feeling of oppression borne with anxiety. Parents worried about encumbering their young adult children; young adult children worried about taxing their parents.

When they imagined themselves as burdens, parents and young adults expressed concern that they might be a weight that the other should not have to carry. Using the anthropologist Mary Douglas's classic formulation, being a burden figured parents and young adults as "matter out of place" within the other's sphere of independence.[19] As a burden, the parent or young adult crossed an essential symbolic boundary, posing a danger to family members whom they otherwise seek to protect. Most troubling to parents was the possibility that their financial situations would threaten their young adults' development. They feared that their children would have to carry them not across space, as a physical load would require, but across time. They wanted to avoid becoming a drag on their children's futures. Burdens work explicitly against open futures; they bind young adults to the weight of their parents' pasts.

## Burdens of History

The burdens of the past can come from personal limitations, such as the financial straits that come with divorce, or from failures to support a family in the manner a parent would like. They can also come from outside, from histories of discrimination and inequalities that have shaped the economic conditions of a family's life across generations. Parents look to release their children from the restrictions their histories can impose.

The Baker family has managed to do so for their daughter, Karen, who attended Princeton University. She is the first in her family to attend college right out of high school, let alone an Ivy League school. Karen's younger brother, Owen, is also now in college. Their parents—Donna and Russell—have structured their family life to protect their children from the burden of their histories.

Donna expressed their strong, shared belief that their core job as parents was to support their children's launch into autonomy. As with so many parents we interviewed, she saw a commitment to funding a college education as vital to that mission. Donna and Russell have themselves used college degrees as stepping stones, and they hope their children can rise even further. Both Donna and Russell are African American, and their story illustrates both the strains that middle-class families endure under enmeshed autonomy and the especially acute problems the history of discrimination against African Americans imposes.

Neither Donna nor Russell took a direct route to college. They met in high school and married shortly after, and Russell quickly enlisted in the Army. They moved regularly, at the whim of the Army, and Donna found whatever work she could and picked up credits at local community colleges along the way. She had Karen five years into their marriage and Owen two years later. Even as a young mother, Donna earned enough credits for two associate's degrees, which she eventually parlayed into a career as a paralegal. Russell took advantage of the Army's higher education program after he had served in both Operation Desert Shield and Operation Desert Storm. He completed his associate's degree while they were stationed at Fort Bragg in North Carolina, and earned his bachelor's and master's degrees later.

The Bakers instilled their commitment to education in their children. Donna described the importance of education in their family by relaying the lessons she taught her children, that college would open possibilities and the degree would bring independence: "Karen and Owen knew that they had to make the best grades that they could make so that they could have the most options that they could get. Then they could help define their own futures. It wouldn't be dictated." Having grown up in the South as Jim Crow gasped its final breaths, the Bakers understood how their families and communities had been systematically denied the ability to direct their own affairs. Autonomy was essential to Donna and Russell.

Karen and Owen understood that getting good grades would be key in pursuing this freedom. Their father's Army pension and their mother's earnings from her paralegal job provided a good income, but like many first-generation African American professionals, Donna and Russell had no inherited wealth and little savings to draw on.[20] The children would need to earn scholarships, and that meant hard work. When Karen was accepted to three institutions—Florida State University, the University of Florida, and Princeton—her father balked at the prospect of paying for the Ivy League school. Even though Karen received a generous financial aid offer, including a healthy grant for tuition, her living expenses would be high. She would have to take out loans and get a job, and that would mean less time to study.

Donna and Russell were concerned about the cost of school because in two years' time, Owen would also be going to college. Since his grades weren't as strong as Karen's, they reasoned, Owen would likely require more financial support from the family. Karen disarmed her parents by arguing for Princeton on the basis of the values they had instilled in her, telling them, "If I go here I'm going to get this amazing Ivy League education and I'm going to be able to do whatever I want with it." How could they argue with that?

As Donna and Russell considered how they could afford to let Karen attend Princeton, they were determined to shield her enough from financial responsibilities that she could keep her focus on her studies. Paying, they believed, was their responsibility as parents. They would have preferred that Karen didn't have to take out any loans or work outside of her classes' demands while in school, but that possibility was not on the table given the costs of living in the Northeast.

Their commitment to separate generational responsibilities would leave the parents responsible for financial support while the children focused on their studies. Teaching young adults the value of work meant encouraging them to put everything into their assignments. Education, parents including the Bakers would say, was their children's job. Self-development was the most important responsibility of a student, and it should be primarily the parents' job to deliver financial support. Donna and Russell wanted that for Karen, but going to Princeton made it impossible. To get the education that their child wanted, they would have to compromise this commitment.

Today more than three-quarters of college students work during the school year or during school breaks, almost two-thirds in food service, retail, or campus employment.[21] Their earnings are generally modest, however, and they usually do not cover a substantial portion of expenses. According to Sallie Mae, in the 2015–2016 academic year, student income and savings covered on average just 12 percent of college costs, while parents on average footed 29 percent from their income and savings. Loans paid for another 20 percent, with the remaining costs covered by scholarships and grants (34 percent) and relatives and friends (5 percent).[22]

Paying for education is even more stressful in families whose pocketbooks are already stretched by the costs of discrimination, past and present. Typical African American families, for instance, have significantly less wealth than white families, and that means significantly less savings—in both the nuclear and extended family—to draw on for school. Despite the financial inequality they live with, the African American families I interviewed shared the middle-class desire not to burden their children. Across the board, parents expressed their determination to spare their children from their stress about college costs. In practice, that meant keeping silent about their financial struggles.

## Nested Silences

Frank conversations about the financial costs of college were remarkably uncommon in the middle-class families I interviewed, though some families did discuss the particulars. Most parents did not want their young adult children to feel burdened by knowing how much they would have to pay for college or how the costs might affect their futures. Even though college is now the second largest expense that typical American middle-class families pay for in their lifetimes (after their home), parents rarely disclosed to their children the financial sacrifices they faced. They obscured their struggles to allow their children to imagine their own futures freely. Children, for the most part, willingly participated in the silence. They avoided asking their parents about the financial strain of college expenses. They valued the freedom to pursue their futures on their own terms, and they wanted their college choice to be made on the basis of noneconomic matters, such as the educational and social opportunities a school could provide. They understood that college was expensive, and that paying for it was a challenge for their family, but when they discussed where to go to college and what being a college student meant, the finances were not the central themes.

These tacit agreements to keep quiet, which I call "nested silences," preserve essential middle-class boundaries.[23] First, American middle-class families keep financial information to themselves; they do not share how much they make or what they owe with outsiders, insulating the household from the world beyond. This norm creates a zone of family privacy, and discussing finances breaches this sacred boundary of middle-class life. Many parents enforce silence inside the family too. They create a second, internal boundary between generations, across which they do not share financial details. This divide maintains the separation of responsibilities. Silence between parents and children around paying for college supports parents' moral commitment to shoulder their payments willingly. At the same time, ignorance of their family's finances gives young adults the freedom to move forward without inheriting anxiety or worrying that they might need to care for their parents in the future. Nested silences govern family discussions around college.

Donna and Russell were exemplary. They never discussed their finances in front of Karen and Owen, and they didn't believe they should start when it came time for college. Donna recounted that her own parents had never allowed her to know about their financial troubles, even though they did not have much money and supported nine children. During Donna's childhood, her father worked at first as a custodian, then as an insurance salesman, and, finally, in a car parts plant. Her mother was a hospital orderly, a stable job if not a well-paid one. Donna's father died when he was in his thirties, and after that her mother struggled to support the children. "She put us through the rest of school—through high school—and did the best she could to make ends meet," Donna told me. "We didn't grow up with a whole lot, but we didn't go hungry and we didn't go without clothes. But we didn't go on Disney trips either."

Throughout, Donna's mother shielded her children from her financial stresses. "That was grown folks' business," Donna explained, "and you would have to go outside when it was being discussed. My husband's family didn't discuss money either. . . . There wasn't really any money to discuss. Bills got paid as they could get paid and they did the best that they could do."

I was surprised by just how important it was for parents to keep the full picture of their financial lives from their children. Before the interview began, parents would often ask for reassurance that I would not disclose the details that they shared with me to their children. (I have kept that promise.) One mother aptly expressed the concern succinctly: "It's not really part of a conversation that [my daughter] needs to be in."

Reflecting the silence imposed between generations, children knew little about their family finances. They did not know their parents' salaries. They did not know how much their parents held in savings or how much debt their parents carried. Often they did not even know how much their family was paying toward their college education or how much college debt they carried in their own name.

Rather than apprising them of the family's finances, many parents taught the value of fiscal prudence. Parents communicated to their children that they would need to make trade-offs among their desires. Donna related that she had been explicit about achieving this balance with Karen and Owen, telling them that "they couldn't have everything that they wanted to have, and they had to make choices." The lessons of prudence allowed parents to teach moral lessons about household management while maintaining silence about their own finances.

Many children understood that their parents were hiding their concerns and struggles. Olivia Garcia, a child of middle-class immigrants, reported, "I think my parents shelter me a lot from the finances. They don't like to talk to me about where our family is financially." Some parents even sheltered their children when they faced extreme stresses. Another student, Sophie Slater, described discovering the gap between her parents' true financial situation and what they had discussed with her. "I don't think they know that I know this, but I remember seeing a document that said how much debt we owed. It was over $175,000." Her father had been out of work, and her mother had gone through an illness for which treatment had been expensive. Sophie remembers her shock. "They were acting like everything was normal. My parents protect me and my sister. They don't want us to know those things."

Parents also did not want their children to suffer from comparing their family situation with those of their friends. Karen got the message loud and clear from Donna and Russell. "I think my parents have always wanted me to not worry about money at all. So they've never really wanted me to think about finances, compare myself to other people, to feel like I didn't have anything. They also didn't want me to feel better than other people." Olivia Garcia's parents also impressed on her that knowing their financial situation could serve to make her "feel bad" in comparison to others with more robust family finances. They also didn't want her to feel superior to those who had less than she did, for fear she might use the knowledge of her family's status to put down a friend.

Parents worried that knowing about their finances would lead children to see themselves within a social hierarchy, and parents feared that this knowledge could hinder their children's feeling that they are free to make their own way as adults. Just as their children were stepping onto a playing field that should be level, they would find it slanted by their parents' histories. Maintaining this commitment to abstract equality marks families as middle class even when young adults face social and economic obstacles beyond their control.

Donna and Russell were explicit with Karen and Owen about the ways their family legacy would have an impact on the children's financial lives. They wanted them to understand that they would face racial and gender discrimination, and that getting ahead would mean surmounting prejudice. African Americans and women face hurdles others do not, they wanted Karen and Owen to know. To make this point, Donna told a story of having learned that she was being paid far less than a white male coworker. When she took her discovery to her boss, the white male attorney told her that her performance was strong, but, "You know, this guy has a family to feed." She recounted, "I started laughing, like 'Are you kidding?' I said, 'I have a family to feed.' And he says, 'Yeah, but you have a husband.' I said, 'He has a wife.' So every time he said something I came up with just the same thing, you know? And, finally, he said, 'I sound pretty stupid right now, don't I?' " Donna summed up the larger problem, "As a black woman, I make less money than other people, and I know this to be true."

She's right. Reporting on the gender and racial wage gap in Bureau of Labor Statistics data, the Pew Research Center found an almost 30 percent gap between white male and black female workers (black women made sixty-five cents on the white male dollar).[24] Donna made sure her children were aware of this discrimination, and so did other African American parents we talked to. They explicitly taught their children about the limitations of the American fiction of equal opportunity. White parents, however, did not discuss their own privileged social positions or suggest that they conveyed such an understanding to their children, a silence that upholds the mythology of the level playing field.

## A Student's Obligations

No matter how much they tried to shield her from their financial situation, Karen worried about adding to her parents' economic obligations. She didn't know the specifics of what her parents were paying in college costs for her and her brother, and she was only vaguely aware of how much she had taken out in direct loans, even though she had signed for them and despite the fact that they were in her name. But she knew the expenses were considerable. She told me that in arguing for attending Princeton, she had made a promise not to ask her parents for any more money for her daily living expenses than they were already committing to her room and board. "I promised my dad when I got started that I wouldn't make it a burden on him," she recounted. Despite her parents' ideals and aspirations, for Karen, going to Princeton would mean paying for daily living expenses through work.

For the most part, Karen kept the promise she had made. She did ask her mom for a little bit of money here and there, "like $200 for toiletries and laundry detergent and stuff like that from Walmart." Otherwise, she relied on her jobs, at the library and the university public safety office, to make ends meet. "I mean I obviously wasn't shopping at J.Crew," as lots of other Princeton students were doing, she reported. "But I could get dresses and things at J. C. Penney's and go to parties. I could go out to eat every once in a while."

Despite their concerns about the financial toll, most students accepted that it is their parents' responsibility to support them in college. Not only did they believe that parents should pay for the family's required share of tuition and living expenses, but generally they also thought that their parents would—if they could—take on the responsibility of repaying their student direct loans. In this way, parents and their young adult children extended the household to college and beyond; they made stretching family obligations into young adults' college years seem natural, mirroring what the policies of the student finance complex expect of them.

Silence about finances maintains the separation between parents' and children's responsibilities under these conditions of intense and extended familial connection. This ring-fencing of generations can be difficult to maintain, however. Donna and Russell have struggled. As Karen was entering her junior year in college, Owen enrolled in school. He was awarded a partial scholarship, and together he and his parents paid for the remainder by taking out a formidable load of loans. The debts Donna and Russell already carried were significant—a mortgage and car loan, as well as their own student debts, which, at forty-nine and fifty years old, respectively, they were still paying off. They were forced to tighten their belts even more than they had when Karen went to school.

The family cut down on their cell phone expenses and, although they lived in steamy Florida, turned down the air-conditioning in their home. They ate out less, abandoning their ritual of an after-church meal with friends on Sundays. They also refinanced their mortgage, which they were fortunate to be able to do because their home had lost value during the financial crisis, as so many did. When Owen's tuition shot up, Russell tapped his Army connections to bring in more money. They found ways to fill every new gap that opened, but the price was steep and the pressures it generated were heavy.

Donna professed that she looked forward to "getting on track" with her own retirement before long. She expected that Russell's Army benefits would be enough to keep them afloat, but she regretted that she had not been able to contribute to their retirement funds. She had no doubts, though, that she had done the right thing: "I just feel like my job is to be a parent first, and that's what we've been. I think me and my husband both feel the same way." As with so many parents, their commitment will continue past their children's graduation. Donna said of Owen, "Of course, we'll help him pay his loans."

## Success and Social Distance

Parents supporting their children's emerging autonomy has always involved financial strain, and emotional pain too. Even parents who believe that children should rightfully strike out on their own suffer from the absence children leave behind. College educations also can mean that children are ushered into new social spheres, ones to which parents do not have access. This can create tensions across generations, or more subtle distancing, as young adults move into open futures that their parents have wanted and worked for, and that they have tried to protect by staying silent about their finances.

Karen and her parents have had to cope with her entry into a rarefied world distant from her military upbringing. When Karen arrived at Princeton, none of her family and friends had attended such an elite university, and she had little understanding of what the experience would be like. She had to figure out for herself what she needed to know and how to negotiate social life there; her parents would not be able to help her.[25]

She managed the feat well, figuring out, for example, what "eating clubs" were and learning about Princeton's socially exclusive student associations that admit members through secretive deliberations. She decided to reject them, though, and instead found a group of friends who were focused on their academic work, rather than worried about their social standing as she felt the club members were. She has also stayed close to her parents, even as she was breaking free from them. Today she is enrolled as a graduate student at another prestigious university and is poised for success in professional spheres in which neither her parents nor her Florida community can participate.

Children's autonomy has always carried the poignance of letting go of those we love most dearly. The conditions of the student finance complex have deepened the sacrifices parents are willing to make for their children's independence and, in the process, reshaped family life, imposing silences between generations as parents and children try to shield each other from the damage it inflicts.

# CHAPTER 5

# Race and Upward Mobility

...

To catch his first glimpse of Howard University, Stanley Gates II, age ten, strained to see out the window of the rented bus his father was driving. Stanley recalled sitting between two teenagers who were antsy from their many hours driving on eastern highways to visit colleges. As they passed the Capitol Building in downtown Washington, DC, the Founder's Library clock tower on the Howard University campus peeked out above the buildings, giving Stanley his first view of the Mecca, as the historically black university is known to its devoted students.

For years, Stanley II's parents, Ramona and Stanley Gates, rented a bus for a week in the summer to take African American teens from their community in Columbus, Ohio, on a college tour. As graduates of Mississippi Valley State University, a public, majority-black institution set among the Delta cotton fields, they had leveraged undergraduate degrees in social work to escape the limited opportunities of the poor and working-class Mississippi communities they grew up in and join the middle class. They met in college, and shortly after graduating, they married and moved to Columbus.

Ramona continued her education there by earning a master's degree in social work from Ohio University, and then took a job at Franklin County Children's Services, where she's worked for more than twenty years. Stanley Sr. has also always worked with young people. Today he runs a last-chance program for kids on probation. He picks them up after school and keeps them busy in the late afternoon hours when most trouble happens. He has a bigger goal than just keeping the kids away from trouble, though. He wants to widen their vision. He takes them on field trips, like to the airport. Watching the planes take off, Stanley asks them to imagine their futures and tell him where they want to go. In their work, and in their community, Ramona and Stanley Gates have devoted themselves to opening young people's imaginations to their possibilities.

At home, Ramona and Stanley were determined to instill their passion for education and its promise in their boys. College, they knew, would enable Stanley II and his younger brother, Ethan, to develop their potential and pursue their own successes both in serving their communities and in achieving economic security. They organized their bus tours in the hope that they would also inspire their young neighbors to educate themselves and expand their horizons beyond the borders of Columbus. Committed parents and educators had done that for them, and they wanted to give this gift to the next generation.

Upward mobility is most often discussed in economic terms. But it is also a moral project, one in which a generation of parents and community members devote themselves to helping young people make the most of themselves in ways that will ready them for the great possibilities of their futures. For Stanley and Ramona, and for many black middle-class Americans, historically black universities have a special role to play. They organized their tours to make sure their young charges understood that these colleges and universities represent an honored piece of their cultural legacy and that they offer special opportunities. Black colleges and universities are places where they can thrive, the Gateses wanted Columbus's young people to know. Ramona and Stanley Sr. made it their mission to help children envision themselves as part of the intellectual and social life of these campuses and begin imagining where their time there could take them.

The historically black colleges and universities (HBCUs) are of particular importance in the history of African American education and social mobility. Most of these schools were founded in the decades following Emancipation, with the mission to educate the formerly enslaved. While the slave system reigned in the US, most enslaved people were denied educations. Southern states legally prohibited enslaved people from learning how to read and write, and their enslavers from teaching them. The laws codified the fear that education would empower slaves to rebel and motivate them to escape. Some enslaved people managed to learn nonetheless, and some slave owners taught them to read and write. After all, the skill would allow them to labor in highly skilled work that would be valuable to their owners. However, in the Southern states at the end of the Civil War, where most of the black colleges and universities would be located, 90 percent of former slaves were illiterate.[1]

During the years of Reconstruction, religious groups, the Freedmen's Bureau, and formerly enslaved people worked together to found private institutions of higher education across the Southern states and in the Midwest, many of which began as vocational training programs, like Hampton Normal and Agricultural Institute and Tuskegee Normal School for Colored Teachers, which have now evolved into prestigious four-year universities. These private schools were joined by state institutions. In 1890, Congress passed legislation that required states to either admit blacks to their federally supported universities or establish separate institutions. The Southern states chose the latter.

From the late nineteenth century until the decades following the *Brown v. Board of Education* decision, which legally abolished school segregation, the historically black institutions awarded the vast majority of higher degrees earned by African Americans and established a class of African American professionals, from doctors and lawyers to ministers. The greatest number of graduates, though, became teachers at segregated grammar and high schools across the South, where most African Americans lived.

As was the case for segregated schools generally, black institutions of higher education were underfunded and forced to operate with insufficient facilities compared to white schools. Their graduates, too, did not receive the same economic benefits as whites with similar educations.[2] For instance, in 1941, African American teachers earned only 40 to 50 percent of white teachers' salaries.[3] Teachers' education and work earned them status and respect in their communities, but school boards openly discriminated against them in pay. Still the black institutions held a special place as the training ground for those who would help educate others and tend their potential. The segregated black colleges and universities, like Ohio's Wilberforce University, Kentucky State, Louisiana's Grambling State, South Carolina's Morris College, and national beacons like Virginia's Hampton University, Alabama's Tuskegee University, and, of course, Howard, led the way for African Americans to study and to serve their communities while moving up socially, even though the economic, social, and political benefits continued to be limited by Jim Crow.

The Higher Education Act (HEA) signed by President Johnson in 1965, the year after the Civil Rights Act outlawed discrimination based on race, was a landmark for both African Americans seeking higher education and the institutions that served them. The HEA contained two critical provisions. First, it established the Basic Educational Opportunity grant, now known as the Pell grant, which provided funds for lower-income students of all backgrounds to attend college. The HEA also directed federal dollars to African American institutions of higher learning to enhance the educations they had provided on a shoestring. Opportunity grants awarded to students strengthened the historically black colleges and universities through funding their tuition dollars, and the HEA also established direct federal financial support for historically black colleges. These provisions recognized that the schools had been deprived of resources and sought to correct the imbalance. Since blacks were overwhelmingly lower income, the Act opened up possibilities for earning a college education that were previously hard for many to imagine. Like so many others, Ramona and Stanley Sr. had relied on this aid to achieve their educations and social mobility.

On signing the bill, President Johnson articulated a foundational piece of twentieth-century American political morality. Standing in the gymnasium of his alma mater, Southwest Texas State Teacher's College (today called Texas State University), Johnson delivered a speech about the legislation, pledging the federal government's commitment to supporting higher education as the path to fulfillment and mobility for all Americans (figure 5.1). This was a moral as well as economic commitment, he said. "To thousands of young men and women," the president declared, "this act means the path of knowledge is open to all that have the determination to walk it. It means a way to deeper personal fulfillment, greater personal productivity, and increased personal reward."[4]

Today historically black colleges and universities include many different kinds of schools and serve students from a range of racial and ethnic backgrounds. The majority of their students are still African American, though, and face the particular challenge of race in paying for school. Black students carry almost 70 percent more debt than white students.[5] Even when they

FIGURE 5.1. Lyndon Johnson heralds the Higher Education Act's financial
support for low-income students.

attend public universities, like Ramona and Stanley's alma
mater, Mississippi Valley State University, four in five black
students graduate with debt.[6] These numbers do not reflect the
full burden, though; they don't include the loans that parents
themselves take out.

Like their college-going children, African American parents
on average carry more debt than white parents. Take the Department of Education's PLUS Loan Program, which extends credit
specifically to parents. The Parent PLUS Loan Program lends an
average of $13,000 per year per borrowing parent.[7] But the bor-
rowers are allowed to take out much higher sums—up to the full
college costs—and they pay higher interest rates and benefit
from fewer protections.[8] That makes PLUS loans the riskiest
ones offered by the federal government. Of the families with students at the colleges supported by the United Negro College
Fund (a subset of the historically black institutions), almost

10 percent borrow parent PLUS loans. At non-HBCU schools, they number 6 percent.[9]

Credit exposes parents of all backgrounds when they face a dip in their finances or lenders change the terms of borrowing; African American families, however, are particularly vulnerable. The country's long history of discrimination in wages and in the opportunities to build wealth have left African American families with limited assets and weaker credit ratings than white families. African Americans are more likely to be denied loans or are offered them on less favorable terms. Their vulnerability leaves historically black colleges and universities exposed too, since they are dependent on the funds students bring with them to school. When loans to students and families are compromised, the institutions that serve them are compromised as well. Funding higher education through credit leaves both students and schools at risk; even seemingly small and obscure changes can cause massive disruptions.

The vulnerability of African American families and the historically black schools was laid bare in 2011. Without consultation and without announcing the modification, the Department of Education revised its terms for parent PLUS lending, lengthening the time frame for the credit history required for PLUS loans from ninety days to five years. Many parents who expected to receive PLUS loans were turned down, even those who had been approved in years before and whose finances remained steady. In the year following the silent change, federal loans extended to parents dropped by 11 percent after more than a decade of skyrocketing growth.[10] Many students who had won admission or who had already worked years toward their degree could not enroll or return.

The Department of Education changed their lending rules because defaults had been high, and the department was rightfully concerned. But instead of taking a closer look at how the problem of payment could be addressed, the department simply tightened the lending standards, bringing them closer in line with private lenders' requirements. This was at a time when, in response to the 2008 financial crisis, private loans were also more difficult to come by, especially for those lower-income families of color who were more likely to carry compromised credit histories. The Department of Education was operating much as a bank, and the fallout underscored just how disparate the benefits and punishments of the credit system can be, particularly for people of color, and even when the loans come from a government tasked with treating its citizens equally.

The changes hit hard across universities and colleges, especially those that served lower-income students. The historically black institutions bore the greatest impact, however. The schools lost 36 percent of the PLUS funds that they had taken in the year before—a decline that significantly outpaced the losses at other colleges and universities, even ones that served primarily low-income students from more mixed racial backgrounds. The impact on families was immense. The number of African American families receiving parent PLUS loans fell by nearly half.[11]

Looking closely at the parent PLUS debacle highlights not only the vulnerabilities to which the student finance complex exposes families across races but also that the legacy of discrimination continues to shape educational opportunities for African American young people, often in ways that are difficult to see. Although many families borrow to pay for college educations, economic discrimination across generations has created a particularly acute need among black parents. Higher education is supposed to be a boost to a secure future, but by tying access to college to parents' credit, the student finance complex leaves African Americans particularly exposed.

With, on average, much less wealth to draw on for college expenses and credit scores that limit their borrowing potential, African American families have less margin for error in their budgets than white families. As a result of the legacies of discriminatory practices in education, housing, and pay, the median net worth of white families is $171,000, about ten times the size of blacks'.[12] Although the families of black college-educated parents do better, they still have far less wealth than college-educated white families, and the gap is growing. This means that African American children are far less likely than white children to get a transformative inheritance, the kind that can help them pay off their debts and use their income in more productive ways.[13]

The Gateses were among the families whose plans suffered a shock when the Department of Education changed the PLUS loan rules. Ramona and Stanley Sr. had been delighted, although not surprised, they confessed, when Stanley II was admitted to Howard eight years after his first look at the campus. He had worked hard in school, earning excellent grades at the majority-white school he attended, Central Crossing High in Grove City, a suburb just outside Columbus. He had even brought some black history to Central Crossing's students. *The Tom Joyner Show*, a staple of Gates family car rides, provided a model. Joyner, a graduate of Tuskegee University, delivers a "little-known black history fact" to his listeners each day. During February, Black History Month, Stanley II took to the school's airwaves each morning to report his own research on history and culture. He told students about the first black superhero, the Green Lantern; and informed them that despite its name, the White House had been built by slaves.

Attending Howard was his dream, but by the time he was admitted, the cost of attending had risen to $32,000 a year. When

Ramona and Stanley were denied a parent PLUS loan, they were unable to come up with the funds to support his enrollment on their own. With their son's dream on the line, they went into overdrive. They rallied their family and strong circle of friends, and between their herculean efforts and substantial luck they were able to raise the needed funds. Once at Howard, Stanley II contributed too.

He flourished, earning a 3.6 grade point average his first year, which afforded him a spot in the Howard Honors Program and $10,000 of financial support from the university. Still the family's financial challenges continued. That summer, and all the rest of his years in school, his parents were again denied a PLUS loan. Each summer brought uncertainty and stress as they turned their energies toward getting him back to Howard. Stanley II took on both subsidized and unsubsidized loans in his name. Ramona and Stanley Sr. set aside their tax refund to apply to tuition. They checked in with family members, letting them know about Stanley II's honors, his plans to go abroad to study, and about his bills to come, and every summer family and friends continued to chip in, even though they could have used the money themselves. Stanley II recognized that money wasn't flowing easily for the family members who had gotten behind him. "Everyone's been sacrificing the last four years just so that I can get this degree," he explained.

Ramona and Stanley did not predict their trouble paying. Their experiences in college during the late 1980s and early 1990s had been very different. They had expected that their steady middle-class jobs would provide adequately and that Stanley II would have the opportunity to rise even further. Then the student finance complex complicated the neat story of their mobility. Their experience showcases how the student finance system can perpetuate the history of discrimination that has made upward mobility for African American families particularly difficult.

Although the HEA promised intergenerational freedom, allowing children to break from constraints that had held their parents back, today the student finance complex violates the foundational political morality that President Johnson laid out. Even with the difficulties they've faced from programs that were supposed to assist them, however, the Gateses' commitments to both education and upward mobility have only grown deeper.

## Race and the Ideal of Upward Mobility

Pursuing upward mobility has long been a core feature of American middle-class life, and getting a college education has been a primary vehicle of that social and economic advancement. From early in the nation's history, assuring that children receive an elevating education has been a central responsibility for American parents. Indeed, doing so has been seen as a moral obligation. Upward mobility has been characterized not only as an economic aspiration but as an indicator of virtue, although one available only on distinctly different terms for African Americans.

Beginning in the 1830s, a growing economy established the conditions for the white middle class to begin to grow. A thriving economy gave birth to new occupations, like managers and clerks, associated with the country's burgeoning industrial enterprises. White male employees of these establishments were well paid, earning steady salaries that enabled them to reside in neighborhoods of central towns and cities, far from the farms that had supported many of their parents and grandparents. In urban centers, their salaries also supported independent shopkeepers, who made up another wing of the growing middle class. Together these men and their families established a new way of living, one organized around a morality of aspiration and respectability. Their new American middle-class way of life included seeking out explicit instruction in how to conduct their lives and manage their households in light of their novel prosperity. Popular domestic manuals laid out in great detail specific practices for managing the family, the household, and finances, all organized around social, economic, and moral aspiration.[14]

Books like Catharine Beecher's 1841 best seller, *A Treatise on Domestic Economy*, instructed newly minted middle-class housewives in how to organize their families' lives to reflect specifically Christian values, which she linked to moral aspiration and growing prosperity. Beecher urged her readers to become "systematic economists" in the name of honoring the time on earth and the property that God had provided them.[15] That effort, she instructed, began within the family. Beecher directed her readers to submit to the discipline of economizing in pursuit of the moral goal of family elevation.

As careful management propagated their resources, families obtained higher community standing, and their growing status and wealth were seen not only as ends in themselves but as proof of strong moral character. An ordered and nicely appointed home, properly cleaned and mended clothes, and perhaps even a well-mannered housekeeper, marked the virtue of the woman of the house. Beecher directed that such aspiration should also be a project for the whole family. Children should be taught to conduct themselves to achieve superior moral standing. Education, both in school and at home, Beecher taught, was the foundation upon which children could rise beyond their parents' achievements. Parenting toward these aspirations was a mark of devotion.

Aspiring families not only served themselves and God, however; they enhanced the moral standing of the nation, Beecher asserted. Virtue at home raised the United States to its rightful place as a world beacon for democracy and Protestant Christianity. Family aspiration proved the righteousness of the US and its democratic political system, and rising standards of living gave families membership in the moral community of the growing middle class. Although the overtly religious language has been left behind for the most part, aspiration to upward mobility still carries strong moral power. It has also become enshrined as a sacred promise of American middle-class life.

In the 1990s, at the time Ramona and Stanley Sr. graduated from college, sociologist Jennifer Hochschild documented that blacks and whites alike overwhelmingly agreed that "America should promote equal opportunity for all" and that "everyone should try to amount to more than his parents did." In fact, her respondents expressed that this effort made a person a "true American."[16] African Americans were almost as likely as whites to agree with these sentiments, despite the legal sanctions and unspoken discrimination that had suppressed their ancestors' and their own prospects. By any measure, Ramona and Stanley honored this morality. They had educated themselves and made it to the middle class. And they passed those aspirations on to their sons. They were counting on Howard to help Stanley II make the next leap.

But upward mobility has never followed the same script for African American families. The history of discrimination has weighed heavily on their prospects as they worked to become prosperous and accepted as morally upright citizens, as white middle-class families had been. This has meant that for African Americans upward mobility has always been a collective enterprise.

In the decades following the success of Catharine Beecher's *Treatise,* African American women activists came together to form the National Association of Colored Women's Clubs, creating an umbrella group for local organizations across the country. In 1896, when they founded the association, the educated and largely middle-class activists represented a generation that had benefited from the successes of formerly enslaved people who had founded schools and colleges. Education had already played an important role in their rise.

Like Beecher's white readers, NACWC activists saw themselves first as leaders of their families. "We are daughters, sisters, mothers, and wives. We must care for ourselves and raise our families, like all women," the activist Mary Church Terrell argued in 1916. Activists like Terrell understood that their educations and positions in their communities gave them special responsibilities, the historian Deborah Gray White has written in her history of the group. "We have to do more than other women," Terrell argued on behalf of the NACWC activists. "Those of us fortunate enough to have an education must share it with the less fortunate of our race. We must go into our communities and improve them. We must go out into the nation and change it. Above all, we must organize ourselves as Negro women and work together."[17]

NACWC activists lay claim to political voice by appealing to the idea of women's moral purity that advocates of white aspiration also evinced. The NACWC also paralleled white women's groups in their support for causes like temperance and suffrage, but they framed the issues differently. Adopting the motto "lifting while we climb," NACWC activists saw their organization as the leading edge of advancement for their race. Organizing for suffrage, for NACWC leaders, meant pressuring states and the federal government not only to enfranchise women but also black men, whose ability to vote was nominal at best in many states. The activists had to reckon with their collective history as formerly enslaved and currently subjugated citizens; they could not focus solely on a neat and efficient layout of their home or simply educating their own children.

With the history of African American oppression came white claims that black women and men were morally corrupt, which was a tool for silencing them as they fought inequities. NACWC activists responded with strategic displays of female propriety, dressing carefully in skirts and heels and parading impeccable manners. They adhered to the standards of white decorum with meticulous attention and adopted its aspirations with calculated fervor. The advancement of African American interests, this political strategy displayed, would be premised on asserting a moral image of the race that included an intensive focus on education and upward mobility, the paramount white middle-class virtues.

Any personal advancement would come with improvement of conditions for African Americans as a group. Where Catharine Beecher advised her white readers to focus their energies on the moral improvement of their own families, ascent for Terrell and her compatriots was always premised on reckoning with racial suppression. The history of enslavement and its legacies would play out both within and across family lives unless activists like her addressed them head-on, changing the politics and institutions that were, too often, designed to stop them from rising. Thus, for African Americans, upward mobility has always been a parallel project of individual families and a political endeavor tied to their collective history.

When Ramona and Stanley Sr. organized their bus tours, bringing their young Columbus neighbors to see the HBCUs, and when they educated their sons to expect a high-quality education that would boost their aspirations, they joined in the long lineage of this project. They too believed that they had an obligation to lift others up while they climbed, and to embrace the history they shared as African Americans. They could never leave this history behind. The challenges they faced in supporting Stanley II's dream of graduating from Howard were part of the legacy of that history. The aspiration of upward mobility has been threatened in recent years for lower- and middle-income families across the board, but it's become especially threatened for African Americans.

## The Realities of Mobility

Today's reality of upward mobility departs substantially from the ideal of children doing better than their parents, but the aspiration middle-class Americans have inherited remains strong. The early 1900s brought the great expansion of middle-class life to white Americans. An expanding industrial economy provided them with what have become the signal markers of middle-class life. More and more white Americans moved to the suburbs and organized their families around bettering their social and material lives. As the twentieth century wore on, frugal household management no longer gave access to these cornerstone achievements; instead the middle class began to rely on debt. With credit, white families—especially those who were newly arriving in the middle class—could more readily buy homes, cars, and clothes, and borrowing became both normal and essential.[18]

At the same time, more and more Americans began attending college, giving higher education its place as a middle-class pillar.[19] The growing middle class propelled a mass movement for higher education early in the twentieth century, but it was the end of World War II that brought new energy to upward mobility. During the 1940s, the federal government explicitly set out to expand the American middle class. White American mobility got a big boost when the federal government started to back housing loans and funded education for the returning GIs through the Servicemen's Readjustment Act, or GI Bill, which paid for them to attend college. The government then extended support for the growing number of white nonmilitary families as well.

The government backed home ownership by supporting both the large-scale real estate developers and the white families that would buy their properties. The Federal Housing Authority (FHA) guaranteed business loans to real estate developers like William Levitt, who spread his name and Cape Cod–style homes across the East, and Philip Kluznick, who owned American Community Builders in the Midwest. With the government's guarantees, banks could lend the builders money for their enormous projects with little risk, and the Veterans Administration and Federal Housing Authority guaranteed loans for the buyers. This government support brought down the cost of borrowing and made home ownership available to for more and more Americans.[20] These federal programs, which set up white families with assets in homes and in educations, have been responsible for establishing families' wealth across generations.

The gains in mobility were heavily skewed by race, however. The government support for home ownership extended to whites was denied to African Americans, who were systematically "redlined." The Home Owner's Loan Corporation (HOLC), a government-sponsored entity, literally drew red lines through maps of city neighborhoods where African Americans lived, showing banks the areas where they should avoid lending to potential buyers. Even a single black resident would turn a neighborhood from a good risk to a bad one on the HOLC map.[21] Builders and neighbors alike established racial restrictions, and most African Americans could not access the government-supported funds necessary to buy homes. Meanwhile, within segregated neighborhoods, African Americans could buy only "on contract" with usurious loans from shady operators, who could evict a borrower for a single missed payment or other minor infractions. Today owning a home is the single biggest contributor to the transmission of intergenerational family wealth, and African Americans have been systematically excluded from the benefits of this essential asset.[22]

In the middle of the twentieth century, as higher education joined home ownership as an essential stepping stone to middleclass life, it was also more difficult for African Americans to access. Universities expanded rapidly after World War II to accommodate the GIs enrolling. But African American GIs were funneled mainly into vocational training programs.[23] African Americans, in fact, did not benefit widely from higher education until the decade after the Civil Rights Act and the Higher Education Act brought access and affordability. [24]

Then just as African Americans were finally gaining mobility from higher education in large numbers, overall mobility in the US began to decline. Research conducted by the Equality of Opportunity project, headed by economist Raj Chetty and sociologist David Grusky, shows that, overall, American children born in 1940 had a greater than 90 percent chance of earning a higher income than their parents in adulthood. Children born in 1980 had less than a one in two chance of making more money than their parents by age thirty.[25] This decline has led to a widening gap between the ideals of American life and the ability to achieve them. Parents still believe it to be their responsibility to give their children opportunities that they did not themselves enjoy, but this moral commitment pays off for fewer and fewer Americans.

Both legacy and contemporary realities of discrimination make it especially difficult for African American families to rise into the middle class and to pass on that status to their children. Sociologist Mary Pattillo has pointed out that many black middle-class families live in an uncertain position between "privilege and peril." They have advantages in relation to many poorer African Americans, but they generally hold lower-paying jobs than white middle-class workers, many in clerical work, government jobs, teaching, and social work, as is true for Ramona and Stanley Sr. They also experience more difficulty moving into better-paid positions than whites.[26]

Accumulated family wealth, including wealth inherited from parents, can provide a bulwark against downward mobility, and whites have more of it—much more—than African Americans. In 2013, the Pew Research Center reported that an average white family possessed thirteen times more wealth than an average black one. Latino families fared only slightly better, with ten times less wealth than white families on average. Both African Americans and Latinos have also seen their finances recover more slowly in the wake of the 2008 financial crisis. With less wealth invested in securities, they have not benefited nearly as much as white families from the rise in the stock market, where most of the gains have come.[27] Black middle-class parents are now more likely to see their children move down the income ladder rather than up.[28]

Even when they've established themselves, most middle-class African American families face financial situations that now make their college aspirations fragile. The student finance complex has exacerbated the difficulties that families like the Gateses and

Stanley and their sons already faced. Today federal funding for higher education is built on a political morality very different than the one the original HEA espoused. Federal funding is no longer offered as an explicit effort to free young adults from legacies of discrimination their parents might carry. Instead the federal government delivers a different instruction: once families have arrived in the middle class, they should bear the costs of their own children's aspirations, no matter what their collective histories may be. The changes in the terms for parent PLUS loans quietly tightened the links between the aspiration of upward mobility and narrowly personal histories of credit.

## The Road to the Middle

Ramona and Stanley Gates committed themselves to helping African American children in their community visit colleges because they benefited so substantially from their own higher educations. Each spring while their sons were growing up, they would start to field calls from parents asking when they were scheduling their yearly summertime swing. Once they set the date and itinerary, they mobilized the kids to help pay for the trip, which was expensive considering the hotel costs. They held bake sales and car washes and mounted step shows. On the road, they might stop at universities like the University of Virginia or Emory, but always at the historically black colleges and universities, like North Carolina A&T and Xavier. There the kids could see black intellectual life in its greatest concentration of young achievers.

Ramona and Stanley had been raised, respectively, poor and working class in Mississippi, and on each of these trips, they retraced the steps of their own journey from the working-class South to the middle-class North. Clarksdale, Ramona's hometown, was among the very poorest areas of the country during her childhood, and the area remains that way today. In Coahoma, Clarksdale's county, 35 percent of the residents live in poverty and three-quarters of the population is black.[29] Ramona's mother, Mamie Lee Hinton, was a nurse's assistant and a single mother for much of her child-raising years. Her grandparents were sharecroppers and her ancestors before them had been enslaved. Growing up in the 1980s, the Hinton children cleared weeds from the cotton fields as day laborers in the summer months.

For Southern African Americans in particular, social advancement has been historically tied to geographic mobility, particularly moving from the rural South to northern cities in the Great Migration, which spanned from 1914 to 1970. Ramona's father made the move, the first in her family to leave Clarksdale. The routes of migration followed the train lines, with most of those leaving Florida and the Carolinas traveling to cities along the East Coast, like Baltimore, Newark, and New York, and most of those leaving the Mississippi Delta settling in Chicago, as Ramona's father did.[30]

Ramona's mother, Mamie Lee, needed to care for her parents, so she stayed behind with the kids. But she emphasized the need to leave Clarksdale to her seven sons and daughters, and she showed them the world beyond the Mississippi Delta, taking them to visit her sister in Indiana and St. Louis as well as to visit their father in Chicago. They always returned to Clarksdale, though, and soon Ramona's father did too.

At first, he returned for visits periodically, but the time in between visits began to grow longer and longer, and when he was in Clarksdale he drank and gambled too much too often, and his visits became stressful. Then they stopped. But he returned permanently to Clarksdale after a stroke, which left him permanently dependent on Mamie Lee and added another person to care for in her home.

Mamie Lee understood that her children's best chance at a better quality of life lay in getting a higher education, and she impressed upon them the necessity of going to college. She believed her children could and would do better.[31] When her first child, her oldest son, was admitted to Mississippi Valley State University, or Valley as it's known in the area, she dragged a trunk into the hallway to fill with clothes and supplies. The university, which was an hour south of Clarksdale, was the newest addition at the time to the Mississippi public higher education system. The school, originally known as Mississippi Vocational College, was founded in 1946, the last black college established before *Brown v. Board of Education* put an end to the legal doctrine of school segregation.

Facing an enrollment explosion in the wake of World War II and anticipating that segregation would not last forever, the Mississippi legislature established Valley and located the school in the heart of the Delta, where the population was largely black. The college was founded with the expectation that it would offer African American students vocational training for blue-collar and teaching careers. The legislators also expected Valley would alleviate mounting pressure on white institutions, like the University of Mississippi, to enroll black Mississippians.[32]

When Ramona's oldest brother enrolled at Valley in the 1970s, legal segregation was more than a decade gone, and more African American students were going to college. Valley still enrolled African American students almost exclusively, and the school continued to struggle for funds and support from the Mississippi legislature. Still Valley administrators and advocates had won it the status of a university and expanded its higher education mission beyond the limited horizons of a vocational college. More

African American students were enrolling at the majority-white colleges too, part of a surge in higher education for Americans around the country.

President Johnson's Higher Education Act had completely transformed the American landscape of higher education by that time, particularly the way college administrators crafted their student bodies and financed their schools, as historian and public policy scholar Christopher Loss has shown. By the mid-1970s, 1.5 million students, about 10 percent of the total enrolled at universities, were lower income and received federal funding. Ramona's brother was among them. Black student matriculation tripled between 1968 and 1978, and earning a college degree had become the cornerstone of African American upward mobility that the HEA had intended.[33]

Federal support for lower-income students was a boon for the black colleges and universities too. State legislatures had always directed more funds toward majority-white schools, so the federal tuition dollars lower-income students brought with them were essential to their colleges.[34] By the 1980s, a report from the Department of Education observed that "the high degree of reliance of TBI [traditionally black institution] students on Federal financial aid makes these programs vital to the institutional stability of TBIs, even though they are not institutional assistance programs."[35] This dependence on federal funds also rendered them vulnerable to a reversal of fortune.

Ramona recalled that the trunk Mamie Lee filled for her son was a marker of his accomplishment and a statement of her support for him leaving Clarksdale to make a new and better life for himself. Ramona remembered that it sat there for weeks as her mother added to it little by little. The sheets, soap, lotion, and other basics appeared slowly, as she could afford to purchase them. Over the next several years, Ramona's mother packed trunks for each of the next six siblings as they made their way southward to Valley. Although she worried about how they would get along on their own, whether they would eat right, keep their rooms in good order, and keep themselves safe, one thing she did not worry about was how to pay for tuition, room, and board. All through the 1970s, 1980s, and into the 1990s, when Ramona and her siblings graduated from Valley, federal grants and support programs, combined with inexpensive tuition, meant that Mississippi residents could attend Valley with almost full support.

Stanley Sr. also relied on federal aid to attend Valley. His father, along with many neighbors, worked in a furniture factory in their northeast Mississippi working-class town, where they built tables and sofas and shipped them across the US. His father's job was steady, but the family finances required that Stanley get assistance to attend college. As for many students, including Ramona and Stanley, Pell grants were the essential piece of funding, but they didn't cover all the costs. He and Ramona also both got work-study support, and they worked additional jobs too. She waited tables and assisted residents in a public housing office. He picked up odd jobs at a grocery store and a hotel, cutting the grass and sweeping the parking lot. During his senior year, he worked in the health center at the nearby Mississippi State Penitentiary, the infamous maximum security prison also known as Parchman Farm.

## Dangerous Credit

It was during the years Ramona and Stanley were in college, in the 1980s, that the Department of Education began to advance loans over grants for college support. The shift hit lower-income students hardest, and African American students bore the brunt of the change. Drawing on data from the United Negro College Fund, the sociologists Julian B. Roebuck and Komanduri Murty have observed that, in 1980, more than three-quarters of students at black private colleges relied on financial grant aid to attend, with only 4 percent having taken on federal guaranteed loans. Close to half of these students had grown up below the poverty line. By 1987, the number taking on loans had climbed to nearly 50 percent.[36] Although lower-income students were the first to be drawn into debt, middle-class students and their families would also be squeezed in the decades to come.

The parent PLUS loan was one of the vehicles by which the federal government shifted the burden of responsibility for paying for college onto middle-class parents. Created by the Department of Education in 1994 and officially called Parent Loans for Undergraduate Students (PLUS), they are specifically designed to help parents pay their expected contribution when their funds fall short and after the family has exhausted all other aid resources. Today the PLUS Loan Program extends loans for 13 percent of full-time dependent undergraduates. Families making use of the program take on an average of $13,000 of debt per year, paying considerably higher interest rates than those for student loans (as of this writing, 7 percent as compared to 4.5 percent for loans to students).[37] Payment also begins as soon as a loan is approved rather than being deferred until the student's graduation. In addition, parents must pass a credit check in order to be awarded these loans, unlike loans to students. PLUS loans therefore tie student's college prospects to their parents' credit history, which, for African Americans, reflects their collective history of discrimination in jobs, pay, and wealth accumulation. This historical disadvantage is not considered in the approval process, however; credit is extended based only on an individual's record.

This means that the Department of Education acts much like a private bank, complete with local branch bankers, in this case universities' financial aid officers. Parents are not left on their own to make their case for loans. Financial aid officers mediate between the family and the student finance complex in the PLUS loan process, just as they do with verification. They play an important role in informing parents about PLUS loans, providing advice about how to apply and facilitating applications. College aid offices can recommend that a family turn to the Department of Education for a PLUS loan, and they can specify just how much the government agency should approve.

Financial aid offices also explain the lending rules to parents and dispense advice on how to comply and take advantage of them. Pennsylvania State University offers particularly elaborate support, explaining the process on its website and presenting a PLUS worksheet that helps parents make three calculations that show how much they should ask to borrow. After adding in the fee that the government charges for making the loans (called an *origination fee*, as with private loans), the calculations result in a recommended sum that the school, on behalf of the family, can request from the Department of Education.

Voluminous additional advice is available to families, and its scope reflects the complexity of funding a child's college education. Each source gives a variation on predictable themes set by the Department of Education's terms, but with its own twists on how to make it work. Take *US News & World Report*. Their primer "How Do I Get a Parent PLUS Loan?" counsels that, once parents have determined they are eligible, they might want to consider alternatives to the PLUS loan. A home equity or second mortgage might provide a lower interest rate, and private loans—from a bank or even loans from friends or other family members—might also be preferable.

*US News* balances a sober approach with the gamesmanship to which a family might need to resort. If an application is rejected, they counsel, families should take that as a data point for their calculations and "reconsider the children's college choices and costs."[38] Still, if parents want to proceed as planned, *US News* tells them that they have the option to engage a cosigner. The Department of Education also offers an appeal process for those who believe they've been turned away unfairly. It allows parents to ask for more support in PLUS loans or to request that their child be granted more in direct loans. Parents can even ask the college aid office to step in and ask the Department to alter its decision, offering what's referred to as a *professional judgment*. But the professional judgment carries little authority. In the financial aid system, college officers work primarily as intermediaries between the family and the federal lender. They cannot change or adjust the results of the core federal formula, and—since they are advocating for families as well as for their own institution—their interests are divided.

## A Shock to the System

Although Ramona and Stanley Gates had expected their son to be accepted to Howard, the cost they would have to pay out of pocket to send him there was a shock. With the full cost at about $32,000 that year, they were informed that their Expected Family Contribution was $25,000, considerably more than they had anticipated. When they reached out to the Howard financial aid office for help, the aid officer suggested that they apply for a parent PLUS loan. Howard's student finance director contacted the Department of Education, recommending a $25,000 loan for them, and Ramona and Stanley fully expected approval. After all, they both had steady-income jobs that they'd held for years. But they had run into financial trouble in the past. They hadn't always kept current on their bills, but they had managed to avoid major problems by watching their money and paying down their credit card debt when they could. When they suffered some unexpected misfortunes—medical bills and car repairs— those expenses pushed them into bankruptcy. Afterward, Stanley Sr. took on a second job and worked overtime hours, and they climbed back to solvency. By the time Stanley II was admitted to Howard, they thought their financial troubles were behind them. They had even recently been approved for an FHA-backed home loan to move to a nearby suburb.

When they were turned down for the $25,000 loan, the financial aid director advised them about their options. The first step was to find a family member or friend willing to cosign for the loan, ensuring that, if they failed to pay, the Department of Education could bill the cosigner. Ramona's sister agreed to help, but even with her sponsorship, the Department continued to deny the loan. They couldn't get private loans either.

Flummoxed and frustrated, Ramona prayed, turning to her faith to help them find a way. She and Stanley Sr. started ticking through the rest of their options, asking other family members for help. An aunt who worked as a corrections officer, a cousin who worked as a supervisor at Walmart, and another cousin who worked for a railroad company came through with some support, but it didn't cover the full $25,000.

Two weeks before Stanley II was supposed to arrive in front of Founder's Library, "we pretty much had exhausted every option that we had," he remembers. Reluctantly, Ramona turned to their "church family" at Columbus's Oakley Full Gospel Baptist, who cobbled together an impromptu scholarship of over $3,000. The father of a friend, a judge in Chicago, handed them an additional $1,000. Ramona and Stanley Sr.'s hard work registered with

Stanley II as magical. He remembers, "So, really, like out of nowhere money just started to pour in." Still it was not enough.

The Gateses contacted Howard's aid director again, informing him of their newfound funds, and he was able to arrange a grant to cover the remaining expenses for the fall. The office also worked out a payment plan for them for the rest of the year, with Ramona and Stanley Sr. committing to pay $1,700 per month. Stanley Sr. picked up a second job, again.

Thanks to his family's extraordinary efforts and the remarkable contributions of a tight network of supporters, Stanley II made it in just under the wire.

■ ■ ■

The United Negro College Fund (UNCF) estimates that as many as 400,000 students were adversely affected by the parent PLUS rule change; those attending majority-black colleges and universities were particularly hard hit, with more than 128,000 affected at UNCF member schools. In the 2013 enrollment season alone, 39,000 were denied access to parent PLUS loans.[39] Lower-income families of color were most impacted, as many of their children, often the first in their families to attend college, were enrolled at historically black colleges and universities.

With scant state funding and alumni whose incomes mirror the American racial wealth gap, these colleges and universities rely more heavily on tuition for their operating expenses than majority-white ones. Their endowments are also smaller and cannot sustain them, so the funds students and their families contribute fill a critical hole in their budgets. The tightening of credit standards hit these schools hard, removing their tuition dollars from their colleges' coffers and threatening much more than these students' educations.

The majority-black colleges and universities asked representatives in the Congressional Black Caucus (CBC) to press the Department of Education to change course, and in August of 2013, Marcia Fudge, the representative from Ohio's eleventh district and the CBC chair, moved the issue from family checkbooks to the public arena, blasting the Department of Education and demanding that it suspend its new "adverse credit" rules, as the Department called them.

The Department averred surprise at the damage the new rules had inflicted, and it began to review the files of those denied. It then reached out to a select set of families it had turned down, suggesting that the families submit an appeal, and after review of the details of their histories, almost all of these handpicked families were then quietly approved.[40] In the student finance complex, justice is administered obscurely, from deep inside its bureaucracy, and is extended or denied just one petition at a time.

By treating families individually, with each required to ask the lender to consider their particular circumstances, the appeal process regards each as unique in its constraints and in the qualities of its misfortune. Within this framework of creditworthiness, deserving is calculated by family responsibility and attendant riskiness.[41] In this way, the system turns a blind eye to the fact that African Americans and other families of color have been caught in the net of economic and social discrimination.

Creditworthiness binds families' possible futures to their collective pasts. When the federal government is the lender, it also determines access to a benefit of citizenship, and a highly consequential one. The current federal approach to parent lending acts in keeping with the norms of private banking and shuts out those whose creditworthiness has been compromised by the injuries of racism, those who have miscalculated their life chances and fallen behind, and those who have made mistakes that have placed them outside the moral mandates of the student finance complex. In the parent PLUS wing of the complex, history has become primarily a matter of credit, and the benefit of citizenship goes disproportionately to those who have already benefited most fully from it.

The outcry from the Congressional Black Caucus, the United Negro College Fund, and the historically black colleges and universities exposed the veiled change in the moral politics of the student finance regime, but proponents stood by the new guidelines. They maintained that, out of responsibility to taxpayers, the Department of Education should not lend to families who might not be able to repay. Why should taxpayers have to foot the bill for defaults? Proponents also argued, paternalistically, that denying loans to would-be borrowers who didn't measure up to the Department's standards was for their own good. When families rely on credit to build their futures, they are subject to market reasoning that couches political judgments in technical financial garb. This masks consequential decisions from broader citizen oversight and shields them from the political process.

The Department of Education did change the rules, and the secretary of education, Arne Duncan, apologized. But both the assurances he offered and the solution he authorized reiterated the financial morality that had generated the crisis:

> The Obama Administration is committed to keeping college accessible and affordable and helping families make thoughtful and informed choices to fund a higher education in today's economy. These changes allow us to continue to be good stewards of taxpayer dollars and open the doors of college to ensure all students have the opportunity to walk through them.[42]

The changes announced that day focused on redefining the Department of Education's lending standards for parent loans.

Following Duncan's announcement, it would consider only the past two years, rather than five, of a parent's credit history when assessing creditworthiness.[43] The new regulations also required that families on the border—who, even with adverse credit, would be extended loans—submit to mandatory counseling, implicitly characterizing their financial deficits as the product of personal miscalculations. The Department of Education would make sure that these families understood how to weigh the debt on their own books. The counseling delivers a lesson that layers morality on top of math: with credit comes responsibility, which includes an obligation to pay without consideration of collective histories.

Internally, the Department of Education examined its misstep. In 2015, its research wing released a study, noting that the number of PLUS loan families enrolled at black colleges and universities dropped by almost half in 2012–2013. The effect on schools outside the HBCU system that also served many low-income families was significant too; the number of PLUS loan students in their classrooms declined by almost one-third. Those statistics represent a lot of pain for students and their families, and for the schools as well. The HBCUs lost more than 35 percent of their PLUS funds in 2012–2013, a number that had otherwise been increasing rapidly since 1999, tripling from $152 million to $450 million before the 2012–2013 drop.

Acknowledging the particular vulnerability of African American students and families in the credit system, the Department of Education research team determined that race was the critical factor in the rout at the HBCUs, a finding few black families would themselves deem surprising. The Department should have understood in advance that the change would hit them hard. Indeed, just before the 2008 financial crisis, the Federal Reserve released a report showing that African Americans suffered from worse credit histories than all other groups, even when accounting for family incomes.[44] The Department of Education report concludes that "the demographic characteristics of the student body fully explain (statistically) the disproportionate change in PLUS recipients at HBCUs."[45] In other words, being black and lower income downgraded credit scores, a condition that left African American families more vulnerable to the PLUS loan crisis.

A clue to this process lies in the meaning of a powerful word within the credit system: qualify. It appears most often in descriptions of financial assessment; qualifying for a loan is a matter of assessing families against a compulsory standard and evaluating whether or not they measure up. The word *qualify* carries another implication too. It means investing a subject with particular characteristics, and in the case of PLUS loans, the process of qualifying for a loan identifies families' financial successes and failures as a result of their private actions. Ultimately, qualification restricts how government views families who have applied for loans. Instead of citizens among many with equal claim to government resources, the private financial histories rendered in the process of qualification marks families as particular and either deserving or undeserving of government assistance. Hopeful borrowers move from a general belonging as Americans to their individual ratings, a process that hides the collective histories that have produced the status they are assigned individually. This pattern, and the exclusion they often face as a result, is all too familiar to African American families.

■ ■ ■

Stanley Gates II thrived both in class and outside at Howard, even getting involved in campus politics to bring presidential candidates there to speak. After graduating in 2016, he moved back to Ohio, carrying a debt burden of $44,000. Stanley II proceeded to pursue a master's degree in public policy and education, his family's wrenching experience with the Parent PLUS Loan Program at the front of his mind.

# CHAPTER 6

# Cultivating Potential

...

Among all the things that middle-class families consider when choosing a college, none is so important as which institution will best cultivate their children's potential. In my interviews, parents and students told me that finding the right college was essential, because only in the proper environment could young adults explore and develop themselves. Although college is, of course, also about preparing for work life, parents and students alike spoke about self-cultivation as the main reason for pursuing higher education. The college years are a unique time, they said, during which students have the freedom to discover interests and nurture talents; they can develop as whole people—not just as budding employees—and make their own choices about their futures. The college campus is also a unique place, one where students can come together in pursuit of fashioning themselves and their new collective futures.

Both parents and students saw young adults' potential as still largely unrealized as they enter college. They might have plans for their future and interests they've developed, but they also have talents yet to be drawn out and unidentified interests to be sparked. Because their potential is inchoate, college gains a special significance. It is a critical time and place of exploration, allowing students the latitude and autonomy needed to tap into and develop their capacities and to find like-minded peers who will engage with them in the process of making themselves and their world anew. This is why leaving home and finding the right environment is so important. College is about so much more than taking courses and gaining credentials; it's also about the people students can meet and the activities and projects they can pursue.

Across my interviews, parents and students described potential not simply in terms of a set of qualities or talents yet to be brought out, raw materials that young adults possess and could shape into something more. The ability to engage in self-cultivation defined potential as much as developing any specific qualities. College is central to this pursuit because it offers the tools—a specific set of relationships and experiences—with which young adults can craft themselves. Potential is the process of bringing interests and talents into being, and it happens only in relation to the environment that shapes those qualities. It is not a thing to be discovered inside an individual, but instead emerges in interactions among peers, professors, and places in which they all meet. When we think about potential as dependent on a young adult's surroundings, families' sacrifices make sense. No wonder they will spend so much time, energy, and money to get the right fit.

This understanding of a young adult's potential and of the value of a four-year degree from the "right" college holds a central place in American middle-class parenting. As a bedrock premise, potential organizes middle-class parents' feelings of obligation to their children, and of their children's expectations for their lives. Parents made clear that they believed they had to suppress their own financial anxieties so that they could allow their children's potential to take precedence. Most often they wanted their children to attend the right college rather than imposing alternatives that might be less expensive. Parents did express unease about the stress on both their own pocketbooks and their children's future finances, however, and some did impose college choices based primarily on cost. The tension between their devotion to potential and their concerns about financial responsibilities structured their decision-making, regardless of what specific path they chose.

Setting economic concerns aside carries its own logic too. Suspending financial constraints proves the value of potential. Families pay to honor their commitment to children's freedom to develop themselves and their futures. When they elevate these possibilities above financial constraints, they lift potential to an inviolable place among American middle-class values. Parents and students alike asserted that their family commitments to the future had to rise above economic concerns. As an organizing value of middle-class family life, potential holds a sacred place: it has to be held apart from the prosaic matters of finance and cannot be reduced to economic value.

Parents most often expressed that they first considered how a college suited their child's hopes and only then grappled with the implications of the cost. Kerry Lynn, the mother from outside Houston we met earlier, is exemplary. She and her son, Caleb, considered first how he was "resonating with" the environment of a school. She told him that college should be a time for "meeting the people that you feel like are like you, that [in college] you're going to be growing to your fullest potential." Kerry Lynn explained that, for her, the bottom line lay with Caleb's ability to cultivate himself in the right environment: "So that's what our value was. If it felt right, we were going to do what it took to get it." Reflecting their parents' principles, students expressed the same concern about discovering and developing themselves. Reflecting on the value of college in that process, Luke, a student from Illinois enrolled at a small private college in Minnesota, described college as a time of unique opportunity because it offered the possibility of "saturating oneself in something and of bringing something to the furthest extent that it could be."

For Luke and others like him, college was a time and place of discovering just what that something might be, on their own, away from their parents, siblings, and hometowns; a time and place not only of personal development but possible reinvention. Finding the right fit between a college and these future possibilities for a life was, therefore, essential. Luke described his desire to find this fit: "I guess when it came down to it, it was, how do each of the institutions feel to me? In what ways were they welcoming to me? And did they have a variety of programs available to cater to whatever whims might arise in the future that I wasn't even aware of yet?"

The expense this would entail was also very much on Luke's mind. Luke and his father considered the finances seriously, evaluating whether a school was "going to make the process feasible in a financial sense." They had to reckon with their larger family picture: Luke's older sister was already in college, and two younger siblings were attending high school and would soon be applying. Luke and his father knew they had to be careful with the family's funds. Together they compared tuition at the University of Illinois—where his sister was enrolled—and the private universities that had admitted him, paying close attention to how the financial aid packages different schools offered weighed out against their costs. At the small liberal arts college he ultimately chose, "the total cost of tuition was more than it would have been had I gone to a place like the University of Illinois." But he and his father deemed that "the financial burden was not insurmountable." Even with aid, federal student loans, and work-study, the family would be on the hook for about $25,000 per year. The cost was "definitely a factor," he told us, but "it wasn't the determining factor." Ultimately, their priority was finding a school that would give Luke the greatest possibilities as he experimented.

Some parents did discuss placing finances before all else, although these conversations were striking because they were so few. Beverly Toni, who lives in New York City and whose son attended NYU, adhered to the advice of DailyWorth, a women's personal finance and self-help advice website. Our discussion focused narrowly on the cost of her son Gabriel's education and the potential payoff of his future job. She was also concerned about saving for her own retirement. She took DailyWorth's advice to heart in Gabriel's college decision, following the instruction for parents to secure their investments first. "I didn't really want to take on a parent loan," she said. "Parents shouldn't do that because they should actually put more money into their 401(k). . . . They should have a good conversation with their children and let them know that they're not going to take on more debt. You know, especially since this will affect their retirement fund." Beverly informed Gabriel that he would attend the school in which the most robust aid package gave him access to the most prestige, and that he could not attend schools outside of New York City. He would live at home and save both of them money. The cost was paramount—an earlier bankruptcy worried Beverly enough that she told Gabriel that she would never qualify for private loans. Gabriel worked his way through college, eventually taking a job as a residence assistant so that he could live in the dorms. Even with his work-study, his job, and his direct loans, he graduated with an additional $10,000 in private loans.

The other two parents, both fathers, who gave financial reasoning pride of place were professionals in business or research, extensively trained to consider economic calculations to be the ultimate authority. They reported that their experiences in the student finance complex were an extension of their regular routines, a straightforward process that followed a logic consistent with their educations and experience. One of these parents pointed out that although he was able to navigate the student aid system, others would not have been so lucky. He explained that student finance should be easier to understand and should benefit a broader range of parents and students more consistently. The other father stressed what he saw as the moral failure of borrowers. This medical professional considered dangerous even those who carry average debt and who haven't calculated the payoff in their future incomes. These students and families are "really going to be a problem for our country in the next couple of generations," he stated, using financial logic to accuse these borrowers of betraying not only their own interests but also those of the nation.

Whereas Beverly Toni discussed following economic advice only in terms of her own family's future, following the self-help script, the fathers with strong financial morality carried clear opinions about how other parents and students should act: more like economists and financial advisers tell them to. This falls in line with findings from experiments designed to ascertain whether students of business and economics make different choices than their peers and may have learned distinct values. Students with economics courses under their belts do indeed maximize their own economic rewards more assertively than other students and place less weight on behaving in ways that take others' interests into account, social scientists have found.[1] Those educated in economics, they have shown, also believe their methods of decision-making to be better than that of those who weigh other matters first or who disregard economic benefit. Financial morality is distinctly hierarchical; some social scientists even see "acting like an economist" to be a marker of high intelligence, disregarding why others might honor competing systems of value.[2]

Whether students with such dispositions select business and economics courses, or whether these courses instruct students to prize financial logic and rewards, is a matter of some debate. What is clear, however, is that a value system that elevates self-interested financial calculation above other considerations is associated specifically with business and economics education.

## The Ritual of College Selection

No matter how much the finances weighed on their minds, families carried out the process of selecting a college through tense and caring conversations, which they often recalled in vivid detail. My interviews confirmed that these conversations composed a core middle-class ritual, a scripted event that takes participants out of the stream of everyday life and that stages key cultural contests. Rituals can make explicit conflicts that are suppressed in everyday life, and for middle-class families, they force the moral contest between the values of finance and potential into the open. Rituals also repeat across time and location. Reflecting this form, families from across the country told stories about these conversations and, in fact, restaged their moral conflicts by discussing them again in our interviews. Rituals can involve small numbers of people—they might even take place in private, as with the college selection conversation—but they are shared widely, uniting otherwise disparate individuals. Families' ritual conversations around the college decision accomplished important cultural work: they sanctioned potential as the prevailing victor again and again and made the act of accepting that outcome a mark of families' middle-class standing.

Parents' and young adults' explanations of their particular college choice were also ritualistic. The content was predictable, as rituals prescribe. Parents proceeded through a familiar script. They first described the value of the classes students could take, their interactions with future peers, their opportunities to join teams and clubs, their chances to train on sports fields, their prospects to travel and to engage in politics, arts, and work outside the school. Then they discussed how the price became a factor in their discussions. They described weighing costs, only to follow up quickly with an explanation of how the family sidelined financial concerns and somehow patched together solutions.

The conversations also ritualistically divided responsibilities for voicing the two sides of the conflict. One parent would argue for affordability as the deciding factor; the other made the case for overriding that consideration. For instance, Kimberly, a student from outside Philadelphia, shared that her mother encouraged her from early on to dream about college in New York City. After she got in, her father balked at the cost, arguing that Kimberly should consider Drexel and the other Pennsylvania state options. Kimberly noted the strange feeling of suspension she and her parents shared in the middle of this conflict. She described that "there was this weird moment of them feeling like my potential was going to be limited by their financial decisions and choices." The family came back together in agreement, and she enrolled at NYU.

As with Kimberly and her parents, families would finally achieve a consensus that they must not put a price tag on the value of developing a child's potential. By forcing families to choose, the moral conflict actually strengthened families' commitment to potential and their willingness to pay to honor it.

## Against Potential, For Jobs

In recent years, a chorus of politicians, policy experts, and economically minded columnists have located the value of college in preparing young people for jobs. They argue that college students should spend their time in classes that will further their future careers and that colleges should offer curricula directed toward the positions corporate America can offer graduates. One prominent argument in these discussions is that students should train in science, technology, engineering, and math—the vaunted STEM fields—rather than allowing them, let alone encouraging them, to devote themselves to pursuits seen as less pragmatic and the development of skills portrayed as less in demand. Republican governor Rick Scott of Florida espoused this position in 2011 when he announced his intention to direct state funds toward STEM education and away from the liberal arts and social sciences. In conversation with radio host Marc Bernier, he singled out anthropology for wasting students' time and state monies. "You know, we don't need a lot more anthropologists in the state. It's a great degree if people want to get it, but we don't need them here. I want to spend our dollars giving people science, technology, engineering, math degrees . . . so when they get out of school, they can get a job."[3]

A political proposition that college should be considered primarily a route to a job hides under the economic veneer of such arguments. Proponents of this perspective hand the reins of college students' futures to the corporations that can hire them, wresting them away from students and steering students away from the open future that they and their parents value. The proposition can be summarized this way: The children of middle-class families, who need the government's support to go to college, should consider pursuing their own interests in college to be a luxury. Higher education should be for buckling down and studying the material that will bring solid salaries and help them pay their debts. Everything else is frivolous. What's more, they should certainly not use their postcollege years to continue with personal exploration. They should commit to a career path and stick with the jobs that corporations need them to do.

College, in this view, amounts to little more than higher-level vocational education for the middle class, anointing them the yeoman workers of the corporate economy. This perspective applies the same fundamental justification for limiting middle-class citizens' educational choices as it does for low-income students. Both should serve corporate interests by pursuing technical educations, whether as undergraduates or in vocational schools; neither should aspire to the broader opportunities college offers.

This morally laden political argument for yeomanship presents itself as hardheaded, but it mischaracterizes the realities of the job market that it vaunts. For one, the presumption that a liberal arts education would prevent students from getting jobs is spurious. Graduates with a broad-based education are in demand. Writing for the National Bureau of Economics Research, economist David Deming argues that employers are currently seeking skills that come from a more exploratory college education, like the one students receive by studying liberal arts. What's more, these workers' "soft skills," their capacity to communicate and work with others, are in short supply. Still further, Deming points out that the income benefits of STEM jobs are in decline. Economists have observed that, since 2000, managerial, professional, and technical occupations have stalled considerably in both the number of jobs and their wage growth.[4] In other words, colleges and universities need to provide the materials for students to cultivate their potential, not just to obtain the kind of targeted, cognitive skills that STEM education offers. The argument for yeomanship also fails to acknowledge that the connection between college and good jobs is not as clear as it may seem. Economists John Schmitt and Heather Boushey found that among twenty-four- to thirty-five-year-olds, almost 20 percent of college graduates "actually do no better than their counterparts who left school after high school," even before taking college debt into account.[5]

The high cost of college makes the return to income less certain, and the nature of employment has become less solid too. Jobs are much less secure now than they were in the post–World War II decades, and they are likely to become even less so in the future. The argument for yeomanship denies the turbulent job market graduates will face. College students will enter a work world in which increasing numbers of jobs are designed to be temporary. Although the corporations of the mid-twentieth century depended on a stable workforce of long-term employees, capitalism in the US today works by assuming that a "flexible" workforce accustomed to temporary and insecure employment will be at corporations' disposal.

The growth of temporary employment has reorganized how Americans both live and work. Because it has coincided with massive technological changes, like the development of the internet, this social reorganization has appeared to be largely a natural consequence of innovation and competition rather than the outcome of human choices.[6] But as historian Louis Hyman demonstrates, the shift was an explicit goal of business leaders. Beginning in the 1970s, corporate heads and their consultants began to look for short-term profits, cutting their commitments to their employees. Workers who might stay for years or decades required promotions and benefits and were protected by unions. Disposing of expensive workers became a key to meeting profit targets. In their place, corporations began to rely on short-term employees who would stay for the job at hand and then leave.

The rise of temporary work means college students can expect to face spikes and dips in income as they lose or finish one job and worry about when the next will come and from where. On top of this volatility, they also have to contend with the rapid transition to automation in white-collar work. Although media discussions tend to pit robots directly against humans in the quest for jobs, today human abilities are more often complemented by automated tasks.[7] Still, together the temporary nature of work and automation undermine arguments for educations that prepare students for specific skills and jobs. If students accept the argument that their college years should be dedicated to job preparation, graduates cannot be certain that the lucrative jobs they envision will even still be available, let alone secure.

The threat of displacement is real too. Technology companies are hard at work attempting to oust white-collar workers by automating their jobs entirely or by reducing their numbers. Venture capitalist Kai-fu Lee, former president of Google China's research arm, has his sights set on jobs that are costly to corporations. Artificial intelligence will replace white-collar workers faster than blue-collar ones, he argues. Loan officers, customer service and training staff, and paralegals are all among the jobs his company has already invested in supplanting.[8] Other firms are investing in technologies designed to ground pilots, sideline journalists, and bench lawyers.[9] Researchers at the Oxford Internet Institute have estimated that 47 percent of US jobs are at risk in the current wave of computerization.[10] Adapt or be sidelined, they warn.[11] Anticipating which specific jobs will be on offer and what they will look like will be increasingly challenging, if not impossible.

The same applies to the jobs advocates of vocational training promote. Career and technical education (CTE)—what used to be called vocational school—in both high school and at the college level can be a path to a good income for those who can't go to college, or wouldn't do well there. Jobs like elevator installer and computer support specialist, for example, can today offer middle-class salaries without a college degree.[12] More than one in three Americans will not enroll in higher education right after high school graduation, and a technical degree may well be a good option for many of them at some point during their work lives.[13] According to the Florida Department of Education, jobs requiring postsecondary vocational training are among the fastest-growing occupations in the state, and that has propelled students into training programs run by community colleges and for-profit schools.[14]

CTE denies students the benefits of a broad education that can't be measured in dollars, however, and the arguments for it also overlook how limited the economic value of the skills taught may turn out to be. Students who enroll in CTE may be training themselves for jobs that are scarce, or will be eliminated in the future, under similar pressures to white-collar ones. Advocates who acknowledge that such skills may become obsolete argue that at least getting the training will provide reliable, well-paying work in the interim; still the development of vocational students' potential gets short shrift.

The benefits of CTE revolve around narrow job training, and debates about its value often skate over a bias: that traditional higher education should be reserved for those who are positioned to develop latent talents and capacities. Potential may seem to come from within individuals, but those students are the ones with the habits and dispositions young adults tend to develop when growing up in middle-class and upper-class families. When experts identify students who should be funneled into CTE programs, they name a distinct horizon for these young people, a framing that can lend legitimacy and reinforcement to hierarchies of class and race as well. It also reinforces the value of middle-class child-rearing practices; by honoring potential, families raise themselves above those who don't have it.

Both advocacy for CTE and the argument for college as preparation for middle-class yeomanship conflict with the traditional American understanding of the value of education, and citizens' rights to it. When politicians and policy experts assert that the primary role of college is to prepare people to perform work the business community needs, they are arguing against the political philosophy set forth by John Dewey: that education should teach students how to fashion novel habits, dispositions, and institutions, serving to advance democracy as circumstances evolve. Education could not be reduced to simple preparation for jobs, he argued, without damaging both students and their country and world. He acknowledged that vocational training could be part of his educational framework, as long as it included social, political, and moral dimensions. But, he cautioned, "The kind of vocational education in which I am interested is not one which will 'adapt' workers to the existing industrial regime; I am not sufficiently in love with the regime for that."[15] Instead he advocated for a vocational education that would enable workers to transform the industrial system, a goal that embraced the rapidly evolving circumstances of the early twentieth century and saw the possibility for justice in them.

Dewey grounded his political philosophy of education in an admiration for human "plasticity," the ability of young people to develop themselves in ways unanticipated by their elders. "The most precious part of plasticity," Dewey contended, "consists in ability to form habits of independent judgment and of inventive initiation."[16] In his philosophy, environment is key, and so is difference. Young people learn, Dewey averred, in interaction with their surroundings, with teachers who conduct themselves with established habits of mind and peers whose ideas and habits diverge. Dewey exhorted his readers to recognize the importance of young peoples' "potentialities," and that these inchoate abilities are more than personal. They transcend the private realm. Democracy is a system that thrives on the renewal that young people will bring if they are taught to fashion themselves, together.

Dewey's argument could not be more relevant today. Rather than impressing on college students that they should commit to particular jobs and the direction of corporate executives, the student finance complex ought to enhance students' ability to experiment; parents and students alike already value this pursuit. Under conditions where students are free to experiment, colleges and universities can prepare students for an open future, even one in which automation may play a significant role. When universities can broaden "their reach to become engines of lifelong learning," education, linguist and Northeastern University president Joseph Aoun argues, they will also "robot proof" education.[17]

Education scholar Cathy Davidson emphasizes that today's students need universities and colleges that will help them "navigate a world in flux" in which constant changes are the norm and learning how to learn, adapt, and understand rapid change is the central problem of living and of citizenship. Only with a college experience that focuses on the cultivation of potential will students be able to become "changemakers," assuming their responsibility to design the future and "serve society."[18] During the college years, students should be learning to direct and thrive in a radically open future. Parents' and students' idea that the college years should be primarily about potential is not idealistic or naive; it is prescient.

# Direct Loans and the Problem
# of Paying Them Back

The federal government supports the message that college students should use their higher educations to prepare for work, and it also sends the message that they should focus on their self-development. The largest student aid program—federal direct loans—expresses both of these mandates.

The conflict comes through in the history of federal college support. Recall that in signing the Higher Education Act of 1965, President Johnson articulated the view that a college education should be an opportunity for young adults to develop their potential, saying federal support was meant to assure that "the path of knowledge is open to all that have the determination to walk it," in the quest of "deeper personal fulfillment, greater personal productivity, and increased personal reward." Although Johnson and his congressional supporters were concerned mostly with access to college for low-income and minority Americans, particularly African Americans, Republican legislators made sure that benefits from the act would also go to the mostly white middle class.[19]

The HEA established the Guaranteed Student Loan Program for these students and gave banks incentives to lend to them; the federal government guaranteed these loans, promising to pay if the borrowers did not. The banks and credit unions could then extend the loans with little risk to their books, keeping interest rates low enough for middle-income borrowers while pocketing the proceeds. The Guaranteed Student Loan Program enshrined debt as the key mechanism for continuing upward mobility while at the same time fulfilling President Johnson's vision of higher education as a path to personal fulfillment and national betterment. Initially, the HEA's loan program delivered government assistance through private institutions and supported those who had already benefited from their social advantages. Today the federal government itself extends by far the greatest number of student loans, and high college costs and insecure jobs mean that what was once a leg up for the middle class now compromises the security it was designed to ensure.

The government's direct loans also foreclose students' futures in another way. The pressure to get well-paid work quickly, and to keep it, comes directly from the Department of Education through the terms it requires of students for repayment. The Direct Loan Program, inaugurated in 2010, requires graduates to start repaying their federal loans six months after graduation and, under standard terms, they must pay back in full during the first ten years of their working lives.[20] The effects of these loans start earlier, however. With repayment looming, students feel pressured to orient their educations around making money, at least enough to make good—monthly—on their student loans. While still encouraging students to view education as a path to pursue self-development, it also applies constraints on their aspirations, officially—though not explicitly—endorsing the message that college should be primarily a means to a job.

Preparing for a career and freely developing one's potential don't *have* to conflict, as John Dewey acknowledged long ago. It is today's rules of debt and the obligations attached to loans that levy the conflict on borrowers. Direct loans privilege the political proposition that students should base their college decisions—where to go, what to study, and how much to pay—on purely economic evaluation, and they no longer adequately support middle-class families' commitment to the enterprise of open self-cultivation.

## Continuous Cultivation

A primary job of middle-class parents, from the beginning of their children's lives, is to cultivate their children's capacities in anticipation of their future schooling and work. Sociologist Annette Lareau names the many ways that middle-class parents fulfill their responsibility *concerted cultivation*.[21] Her book *Unequal Childhoods: Race, Class, and Family Life* shows that middle-class parents talk to their children significantly more than less affluent parents tend to do. Constantly reasoning through problems with their kids, these parents repeatedly demonstrate—in the car on the way to flute lessons, Little League, or church choir practice, and at the kitchen table over dinner—how the central authorities in these children's lives think and argue for their interests. Then these parents encourage their children to negotiate with them using these skills. They also solicit children's comfort with asking for what they want, and they respond to these requirements, delivering key lessons in class expectations to their children. Authorities should be responsive to their needs, and they will listen, seek to understand, and respond to middle-class children's requirements, parents implicitly instruct. Concerted cultivation begins with the notion that these children can and should develop their perspectives and interests, and then builds children's confidence that they will find a welcoming audience for them.

Middle-class children bring these skills, and the beliefs they've been taught about their potential, with them into the wider world of powerful institutions, like their schools. They then fit themselves into these institutions according to the lessons their parents have taught them. Concerted cultivation, Lareau argues, transmits advantages to middle-class children that will benefit them not only in school but also eventually in their workplaces.

Even as young people satisfy powers around them, the distinctive way parents raise middle-class kids enables them to employ their environments in the project of their own cultivation, from disciplining themselves to be productive to managing relationships with teachers, bosses, peers, and colleagues. Most importantly, however, they learn to ask questions about what they need and make use of opportunities to keep learning.

College is the time when middle-class children fully take over the responsibility for their own fashioning, and institutions of higher education have been designed largely to facilitate and to require this. Students are expected to be mostly self-directed. They must learn to define and assess their capacities and deficits, selecting classes from a wide variety of departments and offerings and seeking out peers to assist them in understanding their interests and ideas. Though they may be assigned to academic advisers, they're left largely on their own to determine how well they are progressing and whether their courses are taking them in a valuable or fruitless direction. Colleges and universities supply the framework, and students learn how to use the institution to draw out capacities in themselves. In college, young adults turn from the direction of their parents to learn what I call "continuous cultivation," shaping themselves with the tools of their institutional environment in ways they will continue to pursue into their time after graduation.

Today many young adults see their twenties as a life stage that extends the experimentation they begin in college. In the 1990s, when psychologist Jeffrey Jansen Arnett interviewed young people between the ages of eighteen and twenty-nine in urban centers across the United States, these young people expressed that, in their twenties, they were still forming their identities and taking time to discover who they wanted to be and what they wanted to do. Arnett termed this novel life stage *emerging*

*adulthood*, noting the historically unprecedented freedom it offers.[22] This experimentation reflects unprecedented flexibility
in both personal and work life, some of which is imposed. Rising ages of marriage and parenthood have coincided with recent
college graduates' job instability, a condition that young adults
share with the generation that came before.[23] Student loans mark
a significant difference between young adults today and those
who came of age in the 1980s and 1990s, however. The flexibility
of emerging adulthood today collides with the strictures of
debt, a conflict that plays out as graduates plan their lives.

A student seeking my advice drew this conflict for me in stark
terms. Kimberly always bounded into my classroom, her long red
hair flying behind. Adventurous and gifted, she was the kind of
student whose promise shone. I'd come to rely on her spirit, conviction, and wit in class sessions and relished her probing questions during our one-on-one discussions in my office. In
April 2011, she was about to graduate, so when she knocked on
my door, I expected she would be bringing me news of her next
steps, with her usual energy and excitement.

But when I opened the door, I saw tears on her cheeks. I pulled
out a chair for her and she began to fill in the story of her distress.
Kimberly had dedicated her college years to studying social inequality. She studied the history of urban policy, discovering how
cities like New York and London became playgrounds for high-
income residents and tourists alike, and she worked with street
vendors, learning how they made their small local businesses
work to support their families in the Middle East. An activist by
nature, she had spent her time outside the classroom putting her
studies into practice, working on social justice projects in the city.
She was distraught because she had just been offered a job. The
salary of $45,000 would allow her to start paying down her loans.
But she feared that taking the job—helping companies outsource

work overseas—would betray her commitments to the education she had chosen and the talents she had cultivated. She felt trapped. With unusually high debt from her undergraduate degree, she felt she couldn't turn it down.

Exploring her interests, becoming the person she wanted to be, and pursuing the life she chose for herself were key to Kimberly's decision to attend NYU, and her mother, June, was always deeply committed to providing her that opportunity. June had worked as a waitress when her oldest three children were growing up. Divorced from Kimberly's father, she had long ago put her own dreams in the back of a drawer. When she was Kimberly's age, June had wanted desperately to go to New York City. Her parents had come to Pennsylvania for work in the steel industry in the 1960s. They settled and raised their children there. June had even made it to New York to work for a time. After she graduated from Temple University, a public school in Philadelphia, she moved to New York City to work in a hotel restaurant. Kimberly recalled how these seemed to be some of her mother's happiest times, the stories she always revived.

Kimberly and her mother invited me to their home in the Philadelphia suburbs to talk. The town is the kind of place where middle-class people move to raise their kids, as her father's family had done. Now divorced and long remarried to new partners, June and Dennis—Kimberly's father—still live in the same town, the one that he grew up in. The houses are not fancy, but neat. Families give their uniform style their own twist, with flowers planted in front or a banner fixed to the front porch. Kimberly introduced me to her mother in their sunny kitchen. June opened the refrigerator and brought out the ingredients for hoagies. This was one of Kimberly's favorite foods, June reported, and she was also keen to introduce me to the meat-and-cheese-loaded Philadelphia sandwich. Kimberly's brother and step-siblings kept coming in and out, interrupting, so we picked up our plates and moved outside.

At their metal outdoor table, June described her story. Despite her love for the city, she couldn't stay in New York. Family responsibilities called her back to Pennsylvania, where she married Dennis. June and Dennis had three children before they split. Waitressing allowed June to support herself and her kids and still be available for after-school pickup. She could also swap shifts when a sick kid needed to go to the doctor. Once Kimberly and her two brothers were all in grade school, she was able to parlay her restaurant experience into a sales job in a beverage business. She hated it, and she vowed her own kids would have a chance to make more of themselves. Kimberly, her oldest and most high-achieving child, had what it would take.

Kimberly echoed her mother's desires. "I was focused on New York and I just wanted to be in the city," Kimberly remembered. Specifically, she wanted to go to NYU. "From the time I was eight years old," she recalled. Her mother's stories echoed in a popular television show, *Felicity*, which captured Kimberly's youthful imagination in reruns. *Felicity*'s narrative followed a young woman's development over her college years. It focused on the heroine's drama with dormmates and boyfriends and wove them together with the excitement of debating Shakespeare and vying for faculty attention. It made college—the barely fictionalized University of New York—look great. Looking back at the show in 2011, *Vulture*'s Megan Reynolds reflected, "*Felicity* doesn't nail exactly how college is so much as how it seems like it should feel."[24] *Felicity*, which aired from 1998 to 2002, was a show in which the young woman protagonist strived mainly in the project of making herself into the person she would become. Kimberly was hooked. June took Kimberly to New York City for her first taste as a middle schooler. In the bustle of Times Square, near where her mother had first carried drinks, Kimberly decided that New York "was where I wanted to live, and where I was going to have my perfect life."

During Kimberly's senior year, congratulations rolled in, first from Pitt, which offers tuition discounts to Pennsylvania state residents like Kimberly's family, and Drexel. Kimberly was adamant, though, that she didn't want to stay in Pennsylvania. Then came the schools in New York City—NYU and Fordham. Next they examined the aid packages. Fordham didn't offer much. NYU, Kimberly's first-choice school, offered some, but not enough to dent the approximately $60,000 tuition, room, and board significantly. Dennis was adamant: no to NYU. Kimberly would go to Pitt. June picked up the phone and argued Kimberly's case. Together they would make it work, the exes and their daughter decided. "You've got to go," June told Kimberly. Commenting to me, she reflected, "You don't want to squash your kid, especially when you have a really smart, sharp kid." NYU would give Kimberly the opportunity to make her own path, cultivate her talents, discover the world in the streets of New York. "We'll work it out." June told her, "It will be a challenge, but we'll work it out."

Along with her degree, Kimberly carried away tens of thousands of dollars in loans. Dennis still worries about the choice. After graduation, he tried to convince her to move home to Philly and live in his attic, what he calls her "third floor," where she could settle down to pay off her debts. Kimberly wouldn't consider the offer. "My life is in New York," she reported telling him. "My world is here. I feel alive here . . . I'm not coming home." June is quicker to acknowledge the good NYU and New York City have done for Kimberly. Turning to her daughter, she commented, "One thing that you got by moving to New York is that you got to invent yourself."

Kimberly had all the opportunities that she had imagined as a girl in suburban Pennsylvania, although she could not have envisioned specifically what these would be. On the first day of college, she met a friend she intends to know for life and who became her partner in self-discovery. Diana was from Pennsylvania too, and they were united in their determination to get out. After a year in the dorms, they figured out the social world of NYU and separated themselves from the entitled students and sought out the artists and musicians (and dated a few). They made friends with the working-class young people Diana met at her grocery store job, whose lives in the city were on a far different trajectory than theirs, and they visited with the neighbors when the two moved to central Brooklyn, the first in a series of apartments whose costs the two would share with other students as rents rose and pushed them to move on. Kimberly and Diana invented themselves inside the relationships the city had to offer, all the while reflecting on those experiences in the classroom and in the constant conversation that marked their friendship. Together they learned to cross boundaries between worlds and to value the differences in the city and within themselves that they discovered.

Kimberly had to start paying down her student debt, however, and she felt she had no choice but to accept the same economic yeomanship that had limited her mother's prospects.

Several years after her graduation, the conflict between potential and financial constraints continued to play out in her family. Kimberly's youngest stepsister, Sophie, who had always been a practically minded girl, agreed with her parents that she should apply only to Pennsylvania state schools. Today, unchallenged at West Chester University, Sophie feels stymied and longs for experiences that she cannot access at the suburban campus near her parents' home. She calls Kimberly to commiserate, but sticking to her financial values ties her hands. In fact, the only option Sophie sees is to enroll at Temple, the very university June attended. Her future has begun to look more and more like her stepmother's.

## Profit in the Name of Potential

The conflict between potential and debt is most glaringly exposed in the booming for-profit college industry, which enjoys federal support. The government supports these schools based on the argument that all Americans deserve a chance to go to college and fulfill their potential, even though the results these schools produce for students too often tether them to the disadvantage that they came from. What the schools certainly succeed at, however, is making money from students' federal loans, debt that students will have to repay no matter what the value of their degree.

For-profit colleges and universities do not hide their mission, in fact, their commitment to the bottom line is apparent in the name. Public and non-profit institutions of higher education are required to invest any excess income over operating expenses in the institution and the mission of teaching and research. The primary goal of for-profit institutions, by contrast, is to make money so they can provide a return to investors. Students' tuition dollars generate their cash flow.

For-profit schools have existed in the US since the colonial era. Not until the 1990s, however, did lawmakers commit to expanding the for-profit model as a path for access and inclusion. When they did so, they also exempted the institutions from the kind of oversight that enforces quality of education at public and non-profit institutions. At the same time, they sanctioned student funds as the backbone of their proceeds, granting these institutions the ability to make almost all of their money from federal government loans and grants for lower-income students.

When the National Center for Education Statistics (NCES) assembled a picture of students enrolled at for-profits, the profile looked like the flip side of the middle-class young adults shiny with potential who enroll at public and nonprofit four-year colleges. They reported that for-profit students were likely to be older (above the age of twenty-four) and to come from more disadvantaged backgrounds. For-profit students were likely not to have graduated from high school but to have received a GED credential, meaning they are less prepared for higher education. For-profit students were also more likely to be black and female, which means that many start school carrying economic and social handicaps.

These students are by and large looking for a different kind of education than the middle-class students in my study, aiming instead for careers in trades such as electrical work or cosmetology, although some are looking for a broader education. For-profits offer certificates as well as associate's and bachelor's degrees, with most students working toward credentials other than a four-year degree. They offer students a last resort to gain a higher education. For these reasons, sociologist and former for-profit college recruiter Tressie McMillan Cottom has dubbed the education they offer "lower ed."[25]

Drawing on the work of economists Claudia Goldin and Lawrence Katz and policy scholar David Deming, among many others, the NCES also described how for-profit schools compound the disadvantages so many of their students endure. In comparison with public and nonprofit institutions, for-profits perform badly for their students. They cost more than public higher education, and students take on more debt to attend.

Their graduation rates are lower, and their students default on the debt more frequently. Between 2005 and 2008, students attending for-profit schools received 26 percent of federal student loans but suffered nearly half of federal loan defaults. Students who have attended for-profits are also more likely to be unemployed or out of a job, and, if they do have one, to earn less than students with similar backgrounds who attended public or nonprofit schools.

Sometimes the for-profits commit fraud, giving students made-up data about how well their graduates have performed on the job market, as we learned from the Obama administration's probe of Corinthian Colleges, one of the largest for-profit higher education chains in the US, which shut down in 2015. Echoing Cottom's findings, the Maryland Consumer Rights Coalition identified widespread abuse in their state. In particular, for-profit colleges targeted low-income people and people of color for recruitment, in other words those who would have the fewest options and the greatest need. Once they had attracted potential students to their website, the for-profits buried information about cost, and during the required in-person interviews, admissions officers did not explain how much prospective students would need to pay or how.[26] Even with such revelations, the for-profit sector continues to thrive with federal support. In fact, since the 1990s, for-profits have more than doubled their share of all college-goers, to 13 percent.[27]

By supporting these businesses, the federal government has abetted a process in which, as policy scholar Suzanne Mettler argues, "our system of higher education has gone from facilitating upward mobility to exacerbating inequality."[28] The student finance complex offers students loans to attend these schools in the name of developing their potential. At the same time, it tells them that they cannot expect genuine opportunity. By sanctioning a form of higher education that saddles graduates with so much debt while failing to prepare them to repay it, the student finance complex advocates that students contribute to the economy in a particularly pernicious way, by delivering profits to private institutions that actually put the students' futures in jeopardy.

## Indebted Futures

Even at nonprofit four-year colleges, costs have become so high that middle-class families are coping with a final ironic twist of the federal direct loans' moral mandates. Even if students find a high-paying job out of college, debt can still constrain their lives. Advocates of funding college through student loans underplay the difficulties the current system inflicts on students and their families. Speaking through statistics, they argue that college promises an almost guaranteed economic payoff. Their calculations can be quite precise. For example, some use predictions of earnings to argue that college graduates should expect an education "premium" that makes a four-year degree a good investment, maybe even the best one a young person could make. Between the ages of twenty-five and thirty-two, college graduates can, on average, count on earning about $17,500 a year more at their jobs than employed high school graduates.[29] On this elevated salary, graduates can expect to repay about $103 per month for every $10,000 borrowed if they are enrolled in the standard repayment plan; that's about $308 per month for those who carry average debt.[30]

Such calculations have led economists Beth Akers, Matthew Chingos, and Sandy Baum, among many others, to argue that young adults and their families should adopt a proleptic view, anticipating young adults' future successes as if they are already a given. They should not fear debt, given the high earnings they should assume will be locked in. Under these conditions, "debt is a tool that enables an individual to consume more today by taking money from her future self," Akers and Chingos write. "Of course we can't travel through time to interact with our future selves, so we rely on a third party, the lender, to make this transaction possible. In practice, a loan is an agreement between a borrower and a lender, but it's important to bear in mind that a loan actually is a transaction between an individual and her future self."[31] By reducing debt to a transaction between present and future, Akers and Chingos describe student borrowers primarily as future successful workers, drawing an income that they direct toward their younger, poorer selves.

This reasoning erases the power of the institutions—the federal government, universities, and banks—that give access to needed debt and enforce its obligations to repay. The argument also elides the lived realities of holding a job, one that might end or disappear. Instead the burden of repayment is portrayed as straightforward and simple to manage. Prosperous middle-class graduates will be able to look back and chuckle at their earlier anxieties, this argument implies. Yet many students and their parents worry over debts' constraints on their lives. Debt isn't only a transaction between the present and the future; it requires that money be redirected for many years. And for many graduates it is being directed away from the pursuit of life aspirations.

The effects start early. Recent graduates holding debt are significantly less satisfied than their debt-free peers in their jobs.[32] For college graduates moving across their twenties and into their thirties and forties, research from the Federal Reserve Banks of New York and Boston has shown that those carrying debt are less likely to buy houses, deferring or rejecting this benchmark of middle-class American adulthood. Although college graduates are more likely to buy homes than those without degrees, graduates who carry student debt are less likely than their debt-free peers to buy homes.[33] Graduates with student loans also have less wealth overall than graduates who finish debt-free because, Boston Fed researchers venture, they are spending their money on their debts rather than making other investments.[34] In fact, average student debt will reduce the wealth of college-educated married couples by almost $200,000, the think tank Demos has found. These couples compromise their security later in life, putting less toward retirement savings and gaining less in home equity.[35] For those who carry higher-than-average debt, the effects will be more extreme.

Simplifying economic arguments give support to the current shape of the student finance complex. Worries about the quantity of debt are unfounded in this perspective, and if parents or students have taken on more than they can bear, they should look to themselves and question whether or not they have been irresponsible. In my study, parents and students expressed great awareness of the risks even as they took on debt. Their calculations were both nuanced and robust, and they gave consideration to the possibility that debt would impose future constraints. Their decisions, however, encompassed much more than the statistical probabilities associated with income and debt repayment can convey.

Clarice shared that her mother warned her of the consequences of so much debt, and Clarice was hardly unaware of economic limitations. She worked plating food at a Buffalo-area nursing home to fulfill her ambition of studying abroad during her high school years. At the end of each week, she would walk her check to the bank, dreaming of the world beyond upper New York State her savings would open to her.

Clarice learned thrift the tough way: she had watched when her mother's car was repossessed, and her parents argued about credit card debt and who would take care of the family. Divorce followed. Her father left the house and his two daughters' lives when Clarice was a preteen. Clarice's social worker mother, Linda, counseled addicts at a drug treatment center, so Clarice heard many hard-luck stories. With her mother paying "manimony," as Linda called it, to her unemployed father, Clarice had decided that she would take the primary responsibility for funding her pursuit of the life she wanted. Even though their home was foreclosed on during the divorce and the family could certainly have used Clarice's wages, Linda supported her daughter's plan to put her funds toward her education. For Clarice, her future studies were more important than buying more fashionable clothes or going out for meals with friends. Living with a family in Eastern Europe would enable her to learn as much as she could about the language, the culture, and the people. There she would begin her life's adventures, she fantasized, and she would follow the experience by enrolling in a college far from Buffalo, where her education would take her even farther.

She loved her time in Eastern Europe every bit as much as she'd expected to. The history of the region fascinated her, and after she returned home, she focused her energies on returning, working hard to get the high school grades that would get her into a selective university. College would be her route back, maybe to Russia this time, or Ukraine, and she targeted her college search on schools that could offer strong training in the languages and history that would deepen her involvement there. With acceptances to several colleges in hand, Clarice and Linda weighed the benefits of each. George Washington in the nation's capital and New York University in its largest city rose to the top. After debating the value of education in each place, Clarice and her mother ultimately decided that NYU's programs would give Clarice the best opportunities for "sucking up the world's cultures," as Linda described her daughter's ambitions, and for launching her life.

Clarice and Linda pored over the aid packages the colleges offered just as carefully. They were relieved that NYU extended the most generous financial assistance; they would need it given the school's high sticker price. But even with Clarice's merit scholarship, the family would have to cover about $36,000 for the first year, including tuition, room, and board. Linda had remarried. Clarice's stepfather, Roger, a retired military man, taught ROTC at a nearby college, which brought in money on top of his pension. Money was still a concern, though. On top of Clarice's college costs, the family carried a mortgage and contributed to Clarice's sister's education at Buffalo State. Linda drove an old car, but she also had an eye on retirement down the road; working with addicts was rewarding but emotionally heavy work.

Clarice, her mom, and her stepfather would need to take on substantial debt to make an NYU education work, and direct loans were an essential piece of NYU's package. The financial aid office assigned her the maximum she could take out. But that would still not be enough. The package also included PLUS loans for her mother and stepfather. The family agreed to this plan for shouldering the costs: for the first year, Linda would supplement Clarice's federal loans with the parent PLUS loans and some private loans. In addition to her federal loans, Clarice would take on private debt in her own name to cover the cost of the following three years.

Hoping to bring down the cost, Clarice planned to do well enough in her classes to petition NYU to increase her scholarships. Part of her college selection ritual included coming up with a strategy for how to handle her debt in the years after she graduated. Following school, Clarice might join the Peace Corps; public service could offer delay in paying on the loans and possibly even relief, she and Linda reasoned. With her degree in one hand and her suitcase in the other, Clarice will carry away from college around $60,000 in loans. At home in Buffalo, Linda and Roger will be paying off another $36,000.

Although she encouraged her daughter to say yes to the college that best fit her emerging interests, Linda still worried about the debt, a concern intensified by her own experience with repossession and foreclosure. She warned Clarice about its effects on her future, explaining that her debt load would likely limit possibilities down the road. "Now, we talked about it at great length when she made these decisions," she recounted. "[I told her], you're making decisions today, Clarice, that are going to affect your whole life. You might not be able to buy a home. You might not be able to own a car. You have to make choices." Clarice listened carefully, but ultimately both she and her mother felt that choosing her own path was most important. "I thought [NYU] was worth it," Clarice told us, "and my mother encouraged me to do what I want. She agreed."

## Democratic Obligations

Student debt imperils the fundamental pledge that college education should be a path to self-cultivation, one that will give access to students to join their peers in making a new and open futures for themselves, their country, and their world. Direct loans, as they are designed today, levy conflicting moral obligations on students and their families. With the funds government offers, together with aid from schools and contributions from parents, students should view their college years as a time to develop their capacities, learning from their teachers and peers, to make themselves into the people they want to become. Direct loans carry a conflicting message too—one that denies potential in the way that parents and students envision it. The terms of direct loans require graduates to begin paying six months after graduation and through the most vulnerable decade of their adult lives. The obligation to repay in this way compels students to think about their education differently. They must first consider how they will pay back their loans, directing them to think of education as the means to the well-compensated job they will need to meet this financial requirement. And, as graduates carrying these debts, they will need to focus on earning an income to satisfy their lender before opening themselves up to the exploration young adults believe is most important in their twenties.

The conflicting moral obligations middle-class parents and students confront present a clear problem for our democracy. Bearing the cost of higher education compromises middle-class families' ability to assist their children in becoming the citizens a healthy democracy requires. The federal government, and the broader student finance complex, have an obligation to advance this mandate. Debt is not only a result of economic choices, which families might make either well or badly. The debt loads and repayment schedules with which they contend are the result of political choices. These decisions once might have supported democratic ideals, but they now constrain students more than they liberate them to nurture the "potentialities" John Dewey identified, and to make use of the freedom on which democracy thrives.

# CHAPTER 7

# Conclusion

*A Right to the Future*

...

Every generation must renew the American promise, and within families this means that each set of children has to support the achievements of those who come next. Education lies at the center of this ideal; it carries the weight of both family aspirations and the broader ones of democracy and opportunity on which the United States was founded. Creating the possibility of open futures is an essential part of the American project, but our country is not adequately supporting its citizens in this endeavor. On the contrary: Current policies undermine young adults and their families at a moment of vulnerability—when children are launching into their adult lives.

The tectonic shift in who bears the burden of paying for college—from government to families—goes against long-established national principles. Government support for higher education was once transformative, fulfilling cultural ideals of access and opportunity. Today families bear the financial responsibility for college, a shift marked by a rejection of the long-accepted principle of sharing the costs for young adults' development. Loans are always presented as a choice, but families are compelled to borrow heavily for college, because providing children with a quality education is a sacred value. By refusing to subject the choice of college to economic constraint, families affirm the central significance of children's potential in their lives. Loans may be expensive, but potential is priceless.

In the hundreds of hours I've spent speaking with families about the problem of paying for college, I've learned that, with rare exceptions, students and parents will pursue the college choice they see as best for cultivating young people's open futures. No matter how often, or forcefully, experts tell students and parents that they should make college decisions based on what they can afford, ultimately, middle-class families value their children's potential above all else. If Americans agreed with the idea that they should be thinking of college as if they were investors looking for financial returns, there would be no need for the constant stream of chiding columns and media commentaries about the value of financial prudence in higher education.

A cruel irony of the current situation is that so many experts and pundits condemn parents and students for being financially irresponsible when they fail to save enough for college or spend "too much" on an expensive school. In fact, families make decisions that uphold their sanctioned responsibilities; in the process, they also assure young adults become the engaged and informed citizens that a democracy needs. Rather than supporting this commitment, government's approach to higher education has increasingly undercut it. Moreover, it has failed to acknowledge the moral vise that squeezes middle-class families.

Our social policies and institutions do not need to trap families in moral conflict. With careful thought and political will, government support for higher education can resolve the dilemma and enable young adults to make the most of their educations and their lives as they see fit. It's already happening, just not in the United States.

■ ■ ■

In recent years, protests calling for student debt forgiveness and for free tuition have swelled around the world, and in the US too. Critics have labeled the antidebt activists "entitled," unwilling to pay their fair share of college costs, but protestors' demands are motivated by a different political view of moral responsibility than their detractors see. They are advancing a new idea—or, perhaps more accurately, reviving an old and still compelling one—of why college is important and who benefits from it. College, they argue, is not an "investment" in private labor market value, or "human capital"; this reigning political concept falsely reduces the value of education to pure economic outcomes. Instead the value of higher education lies in the possibility of intellectual growth, solidarity among peers, and, ultimately, in unconstrained prospects. It is both personal and collective, and finding better ways to support it is essential.

These activists demand from their governments what the parents and students in my study assume to be their just inheritance as Americans. They want a right to the future, by which I mean the freedom and capacity to live full, decent lives and pursue their own interests without debts that tie them to inequities and errors of the past. A college education that enables student autonomy, for both individuals and their generation, is one of the fundamental building blocks of this right.[1] But it is only possible when the prevailing political morality of education supports institutions that bring diverse students together to craft new visions of social, political, and economic life. And it only works when these institutions are accessible to everyone, without crippling costs.

Today, however, the student finance complex regularly limits students' prospects by tying them to inherited inequalities. We can see this starkly in the class stratification deepened by for-profit universities, and by the disproportionately high student debt loads that African Americans carry. We can see it in the struggles of indebted black college graduates, because racial discrimination and inequalities in wealth mean that they typically have more difficulty paying back the loans.[2] We can see it in the challenges that all middle-class families face when they grapple with the moral conflicts that onerous college costs impose.

A right to the future speaks to threats that young adults feel beyond higher education too. Climate change, for instance, weighs down young people with an inheritance of destructive decisions that exacerbate existing inequalities. So too does residential segregation by race and class and the continued patterns of gendered wage discrimination in the workplace. The rising generation will need to confront these unequal histories as well as the prejudices of the economic systems that have generated and sustained them. College is not only essential for developing and transmitting knowledge about these problems. It's also one of the few places where young adults can come together and teach each other ways to change the world.

As a key site for securing young people's right to the future, college should foster social solidarity and a spirit of equity among students. It should enable young adults to use their educations for creative, collaborative social experiments. The right to the future is a claim to the possibility of generational reinvention. Today, as democracy and civil society falter, and young people brace themselves for a massive set of social, ecological, and economic challenges, that reinvention is not merely necessary, it's urgent.

■ ■ ■

In the domain of education, the right to the future requires new solutions to the problem of paying for college, ones that honor families' commitments to young adults' open futures. Public re-investment in higher education, particularly at the state level, is the first and most significant policy change that would provide relief to families. During the middle decades of the twentieth century, public support for colleges and universities, in the form of subsidies for research and instruction as well as for tuition and fees, were crucial to the rise of the middle class in the world's most advanced societies. State schools were powerful drivers of local economic and cultural development, helping build industries, support communities, and even create families.

I have benefited from this state support myself. Not only am I a graduate of the University of California (where I met my husband), but my parents met at another one of the great American state universities—the University of Michigan—where my father, the child of a Syrian immigrant, encountered my mother, whose family came to Michigan via rural Kentucky. Many such cross-cultural relationships were forged when young people who would otherwise never have met traveled to places like Ann Arbor because residents in the state decided that public universities deserved big investments, and built them into places that attracted vast numbers of aspiring young adults. These students took risks. They signed up for classes in fields they hadn't heard of before enrolling in college and developed ties to people and places they hadn't known. For students who went to school during the high point of state investment in public universities, the future was as open as it could be.

In recent decades, austerity measures have led to severe cut-backs in public education investments. A recent paper published by the American Council on Education reports that "despite steadily growing student demand for higher education since the mid-1970s, state fiscal investment in higher education has been in retreat in the states since about 1980." With the exception of

Wyoming and North Dakota, all other American states "reduced their support [for higher education] by anywhere from 14.8 percent to 69.4 percent between fiscal 1980 and fiscal 2011."[3] The trend continued in the following years, and according to one recent study of American higher education by the Center on Budget and Policy Priorities, "overall state funding for public two- and four-year colleges in the 2017 school year (that is, the school year ending in 2017) was nearly $9 billion below its 2008 level, after adjusting for inflation."[4]

State university systems that once helped generations of young people achieve success without taking on significant debt had no choice but to raise tuition and slash funds for basic research. The results are apparent in public universities across the nation: students and their parents are stressed, and more places are reserved for out-of-state students who pay full fare, tightening opportunities for state residents. Administrators are scrambling to produce revenue-generating products—such as high-tuition masters programs—regardless of whether they serve the public good and support students in opening their futures. Faculties have less support for the kinds of basic research and innovative teaching that once made college such a valuable experience for students at all levels. It's a vicious cycle.

Today political parties on both the Left and the Right proclaim their commitment to improving the lives of people who are struggling to get by. Reinvesting in public education should be at the top of their list of priorities. In the US, and in other nations where paying for college has become a problem, student-led movements for free tuition are gaining support from a growing number of political officials and candidates. During the 2016 Democratic presidential primary campaign, Bernie Sanders made free college education a key component of his policy platform, claiming that high college costs represented a "shortsighted path to the future [that] must end." Following his example, presidential candidate Hillary Clinton took up the issue too. When the Trump administration stymied or reversed progress at the federal level, state officials—in both blue and red states—picked up the project. In New York, Governor Andrew Cuomo introduced the Excelsior Program, which offers free tuition at the state's public colleges and universities to low- and middle-income students. (When fully implemented, students from families that earn less than $125,000 per year will be eligible.) The University of Michigan announced the Go Blue Guarantee, which commits the university to covering all tuition expenses for students with family incomes under $65,000 per year, the median family income in the state. The Tennessee Promise Program provides all high school graduates with two years of free tuition to community colleges or technical colleges, and, as of 2018, the Tennessee Reconnect Program allows adults to attend tuition-free too.

Some critics complain that free tuition programs are expensive "giveaways" to people who either do not need a public handout or would be better disciplined by a marketplace that demands repayment. But as an anthropologist, I see things differently. It's not only that free or lower tuition represents an investment in the nation's future. It's also that it generates common experiences and social solidarity between the people it serves. It can also foster stronger moral bonds between citizens and the state. What's more, free tuition does not mean that students and families can avoid educational debt. Students also need to pay for books, fees, rent, and other costs of living. It's standard to cover some of these costs by working during college, but even when tuition is low or free, students need to preserve their time for studying, and they borrow (albeit less than they do when tuition is high) to make ends meet. We need a generous and generative system for lending this money—one that doesn't saddle students and parents with anxieties and insecurities, but instead enables young people to pursue their interests without fear of crushing debt. Lending for higher education should launch students into adulthood, not tether them to parents and creditors in ways that compromise their autonomy, as the system does now.

Other nations—including Australia, England, South Korea, and Sweden—are doing this better than the US. In these countries, governments encourage young adults to pursue their personal interests by linking the terms of their debt repayment to the income that they earn after graduation. These systems support experimentation by making higher education loans easy to use and predictable.

Australia has made the strongest commitment to the income-based repayment model, and its programs can help envision a way forward. Graduates of Australian universities are not required to begin repaying their student debt until they earn an annual salary of around US$33,000. Once that happens, they contribute 1 percent of their income as repayment, a figure that rises to 10 percent—but no more—when their income reaches roughly US$97,000 or rises beyond it. The government also automatically withdraws monthly installments from pay, like a tax. There are other benefits as well. College loans increase only to offset inflation, which in recent years has been low, and do not impose additional interest payments.[5]

The US actually has an income-contingent repayment system on the books, though it is a far less generous one than the systems in countries like Australia. In fact, the US Department of Education offers four different income-driven repayment plans: the Pay As You Earn Repayment Plan (PAYE), the Revised Pay As You Earn Repayment Plan (REPAYE), the Income-Based

Repayment Plan (IBR), and the Income-Contingent Repayment Plan (ICR). Too few students and families know about these programs, and too many of those that do have trouble making sense of the offerings. Which of these plans works best for each student and family? When, how, and to whom does a person apply? What are the terms of repayment in each program? The variation in what these programs deliver, from applicant to applicant and from year to year, is maddening, and the process of qualifying, enrolling, and recertifying (which the plans require annually so they can assess changes in reported income and family size) is dauntingly complex.

Ideally, an income-contingent repayment system is easy to understand and is reliable so that borrowers can predict basic terms of the agreement, such as how to remain eligible and what they will repay if their income and family size grows.[6] The government could create and promote a standard income-driven repayment plan that offers favorable terms to graduates. Instead students who do use the programs wind up feeling perplexed about the system or, worse, mistreated by the private sector lenders that get government contracts to manage the programs. Too often these firms take advantage of the student debt system's complexity and extract profit from widespread consumer confusion.

In recent years, major student loan lenders have been sued for practices including "systematically and illegally failing borrowers at every stage of repayment," which is how the US Consumer Financial Protection Bureau described the predatory behavior of the nation's largest student loan servicer, Navient Corporation, in a public statement. The federal government accused Navient, which services more than $300 billion in student loans for more than twelve million people, of giving borrowers vague information about how to reenroll in income-driven repayment plans, and of steering those who struggled to repay their debt into costly, multiple forbearances—special but time-limited arrangements that allow borrowers to delay repayment or pay a temporarily reduced rate—when other, more beneficial options were available. Several states filed similar suits. Of course, this kind of corruption is not the direct result of the Department of Education's actions, but the government's unnecessarily complex and confusing programs for debt relief have created prime opportunities for profiteering at the expense of families and students.

The terms of our current income-based program can be punishing too. A recent article by the higher education expert Jon Marcus explains that, in the US, "income-based repayments typically kick in at $17,820—and take a minimum of 10 percent (and, under some plans, 15 percent or 20 percent) of anything above that." This is an extremely low threshold for demanding repayment, and a punishingly high rate as well. What's more, Marcus reports, "American borrowers are also responsible for the interest on their loans, which also compounds, meaning graduates could end up paying more over the life of the loans than under a conventional repayment."[7]

The Australian system, which most college graduates praise and appreciate, is so easy to use that many students don't think about it much. The expense of college doesn't change the ways they make college decisions, and it doesn't weigh heavily on their lives after they throw their caps in the air.[8] Still the Australian system is not without problems, or critics. One issue that has surfaced recently involves the rise of for-profit universities, which, as in the US, have found ways to exploit public largesse for undue private profits. Australian policy makers have been reforming their system to rein in corruption, but it's not an easy fix. More controversially, graduates now have to begin paying when their incomes are lower than before, because the revenues were falling short of the program's costs. Australia is able to address these problems, though, because they begin from the premise that funding college education is a national priority. In the American system, the benefits and therefore the expense of college education remains framed as a private matter, but the Australian system relies on its citizens' support for higher education and their recognition that it is a collective benefit. Young people are overwhelmingly enthusiastic about the program, but it also requires the support of older voters, who must be convinced that it benefits everyone.[9] As with the extremely popular US Social Security program, one generation must be willing to support the next.

Building and maintaining ties of moral responsibility across generations is a genuine policy challenge, but the benefits of Australia's income-based repayment system far outweigh the costs. It's not only that students are more capable of making crucial life decisions based on what they want to study or do for work. It's also that their families are spared the financial strains that challenge nearly all middle-class American families.

Our nation's higher education provisions should honor the best in our values, and that includes a student finance system that helps the next generation flourish. This is not an idealistic perspective; rather, it is the most prudent strategy because it reflects deep commitments.

Student debt burdens too many families and students. But, as I've argued here, debt need not be so destructive. In fact, as anthropologists have long demonstrated, debt—when it is not excessive or onerous—can be a healthy feature of social life, binding people to one another in social projects that create future possibilities that otherwise could not exist. Today, however, the financial systems we've developed for helping students and families get access to higher education do far more harm than is necessary, and introduce too many difficult tensions into family life.

It's time to renegotiate the terms of this arrangement. The government programs we've designed have made us excessively indebted to the student finance complex, and lenders have not protected us or promoted our interests adequately. We need a new system that genuinely supports families and creates more opportunity. We'll all be better off when we're mainly indebted to each other.

# Family Situations

■ ■ ■

This book is based on a four-year study of how middle-class American families deal with the financial challenges of sending children to college. Of course, defining what middle class means—and, in turn, deciding who to include and exclude from this study—is no simple matter. On the one hand, most Americans, from the affluent to the insecure, refer to themselves as middle class. On the other, social scientists have proposed a variety of ways to identify the group: some by income, some by wealth, some by consumption, some by education, some by profession, some by cultural orientation. Rather than adjudicate between the many competing definitions of middle class, I use a straightforward standard that's immediately applicable for this case: middle-class families are those that make too much (more than about $50,000 as of 2018) to get Pell grants, the federal program for low-income students enrolled in college, and not enough to pay full fare in cash. All of the parents and students in this study carry loans for college. I realize that this may not be as refined a definition as some others, but none of the definitions are perfect or fully persuasive, and this one leverages the problem of paying for higher education to capture both the economic and cultural dimensions of family life in our financial economy.

Like the families in my study, I too participate in the financial economy and am shaped by the governmental imperatives and the moral power of middle-class ideals. As a parent myself, albeit of young children who are five years and eight years away from college (who's counting?), I spend considerable time and energy planning to fund their educations. My husband, our parents, and I have had extensive conversations about how we'll pay. As a married couple with two professional incomes and parents willing and able to contribute, my husband and I are positioned to take advantage of financial supports only a few of the families in my study enjoy. Still we're anxious about the rising cost of higher education, and we feel the imperative to send our children to college—perhaps beyond. We share the problem of financing higher education that my interviewees are struggling to manage. We use the same tools for planning and investing. We draw on the same kinds of family bonds to try to make it work.

As an economic anthropologist, I knew that if I wanted to understand student finance, I first needed to know much more about the place of higher education in the financial economy. I needed to understand its histories, materials, social hierarchies, and moral constitution. Only from within this constellation of reference points could I understand what families who engage in the student finance complex had to say and produce meaningful insights about the common features of their private lives. I read the history of finance and financial capitalism, especially where it came together with family life. And I read policy analyses around the problem of paying for college, diving into economic studies and reports from think tanks and key federal agencies like the Federal Reserve and the Department of Education. I also examined the work of popular media advice-givers, where family members would encounter professional ideas about the problem of paying for college. These sources were important for context, but they are also more than that. Expert advice is part of families' encounters with the financial system; it is where parents and young adults read about the problems people like themselves face. Expert discussions form the public face of the problem of paying for college. The points of contact between families and the student finance complex—the instruments of measurement, and financial tools like loans and investment vehicles—are also important elements in this public face; they create a shared set of references in a process that most middle-class families keep private.

All of this showed me that the financial economy enrolled parents and children as a family. Legal responsibility to repay certain debts might be assigned to individuals by contracts, but families share the burdens and pressures that come from using finance. From child life insurance marketing to home mortgages and credit cards, the financial industry works hard to tell customers that their business is all about helping families aspire. This is an old story and one in which the government also takes part. Since the 1940s, the US government has used finance as a tool for encouraging citizens to build families. Not just any kind of family but particular kinds: middle-class, nuclear ones.

As mountains of social science research has demonstrated, people rarely conform to the models that governments and powerful industries seek to impose, however. Instead they use the tools offered to them in strategic or idiosyncratic ways, advancing their own agendas and crafting their experiences—albeit within limits. Interviews would help me understand what American families actually do with finance as they seek to satisfy their culturally specific sense of responsibilities to each other. The problem with interviewing American middle-class families about household finance is that they generally don't want to discuss it, certainly not with a stranger who's writing a book.

Silence around finances is an important feature of middle-class culture, and the taboo on openly discussing family finances profoundly shaped my research and my analysis. Like most cultural anthropologists, I typically use participant observation to understand people's values, practices, and beliefs and how these draw them into engagement with large-scale, powerful economic systems. But participant observation isn't very useful when it comes to studying how families pay for college. After all, families do not take out their books in public. In many cases, parents don't even share information about their financial situation with their children, which means that people making one of the most important economic decisions of their lives often do so without discussing the numbers as a family—let alone with an outside observer. Americans will sooner talk to you about their sex lives than their salaries, the adage goes, and the same is true for their accounts. They may discuss financial challenges over dinner with friends or with neighbors, but in ways governed by formulas for maintaining privacy around the details. Paying for college placed the privacy of family finances at the center of my study, but how could I research a subject few discuss openly?

The only way to learn about the financial lives of families was to ask for permission to enter their private worlds, and to persuade them that they could trust me to handle their sensitive, personal information conscientiously. Paying for college involved plans and dreams, responsibilities and obligations, and financial schemes that involved both parents and young adult children. Learning how the financial economy fashions family life required understanding how each generation saw its economic and moral responsibilities and reckoning with their failures to fulfill them. It also required gaining a view of how each person in a family understood and engaged with the financial tools they used to construct their lives. I designed an interview study in which I would spend time speaking with people about something so personal, so intimate, that they rarely discussed it with anyone.

I began by interviewing college students. I hired and trained a team of research assistants. We started at NYU, where I work and know the students well. Each student we spoke with carried loans to pay for college. In our interviews, which were open-ended, our questions guided the discussion. We were most interested, however, in where the students themselves would take us. We asked about why they chose NYU, how they paid for school and its related costs (from books to housing and recreation), how they negotiated who would pay for what with their parents, and what kinds of discussions about money they had with their families. We asked students about whether and how they discussed loans with their friends. We asked them about their futures and how they saw their family's finances shaping their possibilities and constraints.

After the first interviews, I realized that talking to students captured only a small corner of the larger picture of student finance. These students, including Kimberly from chapter 6, placed their family at the center of their stories of college and student finance. They were telling me something important: I would also need to understand the experiences that mothers and fathers brought with them to their child's higher education. That meant that getting a fuller story would require interviewing parents as well.

Parents and children occupy different positions with distinctive responsibilities in the student finance complex. Cross-generational interviews promised to help me understand the specific family problems that students and their parents faced. Family life and the problem of paying for college is different today than it was in the 1980s and 1990s, when the parents in my study attended college. These histories and differences would likely shape the way that parents and children perceived student finance and the value of college. The contrasts in their perspectives might generate conflicting understandings of a shared situation, and interviewing across the generational divide would help me flesh out how history plays a part in financing family life.

For me, the next challenge was figuring out how to recruit families into my research project. I began asking each student I spoke with if they would invite their parents to join the study too. Few followed through. Only a handful were willing even to ask. Once I was able to move past frustration, I began to question why this might be. I turned to the students whom I knew and trusted and asked them to explain their reluctance. Their answers were eye-opening. They were afraid that by speaking to me about their family's finances they had broken a sacred trust. They feared that they had given me information that should be restricted to family members. They worried that their decision to participate in our study would anger their parents. The power of this sense of privacy made gathering interviews especially difficult.

It was also revealing—an obstacle to the study that delivered a key lesson. The difficulties of finding students and parents who would open up about their financial situations showed me how important privacy was to middle-class families. Open discussion might reveal just how dependent middle-class families were on assistance, from the government and from each other, and just how dependent they were on the financial industry too. Dropping the veil of privacy, even momentarily and to a stranger who was offering anonymity in an interview, meant compromising their very middle-class status. In American middle-class culture, privacy about family finance is a form of self-defense. Although this meant that interviews were difficult to organize, thinking through and eventually overcoming the challenge of arranging them enriched my understanding of how and why financing education is so challenging. It helped me focus on a problem at the heart of the study: how families use finance to project independence and to generate it for young adults as well.

The secret to getting both students and parents to participate in the study was to build stronger relationships with them, reaching out to those who already trusted us and asking them to refer us to their family and friends. This meant we'd be using what social scientists call *snowball sampling*, which carries one major downside: the risk of bias that comes from speaking only to people who are part of the same network. To make sure we reached beyond any single network or social group, I asked my research assistants to recruit participants from across the US, starting from within their own family and friendship connections and extending beyond them over time. The criteria were that interviewees needed to carry loans for higher education and that the parents' occupations conformed to broad sociological definitions of middle-class work. We recruited from families whose young adults attended four-year colleges, both public and private, some from near their homes and others across state lines. I also understood that starting my interview study at NYU, a costly private school in the midst of the country's most expensive city, as well as my own experiences at the university, could distort my findings. I further diversified the sample by conducting a cluster of interviews in a setting where paying for a private university like NYU would seem to be an unnecessary option.

Michigan has a revered place among the states in US higher education due to the large set of varied and high-quality public institutions that it began building in the late nineteenth century. From the flagship campuses of the University of Michigan at Ann Arbor and Michigan State University in East Lansing to the urban centers of Wayne State University and the University of Michigan at Flint and the farther-flung campuses of Northern and Western Michigan Universities, the fifteen public universities in the state provide excellent choices for all variety of students. Today families in Michigan—and in states with similarly strong public schools, including California, Texas, Florida, and (despite current threats from the state government) North Carolina and Wisconsin—do not need to go outside the public university system to get their children an excellent education. The quality and diversity of these options affect how families in the state thought about the problem of paying for college and shape how they engage with the financial economy. I traveled to Michigan to interview college students and their families about their experiences paying for and financing college, which added depth and heterogeneity to the sample.

This strategy yielded interviews with a wide range of middle-class families across the United States, with particular concentrations of interviews in the Midwest and the Northeast. We interviewed families across race and ethnicity as well as region. Whites made up 68 percent of the families interviewed, followed by African Americans at 10 percent, and mixed race, Latino, and Asian American families making up the remaining 22 percent. These are all slippery categories, but to put the sample in perspective, in 2017 the US Census Bureau lists the "Non-Hispanic White" population of the US at 61 percent, the African American population at 13 percent, the Hispanic population at 18 percent, and the Asian American population at 6 percent.

The interviews also represent a range of family settings. Divorce, remarriage, and single parenthood have redefined family life in the United States. Although the US continues to hold up an ideal of the nuclear family, households with two parents in a first marriage and their children now represent a minority. Adults often move in and out of different situations, choosing marriage, cohabiting or simply staying single. The sociologist and demographer Andy Cherlin calls this the "marriage-go-round."[1] At the time of their interviews, 72 percent of families were in dual-parent households and 28 percent had one parent at home.

Since this is a study about higher education, parents' own college experiences are especially important. Here the college- and graduate school–educated parents are overrepresented. Eighty-five percent had at least a bachelor's degree, which is higher than the general US population. Fifteen percent of parents in our study had no college or only some college. The study is therefore good for talking about what it means to try to hold on to middle-class aspirations, ones that these parents' own parents also aimed for and achieved.

I conducted the first interviews for this study in 2012, and the last of the more than 160 interviews my team conducted took place in 2015. The core of this study consists of 80 interviews, or 40 pairs, each made up of one college student and a parent, who together have taken on debt for the young adult's higher education.[2] Eighty singleton interviews split between parents and college students complete the interview study. In addition, a number of families invited me into their homes and personal lives and allowed me to get to know them better. Peggy, Bruce, and their boys, Tom and Aidan, from suburban Michigan; Kimberly and June from outside Philadelphia; Ramona, Stanley, and Stanley II from near Columbus all belong to this group. In each of these cases, I spent time with the family at home, traveled with them, and kept in touch over several years. This helped me understand more about their situations and observe how they evolved over time.

After all the interviews were complete, my research assistants and I read over the transcripts and reviewed our notes, looking for consistent themes. We worked inductively, developing codes from these discussions and applying them across the transcripts using the qualitative data analysis program Dedoose. I found patterns across all the interviews; the singleton interviews confirmed the patterns that I observed in the family pairs that constitute the core of the study. I was impressed and surprised by the consistency of the responses across the differences of race and region in the study. Although histories of advantage and discrimination divided family paths in powerful ways, aspirations to middle-class status appeared in remarkably similar language and were marked by parallel concerns about young adults' futures.

This was borne out in the Michigan interviews, which closely tracked those conducted in other parts of the country. Although Michigan residents do have access to strong higher education options, they face a financial landscape similar to that of other American families. The state legislature has been cutting funds to public colleges and universities for decades now, and they suffered particularly stringent cuts under Governor Rick Snyder in 2011. Predictably, tuitions have risen. Today the advertised cost of attending one of the four-year campuses for in-state residents can range from $20,000 at Northern Michigan, Western Michigan, and Wayne State to $30,000 at Michigan State University and the University of Michigan. With a median household income of just above $50,000, paying for college in Michigan remains a challenge for middle-class families, and residents rely on federal and family financing like other Americans.

The commonalities I observed across the interviews stem from the fact that the families are similarly situated in their relationship to the student finance complex. American middle-class families are diverse and complex, but they all deal with problems created by the student finance complex, and their class position constrains their set of solutions for sending their children to college. The families were united by their need for federal aid, and sometimes private loans, and they all felt pressure to manage their own savings. They also share common experiences as they move through the student finance complex. Each family with financial need is confronted with the possibility of investing in a 529 plan, compelled to fill out the FAFSA form, nervous to receive (and often baffled by) the Expected Family Contribution, and likely to use loans to cover the remaining costs. The tools of the student finance complex structure American families' lives in consistent ways, even if their reactions and attempts to make them work in their interests differ.

Although particular family circumstances gave shape to their feelings and strategies, the families also drew on a common repertoire of cultural ideas about how and why they made their way through this fixed financial landscape. Across race and region, they described an ambition to create open futures for young adults. This common moral project marked the family as middle class and was central to the ambition to pass class status on to children.

An open future requires release from the patterns of the past. This makes moral orientation even more important to middle-class status, another reason for the commonality among family framings of their situations. Financial reasoning would require families to rely on their histories to anticipate how their futures will unfold. Open futures cannot accommodate being bound to past patterns and explicit calculations. Under the condition of hopeful uncertainty, moral orientations provide a way to navigate.

Interviews are particularly good for understanding moral orientations, as many accomplished interviewers have explained.[3] This is, in part, because the interview represents a shared moral space in which interviewees articulate their aspirations and their sense of what they should do. It's also because interviews, especially when conducted with representatives of respected universities, create a context in which subjects often feel compelled to justify their behavior. The interaction therefore generates strong statements about moral orientations. For this reason, among others, interviews illuminate values and beliefs.

One risk of relying on interviews, however, is that any polite person, especially one who has agreed to discuss their private life, will tell impromptu stories or offer spontaneous opinions about things they haven't thought much about, solely because they want to satisfy the interviewer or meet conversational norms. This is a problem, because the pressure to answer questions might produce answers that are not well thought through or that bear only a glancing resemblance to what interviewees think or what they feel in their everyday lives. Using interviews effectively requires asking people questions about experiences that they have already reflected upon, and they are especially effective if they're conducted at the right moment, when subjects are confronting challenges to their moral systems.

When young adults are enrolled in college is just such a time. The financial trade-offs that families make to pay for higher education force them to assess their own values, weighing them in relation to moral mandates that come from other parts of our shared culture and economy. The problem of paying for college means that families are already reflecting on how they should bring their beliefs—about balancing retirement and their children's education, for example—in line with the possible actions they can take. How much should they borrow to pay for college? Should financial issues affect the school that their child chooses? Who is responsible for the payments? Who, ultimately, gets to decide which place is right? These practical choices require intense moral reflection. As a researcher, I took advantage of the fact that my subjects were thinking intensely about these matters. The interview situation is well suited to draw out these reflections; it produced the best possible evidence for the cultural and economic questions that the study was designed to answer.

# Notes

■ ■ ■

## Chapter 1. Introduction

1. For a revealing, and complimentary, examination of the challenges lower-income students face in paying for college, see Sara Goldrick-Rab, *Paying the Price: College Costs, Financial Aid, and the Betrayal of the American Dream* (Chicago: University of Chicago Press, 2016). As I do in this book, Goldrick-Rab argues that the high cost of college alters family life, particularly by making college a means for students to better their family's circumstances.

2. *Bloomberg*, November 2, 2018; *Fortune*, July 10, 2017; *Knowledge@Wharton*, October 22, 2018.

3. Paula Fass, *The End of the American Childhood: A History of Parenting from Life on the Frontier to the Managed Child* (Princeton, NJ: Princeton University Press, 2016), 9.

4. In its mid-twentieth-century form, the middle class was identified with stability. A central place in the era's corporate hierarchies and the ability of those middling employees to raise children who would be like them gave shape to their in-between social position. This is the middle class that C. Wright Mills and William H. Whyte enshrined and that still anchors both scholarly notions of class and the aspirations of those beyond the academy (Caitlin Zaloom, "What Does 'Middle Class' Really Mean?," *Atlantic,* November 4, 2018, https://www.theatlantic.com/ideas/archive/2018/11/what-does-middle-class-really-mean/574534/).

5. William H. Whyte argued that the "organization man" governed himself by "vows" of upholding the values of the corporate, government, and religious institutions that employ him (Whyte, *The Organization Man* (Garden City, NY: Doubleday, 1956)).

6. The anthropologist Natasha Schüll has named this kind of unequal alliance "asymmetric collusion," to indicate the "tight coupling" between the designs of powerful institutions and the desires of their users that produces a seemingly harmonious relationship (Schüll, *Addiction by Design: Machine Gambling in Las Vegas* (Princeton, NJ: Princeton University Press, 2012)).

7. Elizabeth Popp Berman and Abby Stivers, "Student Loans as a Pressure on U.S. Higher Education," *Research in the Sociology of Organizations* 46 (2016): 129–160.

8. Economist Teresa Ghilarducci has called the 401(k) a "failed experiment." Originally intended to supplement retirement funds for highly paid employees, these investment accounts were a badge of class as well as an economic tool. They were not intended for the widespread use they have come to enjoy. In the 1980s and 1990s, however, corporations began to roll back their retirement supports, replacing traditional "defined benefit" pensions with private investment accounts, or eliminating their commitment to retirement support altogether. Today about one-third of American workers do not have access to a retirement plan and almost half of American workers won't be able to maintain their standard of living in retirement, according to the Center for Retirement Research at Boston College (Alicia H. Munnell, Anthony Webb, and Francesca N. Golub-Sass, "Is There Really a Retirement Savings Crisis? An NRRI Analysis," Center For Retirement Research at Boston College, July 2007, http://crr.bc.edu/briefs/is-there-really-a-retirement-savings-crisis-an-nrri-analysis/; and Teresa Ghilarducci, *When I'm Sixty-Four: The Plot against Pensions and the Plan to Save Them* (Princeton, NJ: Princeton University Press, 2008)).

9. "A Chat with Dave Stockman," *Columbia Daily Spectator,* October 12, 1981. This statement summed up the Republican compromise around aid; those who want assistance from the state must have individual foresight and demonstrate future-oriented self-management that corresponds with the demands of finance.

10. Since the 1990s, the American middle class has been identified with its precariousness. As many scholars have shown, broad economic changes, like financialization, have brought on middle-class instability and cultural anxieties about family life. I refer to this work throughout the book. For starting points, see Stephanie Coontz, *The Way We Never Were: American Families and the Nostalgia Trap* (New York: Basic Books, 2016); Marianne Cooper, *Cut Adrift: Families in Insecure Times* (Berkeley: University of California Press, 2014); Barbara Ehrenreich, *Fear of Falling: The Inner Life of the Middle Class* (New York: HarperCollins, 1990); Rachel Heiman, *Driving after Class: Anxious Times in an American Suburb* (Berkeley: University of California Press, 2015); Karyn R. Lacy, *Blue-Chip Black* (Berkeley: University of California Press, 2007); Michèle Lamont, *Money, Morals, and Manners: The Culture of the French and the American Upper-Middle Class* (Chicago: University of Chicago Press, 1994); Katherine S. Newman, *Falling from Grace: Downward Mobility in the Age of Affluence* (Berkeley: University of California Press, 1999); Joe Nocera, *A Piece of the Action: How the Middle Class Joined the Money Class* (New York: Simon & Schuster, 2013); Elinor Ochs, *Fast-Forward Family: Home, Work, and Relationships in Middle-Class America* (Berkeley: University of California Press, 2013); Sherry B. Ortner, *New Jersey Dreaming: Capital, Culture, and the Class of '58* (Durham, NC: Duke University Press, 2015); Mary Pattillo, *Black on the Block: The Politics of Race and Class in the City*

(Chicago: University of Chicago Press, 2008); Katherine Porter, ed., *Broke: How Debt Bankrupts the Middle Class* (Stanford, CA: Stanford University Press, 2012); Allison J. Pugh, *The Tumbleweed Society: Working and Caring in an Age of Insecurity* (New York: Oxford University Press, 2015); Alissa Quart, *Squeezed: Why Our Families Can't Afford America* (New York: Ecco, 2018); Richard V. Reeves, *Dream Hoarders: How the American Upper Middle Class Is Leaving Everyone Else in the Dust, Why That Is a Problem, and What to Do About It* (Washington, DC: Brookings Institution Press, 2017); Theda Skocpol, *The Missing Middle: Working Families and the Future of American Social Policy* (New York: W. W. Norton, 2000); Rachel Sherman, *Uneasy Street: The Anxieties of Affluence* (Princeton, NJ: Princeton University Press, 2017).

11. "Average Net Price over Time for Full-Time Students, by Sector," Trends in Higher Education, College Board, https://trends.collegeboard.org/college-pricing/figures-tables/average-net-price-over-time-full-time-students-sector.

12. Matthew B. Fuller, "A History of Financial Aid to Students," *Journal of Student Financial Aid* 44, no. 1, issue 4 (2014).

13. This calculation is in 2017 dollars. "Tuition and Fees and Room and Board over Time," Trends in Higher Education, College Board, https://trends.collegeboard.org/college-pricing/figures-tables/tuition-fees-room-board-over-time.

14. This accounts for nonrevolving credit.

15. Consumer debt is also held off the books in asset-backed securities available for sale, which I've estimated at a value of $10 billion (based on https://www.jpmorganchase.com/corporate/investor-relations/document/managements-discussion-analysis-2017.pdf, https://www.jpmorgan.com/jpmpdf/1320746088969.pdf, and Bank of America Q2 Form 10-Q 2018).

16. Of course, some parents and students do subscribe to this morality, but as sociologists Neil Fligstein and Adam Goldstein have shown, thinking about life choices in purely financial terms seems to be most common among affluent Americans ("The Emergence of a Finance Culture in American Households, 1989–2007," *Socio-Economic Review* 13, no. 3 (2015): 575–601).

17. Bronislaw Malinowski, *Argonauts of the Western Pacific: An Account of Native Enterprise and Adventure in the Archipelagoes of Melanesian New Guinea* (London: George Routledge & Sons; New York: E. P. Dutton, 1932).

18. Marcel Mauss, *The Gift: The Form and Reason for Exchange in Archaic Societies* (London: Cohen & West, 1966).

19. Many contemporary anthropologists have also examined the role of debt and speculation in modern economies. Much of their attention has focused on the morality of financial and cultural mandates. In *Debt: The First 5000 Years* (New York: Melville House, 2011) David Graeber argues that modern financial regimes have remade human obligations; in their books *Mutual Life, Limited: Islamic Banking, Alternative Currencies, Lateral Reason* (Princeton, NJ: Princeton University Press, 2005) and *Navigating*

*Austerity: Currents of Debt along a South Asian River* (Stanford, CA: Stanford University Press, 2015), Bill Maurer and Laura Bear have shown that finance introduces conflicts that bring about novel practices in both business and households. Although conventional economic analysis only considers family as peripheral to large-scale economic processes, anthropologists have shown how family ambitions fuel economic activity, from working in jobs that support nuclear households to building globe-spanning firms, as Sylvia Yanagisako did in her book *Producing Culture and Capital: Family Firms in Italy* (Princeton, NJ: Princeton University Press, 2002). In the process, family, and its cultural obligations between parents and children, also makes contemporary capitalism. I build on this long tradition when I argue that college finance steers family life, exercising moral force on families and reshaping their responsibilities and sense of their futures.

20. Throughout the chapters I describe how my interviewees brought faith to economic decisions, especially in the face of vast uncertainties. Sometimes they turned to secular notions, like trust and love, that bind the present to the future, but often this took an explicitly religious form. Religion also provided community resources central to how the interviewees shaped their families. They expressed thinking about and acting on their futures in ways that tied belief and practice. The interviews affirmed a core perspective of cultural social scientists—that economic and spiritual processes are tightly bound, despite the fact that public marketplace and private life of family and church seem to occupy opposing spheres. In fact, this modern institutional separation lays the foundation for the moral conflicts that parents and young adults face. Each, however, remains imbued with the values and processes of the other, and I use language with religious overtones throughout to describe the importance families place on young adults' futures and the financial decisions that enable them.

21. Viviana A. Zelizer, *Pricing the Priceless Child: The Changing Social Value of Children* (Princeton, NJ: Princeton University Press, 1994).

22. Nancy Fraser, "Contradictions of Capital and Care," *New Left Review,* July 2016, https://newleftreview.org /II/100/nancy-fraser-contradictions-of-capital-and-care.

## Chapter 2. Best-Laid Plans

1. US Government Accountability Office, "Higher Education: Small Percentage of Families Save in 529 Plans," December 2012, https://www.gao.gov/assets/660/650759 .pdf.

2. Penn Graduate School of Education Institute for Research on Higher Education, "College Affordability Diagnosis," accessed March 12, 2018, https://irhe.gse .upenn.edu/affordability-diagnosis.

3. Louis Hyman, *Temp: How American Work, American Business, and the American Dream Became Temporary* (New York: Viking, 2018).

4. Jonathan Morduch and Rachel Schneider, *The Financial Diaries: How American Families Cope in a World of Uncertainty* (Princeton, NJ: Princeton University Press, 2017).

5. Patricia Cohen, "Steady Jobs, with Pay and Hours That Are Anything But," *New York Times*, May 31, 2017, sec. Economy, https://www.nytimes.com/2017/05/31 /business/economy/volatile-income-economy-jobs.html.

6. Jamie M. Lewis and Rose M. Kreider, "Remarriage in the United States," US Census Bureau, March 2015, https://www.census.gov/content/dam/Census/library /publications/2015/acs/acs-30.pdf.

7. Jane I. Guyer, *Marginal Gains: Monetary Transactions in Atlantic Africa* (Chicago: University of Chicago Press, 2004), 155.

8. Michael Mitchell et al., "A Lost Decade in Higher Education Funding," Center on Budget and Policy Priorities, August 23, 2017, https://www.cbpp.org/research/state -budget-and-tax/a-lost-decade-in-higher-education-funding.

9. See Jennifer Ma et al., "Education Pays 2016: The Benefits of Higher Education for Individuals and Society," Trends in Higher Education Series, College Board, https://eric.ed.gov/?id=ED572548.

10. Stephen Vaisey, "What People Want: Rethinking Poverty, Culture, and Educational Attainment," *Annals of the American Academy of Political and Social Science* 629, no. 1 (May 1, 2010): 75–101.

11. Chris M. Kirk, "The Role of Parent Expectations on Adolescent Educational Aspirations," *Educational Studies* 37, no. 1 (May 6, 2010).

12. Rashmita Mistry et al., "A Longitudinal Study of the Simultaneous Influence of Mothers' and Teachers' Educational Expectations on Low-Income Youth's Academic Achievement," *Journal of Youth and Adolescence* 38, no. 6 (July 2009): 826–38.

13. Aprile D. Benner and Rashmita S. Mistry, "Congruence of Mother and Teacher Educational Expectations and Low-Income Youth's Academic Competence," *Journal of Educational Psychology* 99, no. 1 (February 2007): 140–53.

14. Higher educations are class-making endeavors in other ways as well. The admissions process can define elite status, as Mitchell Stevens showed in *Creating a Class: College Admissions and the Education of Elites* (Cambridge, MA: Harvard University Press, 2009). College also represents a critical place where parent expectations and visions of an ideal college education come together with student experiences to reproduce parents' class status (and also gender expression), as Laura Hamilton demonstrates in *Parenting to a Degree: How Family Matters for College Women's Success* (Chicago: University of Chicago Press, 2016). Experiences in college—like on the party circuit—can also expose and exacerbate class divides in ways that mark students well beyond their college years, Elizabeth A. Armstrong and Laura T. Hamilton show in *Paying for the Party: How College Maintains Inequality* (Cambridge, MA: Harvard University Press, 2015).

15. The commitment to children's potential is essential to middle-class American parenthood, as I discuss in chapter 6.

16. "Busting the Top 7 Myths About Prepaid Plans," Florida Prepaid College Board, February 3, 2016.

17. This is a problem, behavioral economists Colin Camerer, George Lowenstein, and Matthew Rabin argue, because "most big decisions regarding e.g. savings [and] educational investments . . . have costs and benefits that occur at different points in time" (Colin F. Camerer et al., *Advances in Behavioral Economics* (New York, Princeton, NJ: Princeton University Press, 2003), 23). Behavioral economists say this tendency helps explain why consumers spend now and do not save enough for future goals, like sending children to college.

18. Richard H. Thaler and Cass R. Sunstein, *Nudge: Improving Decisions about Health, Wealth, and Happiness* (New York: Penguin Books, 2009).

19. Annamaria Lusardi et al., "Financial Literacy among the Young," *Journal of Consumer Affairs* 44, no. 2 (June 1, 2010): 385–80; Annamaria Lusardi and Olivia S. Mitchell, "The Economic Importance of Financial Literacy: Theory and Evidence," National Bureau of Economic Research, April 2013, https://doi.org/10.3386/w18952.

20. Marianne Cooper, "Why Financial Literacy Will Not Save America's Finances," *Atlantic*, May 2, 2016, https://www.theatlantic.com/business/archive/2016/05/financial-literacy/480807/.

21. The personal savings rate is calculated as a percentage of disposable income: https://fred.stlouisfed.org/series/PSAVERT.

22. Mishel Lawrence et al., "Wage Stagnation in Nine Charts," *Economic Policy Institute* (blog), accessed March 12, 2018, http://www.epi.org/publication/charting-wage-stagnation/.

23. Allison Pugh, *Longing and Belonging: Parents, Children, and Consumer Culture* (Berkeley: University of California Press, 2009).

24. Daniel P. Moynihan, "The Negro Family," US Department of Labor, March 1965, https://web.stanford.edu/~mrosenfe/Moynihan's%20The%20Negro%20Family.pdf.

25. Carol B. Stack, *All Our Kin: Strategies for Survival in a Black Community* (New York: Basic Books, 1983), 20.

26. Lower-income Americans do turn to some banking institutions, although often ones labeled "alternative" or "fringe," like check cashers and payday lenders. Urban scholar Lisa Servon argues in her book *The Unbanking of America: How the New Middle Class Survives* (New York: Houghton Mifflin Harcourt, 2017) that these institutions are responsive to the ways that low-income work and government benefits schedules determine when and how their customers need their money, unlike the mainstream banks. Customers also find check cashers to be more transparent than larger banks. They know up front what fees will be, rather than being surprised by hidden costs that they cannot afford and that can pile up with no notice.

27. The assertion of low-income Americans' moral weakness laid the groundwork for President Bill Clinton's campaign promise to "end welfare as we have come to know it." In 1996, he signed the Personal Responsibility and Work Opportunity Reconciliation Act, which installed an obligation for aid recipients to work as a condition of their benefits.

28. Nancy Fraser and Linda Gordon, "'Dependency' Demystified: Inscriptions of Power in a Keyword of the Welfare State," *Social Politics: International Studies in Gender, State & Society* 1, no. 1 (March 1, 1994): 4–31, https://doi.org/10.1093/sp/1.1.4.

29. Elizabeth F. S. Roberts, "Assisted Existence: An Ethnography of Being in Ecuador," *Journal of the Royal Anthropological Institute* (N.S.) 19, 562–80.

30. Katherine Edin and Laura Lein, *Making Ends Meet: How Single Mothers Survive Welfare and Low Wage Work* (New York: Russell Sage, 1997). On "secretarial school," see page 139.

31. Sudhir Venkatesh, *Off the Books: The Underground Economy of the Urban Poor* (Cambridge, MA: Harvard University Press, 2009), 22–23.

32. Venkatesh, 379.

33. US Government Accountability Office, "Higher Education: Small Percentage of Families Save in 529 Plans," December 2012, https://www.gao.gov/assets/660/650759.pdf.

34. Jonathan Weisman, "Obama Relents on Proposal to End '529' College Savings Plans," *New York Times,* January 27, 2015, sec. Politics, https://www.nytimes.com/2015/01/28/us/politics/obama-will-drop-proposal-to-end-529-college-savings-plans.html.

35. Pew Fiscal Federalism Initiative, "How Governments Support Higher Education through the Tax Code," accessed March 12, 2018, http://pew.org/2mj7CgJ.

36. College Savings Plans Network, "529 Report: An Exclusive Year-End Review of 529 Plan Activity," March 2016, http://www.collegesavings.org/wp-content/uploads/2015/09/FINAL-CSPN-Report-March-15-2016.pdf.

37. Jens Beckert, *Imagined Futures: Fictional Expectations and Capitalist Dynamics* (Cambridge, MA: Harvard University Press, 2016).

38. Douglas R. Holmes, *Economy of Words: Communicative Imperatives in Central Banks* (Chicago: University of Chicago Press, 2013).

39. See also Arjun Appadurai, *Banking on Words: The Failure of Language in the Age of Derivative Finance* (Chicago: University of Chicago Press, 2015); Stefan Liens, *Stories of Capitalism: Inside the Role of Financial Analysts* (Chicago: University of Chicago Press, 2018); and Caitlin Zaloom, "How to Read the Future: The Yield Curve, Affect, and Financial Prediction," *Public Culture* 21, no. 2 (May 1, 2009): 245–68.

40. Mary Poovey. *Genres of the Credit Economy: Mediating Value in Eighteenth- and Nineteenth-Century Britain* (Chicago: University of Chicago Press, 2008).

41. Thorstein Veblen, *The Theory of the Leisure Class,* ed. Martha Banta (Oxford: Oxford University Press, 2009); John Maynard Keynes, *Essays in Persuasion*

(London: Macmillan, 1931). For more recent appreciations of the role of economic imagination, see Deirdre McCloskey, *The Rhetoric of Economics* (*Rhetoric of the Human Sciences*) (University of Wisconsin Press, 1998); on the evolving imagination of national well-being, see Diane Coyle, *GDP: A Brief but Affectionate History* (Princeton, NJ: Princeton University Press, 2015).

42. Helaine Olen, *Pound Foolish: Exposing the Dark Side of the Personal Finance Industry* (New York: Portfolio/Penguin, 2012).

## Chapter 3. The Model Family

1. Mark Kantrowitz and David Levy, *Filing the FAFSA: The Edvisors Guide to Completing the Free Application for Federal Student Aid* (Las Vegas: Edvisors Network, 2013), 13.

2. In addition to privilege, luck also remains underappreciated in both economic thinking and American culture, as economist Robert Frank writes in his book *Success and Luck: Good Fortune and the Myth of Meritocracy* (Princeton, NJ: Princeton University Press, 2016). Policies and everyday explanations alike assume people benefit from their considered and strategic rational actions, rather than from chance events. Serendipity may be difficult to measure, but it is an undeniable piece of both extraordinary successes, like Frank's own, and more everyday ones, like being employed in a stable industry that allows for regular mortgage payments and saving, not to mention good health and strong marriages.

3. Such discrepancies between precision and accuracy have marked accounting devices like the FAFSA from the very beginnings of their modern history, as the historical scholar of finance Mary Poovey has shown (*A History of the Modern Fact: Problems of Knowledge in the Sciences of Wealth and Society* (Chicago: University of Chicago Press, 1998)).

4. Political scientist James C. Scott argues that such bureaucratic ordering lends much of government its shape and form. In order to tax, conscript, and prevent rebellions, modern state officials "created a standard grid" by which they could record and monitor the complex social practices under their purview. These grids gave states the ability to see and read their populations and to manipulate them (Scott, *Seeing Like a State: How Certain Schemes to Improve the Human Condition Have Failed* (New Haven, CT: Yale University Press, 1998)).

5. Writing in the 1970s, anthropologist Constance Perin noted that middle-class respectability was rooted in the debts of home mortgages. Although bankers and homeowners alike spoke about the freedom that home ownership created, homeowners were valued as citizens based on the very constraints that mortgages required, like consistent and well-paid work. Such cultural creditworthiness continues to

buttress middle-class citizenship (Perin, *Everything in Its Place: Social Order and Land Use in America* (Princeton, NJ: Princeton University Press, 1977)).

6. Matthew S. Hull, *Government of Paper: The Materiality of Bureaucracy in Urban Pakistan* (Berkeley: University of California Press, 2012). For more on the materials that make bureaucracies work, see Lisa Gitleman, *Paper Knowledge: Toward a Media History of Documents* (Durham, NC: Duke University Press, 2014), and Ben Kafka, *The Demon of Writing: Powers and Failures of Paperwork* (New York: Zone Books, 2012).

7. Best-selling author and *Ladies Home Journal* columnist Christine Frederick was one of the most prominent home economists. Frederick, like others, promoted using family money in new ways organized around a home budget. With this novel tool, families could develop shared goals together and allocate their monies to achieve these ever-receding futures. In the home economists' writings, budgeting, especially for higher education, delivered a distinct identity, separating modern, middle-class families from working-class ones. For more historical work on the rise of the middle-class family, see Mary P. Ryan, *Cradle of the Middle Class: The Family in Oneida County, New York, 1790–1865* (Cambridge, UK: Cambridge University Press, 1981); Paula S. Fass, *The End of American Childhood: A History of Parenting from Life on the Frontier to the Managed Child* (Princeton, NJ: Princeton University Press, 2016); Nancy F. Cott, *Public Vows: A History of Marriage and the Nation* (Cambridge, MA: Harvard University Press, 2000); Steven Mintz and Susan Kellogg, *Domestic Revolutions: A Social History of American Family Life* (New York: Free Press, 1988); and Stephanie Coontz, *The Way We Never Were: American Families and the Nostalgia Trap* (New York: Basic Books, 1992).

8. Kantrowitz and Levy, *Filing the FAFSA*, 182–196.

9. In 2017 US dollars. US Census Bureau, "Income in the Past 12 Months," 2005–2015 American Community Survey 1-Year Estimates, accessed May 29, 2017, https://factfinder.census.gov/faces/tableservices/jsf/pages/productview.xhtml?pid=ACS_15_1YR_S1901&prodType=table; US Census Bureau, "Median Household Income in the Past 12 Months (in 2015 Inflation-Adjusted Dollars)," 2015 American Community Survey 1-Year Supplemental Estimates with a Population Threshold of 20,000 or More, accessed May 29, 2017, https://factfinder.census.gov/faces/tableservices/jsf/pages/productview.xhtml?pid=ACS_15_SPL_K201902&prodType=table; and US Inflation Calculator, "Inflation Calculator," accessed May 29, 2017, http://www.usinflationcalculator.com/.

10. Cherlin argues that because fewer Americans are getting and staying married, marriage has become a status symbol; those who have achieved it gain prestige and those who don't or can't lose it and often blame themselves for their compromised social standing (Cherlin, *Labor's Love Lost: The Rise and Fall of the Working-Class*

*Family in America* (New York: Russell Sage Foundation, 2014); "The Deinstitutionalization of American Marriage," *Journal of Marriage & Family* 66, no. 4 (November 2004): 848–61; and *The Marriage-Go-Round: The State of Marriage and the Family in America Today* (New York: Vintage Books, 2010).

11. In 2017 dollars. College Board, "Trends in College Pricing 2016: List of Figures and Tables," December 2016, https://trends.collegeboard.org/sites/default/files/2016-trends-college-pricing-source-data_0.xlsx, Table 2; and US Inflation Calculator, "Inflation Calculator," accessed May 30, 2017, http://www.usinflationcalculator.com/.

12. Andrew Lakoff and Stephen Collier make this point that future scenarios are about governing the present, as do I about futures contracts in *Out of the Pits: Traders and Technology from Chicago to London* (Chicago: University of Chicago Press, 2006). See Collier and Lakoff, "Vital Systems Security: Reflexive Biopolitics and the Government of Emergency," *Theory, Culture and Society* 32, no. 2 (March 2015): 19–51, and Lakoff, *Unprepared: Global Health in a Time of Emergency* (Berkeley: University of California Press, 2017).

13. Teresa A. Sullivan, Elizabeth Warren, and Jay Lawrence Westbrook, *The Fragile Middle Class: Americans in Debt* (New Haven, CT: Yale University Press, 2000). For a more recent overview of the central role consumer debt plays in middle-class bankruptcy, see the essays in *Broke: How Debt Bankrupts the Middle Class*, ed. Kathrine Porter (Stanford, CA: Stanford University Press, 2012).

14. US Department of Education, National Center for Education Statistics, Integrated Postsecondary Education Data System (IPEDS), "'Fall Enrollment' and 'Institutional Characteristics' surveys," August 2001, accessed May 30, 2017, https://nces.ed.gov/programs/digest/d01/dt317.asp, 361, Table 317; and US Inflation Calculator, "Inflation Calculator," accessed May 30, 2017, http://www.usinflationcalculator.com/. In 2017 dollars.

15. US Department of Education, National Center for Education Statistics, Integrated Postsecondary Education Data System (IPEDS), "Fall 2011 and Fall 2012, Institutional Characteristics Component; and Spring 2012 and Spring 2013, Enrollment Component," December 2013, accessed May 30, 2017, https://nces.ed.gov/programs/digest/d13/tables/dt13_330.20.asp, Table 330.20; and US Inflation Calculator, "Inflation Calculator," accessed May 30, 2017, http://www.usinflationcalculator.com/. In 2017 dollars.

16. Eric P. Bettinger et al., "The Role of Simplification and Information in College Decisions: Results from the H&R Block FAFSA Experiment," Working Paper, National Bureau of Economic Research, September 2009, doi:10.3386/w15361.

17. Eric P. Bettinger et al., "The Role of Application Assistance and Information in College Decisions: Results from the H&R Block FAFSA Experiment," *Quarterly Journal of Economics* 127, no. 3 (August 1, 2012): 1205–42, doi:10.1093/qje/qjs017.

18. Susan Dynarski, "An Economist's Perspective on Student Loans in the United States," Brookings Institution, September 18, 2014, https://www.brookings.edu/research/an-economists-perspective-on-student-loans-in-the-united-states/.

19. The principle of "disintermediation"—slimming interaction to create a feeling of direct engagement between user and government or commercial agency—guides interface design. These designs take inspiration from market theories that stress that human and digital brokers alike distort information and prices and, therefore, need to be excised from transactions as much as possible. See Caitlin Zaloom, *Out of the Pits: Traders and Technologies from Chicago to London* (Chicago: University of Chicago, 2006).

20. Many common consumer technologies, like the touch screens of automatic teller machines and internet commerce sites, smooth user experience to capture their labor, attention, and consent; see, for example, Michael Palm, *Technologies of Consumer Labor: A History of Self-Service* (New York: Routledge, 2017).

21. Bettina Elias Siegel, "Shaming Children So Parents Will Pay the School Lunch Bill," *New York Times*, April 30, 2017, https://www.nytimes.com/2017/04/30/well/family/lunch-shaming-children-parents-school-bills.html; and Heather Long, "School Lunch Shaming: Inside America's Hidden Debt Crisis," *CNN Money*, May 10, 2017, http://money.cnn.com/2017/05/09/news/economy/school-lunch-shaming-debt-crisis/.

22. Elana Schor, "Senate Kills Rule Limiting Drug Testing for Unemployment Benefits," *Politico*, March 14, 2017, http://www.politico.com/story/2017/03/drug-testing-unemployment-senate-236049.

23. In her foreword to Marcel Mauss's *The Gift*, anthropologist Mary Douglas deploys Mauss's theory to argue that social assistance damages the status of recipients. There is no such thing as a gift that should not be returned, she points out. To accept a gift without the ability to fulfill the obligation to return one—whether to the original giver or within a wider system of exchange—delivers a moral injury and establishes the recipient as a social inferior (Douglas, "No Free Gift," in *The Gift* (New York: Routledge, 1990)). In this way, state aid does not only give needed support, it also reinforces class stratification.

24. US Selective Service System, "Official Legislation by States, Territories, and the District of Columbia," https://www.sss.gov/Registration/State-Commonwealth-Legislation/Other-Legislations.

## Chapter 4. Enmeshed Autonomy

1. Deepened and prolonged involvement in children's lives inspires other conflicted practices of autonomy too. For instance, professional parents use cell phones to monitor children's initial independent movements. "Tethered independence," as

sociologist Margaret K. Nelson names this use of technology, extends anxiety-driven practices of connection that begin when children are infants (Nelson, *Parenting Out of Control: Anxious Parents in Uncertain Times* (New York: NYU Press, 2010)).

2. Katherine S. Newman, *The Accordion Family: Boomerang Kids, Anxious Parents, and the Private Toll of Global Competition* (Boston: Beacon Press, 2012).

3. Patrick Wightman et al., "Historical Trends in Parental Financial Support of Young Adults," Population Studies Center Research Report, PSC Research Report Series (Ann Arbor: University of Michigan, Institute for Social Research, September 2013), http://www.psc.isr.umich.edu/pubs/pdf/rr13–801.pdf.

4. Robert Fisher, M. D., "Failure to Launch Syndrome," *Psychology Today,* January 20, 2015, https://www.psychologytoday.com/us/blog/failure-launch/201501/failure-launch-syndrome.

5. "The EFC Formula, 2017–2018," US Department of Education, Federal Student Aid, https://studentaid.ed.gov/sa/sites/default/files/2017–18-efc-formula.pdf. It remains a mystery to most families how the government calculates their need, even though the Department of Education's algorithm determines one of the most critical financial events of a family's life. The foundations of the formula can be found in the language of accountants within the 1965 Higher Education Act, Part F, Title IV (with updated computation tables published in the *Federal Register*) if a resourceful student or parent wants to take a look.

6. Lower-income students will receive EFCs that give them access to grants and subsidized loans. Those at the bottom of the scale of income and wealth can receive an EFC of zero, giving them access to maximum federal assistance, which is still not usually enough. Families with incomes above $25,000 receive EFCs that require them to pay.

7. Although merit scholarships are prevalent at some state institutions, private universities also offer them. This type of aid to "deserving" students began to take off in the 1970s, but by the late 1990s private school students receiving merit scholarships crossed the 30 percent mark, the historian of financial aid Rupert Wilkinson explains (Wilkinson, *Aiding Students, Buying Students: Financial Aid in America* (Nashville, TN: Vanderbilt University Press, 2005)).

8. Stephen Burd, "Undermining Pell: How Colleges Compete for Wealthy Students and Leave the Low-Income Behind," New America Foundation, 2013, https://s3.amazonaws.com/newamericacomposer/attachments_archive/Merit_Aid%20Final.pdf.

9. Sallie Mae Bank, "How America Pays for College 2016: Sallie Mae's National Study of College Students and Parents," 2016, 7, http://news.salliemae.com/files/doc_library/file/HowAmericaPaysforCollege2016FNL.pdf.

10. Sandy Baum, *Student Debt: Rhetoric and Realities of Higher Education Financing* (New York: Palgrave-Macmillan, 2016), 17.

11. Matt Phillips, "College in Sweden Is Free but Students Still Have a Ton of Debt. How Can That Be?," *Quartz*, May 31, 2013, https://qz.com/85017/college-in-sweden -is-free-but-students-still-have-a-ton-of-debt-how-can-that-be/; and Alex Usher, "Global Debt Patterns: An International Comparison of Student Loan Burdens and Repayment Conditions," Canadian Higher Education Report Series, Educational Policy Institute, 2005, http://educationalpolicy.org/pdf/global_debt_patterns.pdf.

12. Regeringskansliet, "Financial Aid for Studies," April 22, 2015, http://www .government.se/government-policy/education-and-research/the-swedish-financial -aid-system-for-studies/.

13. For a cross-national comparison of parental responsibilities to pay, see D. Bruce Johnstone and Pamela N. Marcucci, *Financing Education Worldwide* (Baltimore: Johns Hopkins University Press, 2010).

14. Ellen Wexler, "Student Loan Lessons from Abroad: Could Student Loan Repayment Models from Other Countries Work in the United States?," *Inside Higher Ed*, June 14, 2016, https://www.insidehighered.com/news/2016/06/14/what-other -countries-can-teach-us-about-student-loans.

15. Jon Marcus, "How Australia Gets Student Loans Right," *Atlantic*, March 16, 2016, https://www.theatlantic.com/education/archive/2016/03/australia-college -payment-model-exposes-shortcomings-of-new-american-version/473919/.

16. David Brooks, "The Cuomo College Fiasco," *New York Times*, April 14, 2017, sec. Opinion, https://www.nytimes.com/2017/04/14/opinion/the-cuomo-college -fiasco.html.

17. Matthew M. Chingos, "Who Would Benefit Most from Free College?," Evidence Speaks Reports, Center on Children & Families, Brookings Institution, April 21, 2016, https://www.brookings.edu/wp-content/uploads/2016/07/Download-the-paper -5.pdf.

18. Conor Friedersdorf, "Universal Free College Would Be a Regressive Scandal," *Atlantic*, July 30, 2013, https://www.theatlantic.com/politics/archive/2013/07 /universal-free-college-would-be-a-regressive-scandal/278201/.

19. Mary Douglas, *Purity and Danger: An Analysis of Concepts of Pollution and Taboo* (London, New York: Routledge Classics, 2002).

20. According to the Urban Institute, racial wealth inequalities are massive and growing (Urban Institute, "Nine Charts about Wealth Inequality in America," February 2015, http://urbn.is/wealthcharts).

21. Urban Institute, "Nine Charts about Wealth Inequality," 27.

22. Urban Institute, 7.

23. Anthropologists Susan Gal and Gail Kligman introduced the concept of nesting in their research on the political and economic changes in Eastern Europe after 1989. They note that communication practices routinely draw and redraw the distinction between public and private, including within domains already considered on a

single side of that divide. Their conceptualization applies well to the American family; the practice of keeping financial information hidden layers zones of generational privacy into an already private family. Susan Gal and Gail Kligman, *The Politics of Gender after Socialism*, (Princeton, NJ: Princeton University Press 2000), 40–42.

24. Eileen Patten, "Racial, Gender Wage Gaps Persist in U.S. Despite Some Progress," Pew Research Center, July 1, 2016, http://pewrsr.ch/29gNnNA.

25. In *Class and Campus Life: Managing and Experiencing Inequality at an Elite College* (Ithaca, NY: Cornell University Press, 2016), Elizabeth Lee shows how colleges like Princeton bring design campus life to produce "a shared daily life" for students of different social classes, creating a unified identity. In addition to establishing connections among students of the same generation, these new identities also divide them from the worlds in which they grew up, as in Karen's experience.

## Chapter 5. Race and Upward Mobility

1. Eric Foner, *Reconstruction: America's Unfinished Revolution, 1863–1877* (New York: Harper & Row, 1988), 96.

2. James D. Anderson, *The Education of Blacks in the South, 1860–1935* (Chapel Hill: University of North Carolina Press, 1988).

3. Robert A. Margo, " 'Teacher Salaries in Black and White': Pay Discrimination in the Southern Classroom," in *Race and Schooling in the South, 1880–1950: An Economic History* (Chicago: University of Chicago Press, 1990), 52–67, http://www.nber.org/chapters/c8794.

4. President Lyndon B. Johnson, "Remarks on Signing the Higher Education Act of 1965," San Marcos, TX, November 8, 1965, http://www.txstate.edu/commonexperience/pastsitearchives/2008–2009/lbjresources/higheredact.html.

5. Fenaba R. Addo, Jason N. Houle, and Daniel Simon, "Young, Black, and (Still) in the Red: Parental Wealth, Race, and Student Loan Debt," *Race and Social Problems* 8, no. 1 (March 1, 2016): 64–76, doi:10.1007/s12552-016-9162-0.

6. Mark Huelsman, "The Debt Divide: The Racial and Class Bias behind the 'New Normal' of Student Borrowing," Demos, May 19, 2015, http://www.demos.org/sites/default/files/publications/Mark-Debt%20divide%20Final%20(SF).pdf.

7. David Radwin et al., "2011–12 National Postsecondary Student Aid Study (NPSAS:12): Student Financial Aid Estimates for 2011–12," Institute of Education Sciences, U.S. Department of Education, National Center for Education Statistics, 2013, https://eric.ed.gov/?id=ED544184.

8. Rachel Fishman, "The Wealth Gap PLUS Debt: How Federal Loans Exacerbate Inequality for Black Families," New America, May 15, 2018, https://www.newamerica.org/education-policy/reports/wealth-gap-plus-debt/introduction.

9. Katherine M. Saunders, Krystal L. Williams, and Cheryl L. Smith, "Fewer Resources More Debt: Loan Debt Burdens Students at Historically Black Colleges & Universities," UNCF Frederick D. Patterson Research Institute, 2016.

10. Nick Anderson, "Tighter Federal Lending Standards Yield Turmoil for Historically Black Colleges," *Washington Post*, June 22, 2013, https://www.washingtonpost .com/local/education/tighter-federal-lending-standards-yield-turmoil-for -historically-black-colleges/2013/06/22/6ade4acc-d9a5-11e2-a9f2-42ee3912ae0e _story.html?utm_term=.cd6f1df9e069. On "skyrocketing growth," see statistics in Marian Wang, Beckie Supiano, and Andrea Fuller, "The Parent Loan Trap," *Chronicle of Higher Education*, October 4, 2012, https://chronicle.com/article/The-Parent-Loan -Trap/134844/.

11. Matthew Johnson, Julie Bruch, and Brian Gill, "Changes in Financial Aid and Student Enrollment at Historically Black Colleges and Universities after the Tightening of PLUS Credit Standards," US Department of Education, Institute of Education Sciences, National Center for Education Evaluation and Regional Assistance, Regional Educational Laboratory Mid-Atlantic, 2015, ies.ed.gov/ncee/edlabs/regions /midatlantic/pdf/REL_2015082.pdf.

12. Lisa J. Dettling, Joanne W. Hsu, Lindsay Jacobs, Kevin B. Moore, and Jeffrey P. Thompson, "Recent Trends in Wealth-Holding by Race and Ethnicity: Evidence from the Survey of Consumer Finances," *FEDS Notes* (blog), September 27, 2017, https:// www.federalreserve.gov/econres/notes/feds-notes/recent-trends-in-wealth -holding-by-race-and-ethnicity-evidence-from-the-survey-of-consumer-finances -20170927.htm.

13. Joanna Taylor and Tatjana Meschede, "Inherited Prospects: The Importance of Financial Transfers for White and Black College-Educated Households' Wealth Trajectories," *American Journal of Economics and Sociology* 77, no. 3–4 (2018): 1049–76, https://doi.org/10.1111/ajes.12227.

14. Mary P. Ryan, *Cradle of the Middle Class: The Family in Oneida County, New York, 1790–1865* (Cambridge, UK: Cambridge University Press, 1981).

15. Catharine Esther Beecher, *A Treatise on Domestic Economy* (New York: Schocken Books, 1970 [1841]), 188 and 191.

16. 70 percent of African Americans and 80 percent of whites believed that the effort to do better than one's parents was a mark of American character (Jennifer L. Hochschild, *Facing Up to the American Dream: Race, Class, and the Soul of the Nation* (Princeton, N.J.: Princeton University Press, 1995), 55).

17. Deborah Gray White, *Too Heavy a Load: Black Women in Defense of Themselves, 1894–1994* (New York: Norton, 1998), 22.

18. See Louis Hyman, *Debtor Nation: The History of America in Red Ink* (Princeton, NJ: Princeton University Press, 2011), chapter 1.

19. See Roger L. Geiger, *The History of American Higher Education: Learning and Culture from the Founding to World War II* (Princeton, NJ: Princeton University Press, 2014), chapter 10.

20. Many historians have told this story. One foundational book is Kenneth Jackson's *Crabgrass Frontier: The Suburbanization of the United States* (New York: Oxford University Press, 1987).

21. David M. P. Freund, *Colored Property: State Policy and White Racial Politics in Suburban America* (Chicago: University of Chicago Press, 2007); and Ta-Nehisi Coates, "The Case for Reparations," *Atlantic*, June 2014, https://www.theatlantic.com /magazine/archive/2014/06/the-case-for-reparations/361631/. The project Mapping Inequality: Redlining in New Deal America gives access to many redlining maps, city by city. The authors also include the stated reasons for rating an area to be a good or bad risk, including the "great number of fine homes constructed within the last seven years" and "infiltration of undesirables." See https://dsl.richmond.edu/panorama /redlining/.

22. Home equity is essential to American family wealth, but, when black families have it, home equity is even more important to them than to white families, even after their historical exclusion from access to mortgages. Writing in the 1990s, Oliver and Shapiro documented in *Black Wealth/White Wealth* (New York: Routledge, 1995) that real estate made up 63 percent of black wealth, as compared to 43 percent of white wealth. Aspiration to home ownership has not only built wealth for African Americans, however, it has also depleted it. In the years leading up to the 2008 mortgage crisis, African Americans became targets for banks marketing subprime loans. Their history of exclusion from home ownership and the effects of racial discrimination on their credit scores rendered African Americans a lucrative market for these risky products well before the crisis exposed banks' predatory practices (US Department of Housing and Urban Development, "Risk or Race: An Assessment of Subprime Lending Patterns in Nine Metropolitan Areas," August 2009, https://www.huduser.gov /Publications/pdf/risk_race_2011.pdf).

23. African American veterans made significant use of their benefits where they could. Researcher Susan T. Hill documented that "in the black colleges in 1947, veterans composed over one-third of the enrollment and remained a significant proportion of the enrollment through 1950." The public TBIs (traditionally black institutions) were able to offer only limited offerings at that point, however, restricting the educational opportunities of these veterans (Hill, "The Traditionally Black Institutions of Higher Education 1860 to 1982," National Center for Education Statistics, April 1985, https://nces.ed.gov/pubsearch/pubsinfo.asp?pubid=84308, xiii).

24. African Americans began to enjoy substantial benefits from higher education in the 1970s. Bart Landry and Kris Marsh, "The Evolution of the New Black Middle

Class," *Annual Review of Sociology* 37, no. 1 (July 8, 2011): 373–94, doi:10.1146/annurev-soc-081309-150047.

25. Raj Chetty et al., "The Fading American Dream: Trends in Absolute Income Mobility since 1940," *Science* 356, no. 6336 (April 28, 2017): 398–406, doi:10.1126/science.aal4617.

26. Mary Pattillo, *Black Picket Fences, Privilege and Peril among the Black Middle Class* (Chicago: University Of Chicago Press, 2013). See also Bart Landry, *The New Black Middle Class* (Berkeley: University of California Press, 1987).

27. Rakesh Kochhar and Richard Fry, "Wealth Inequality Has Widened along Racial, Ethnic Lines since End of Great Recession," Pew Research Center, December 12, 2014, http://www.pewresearch.org/fact-tank/2014/12/12/racial-wealth-gaps-great-recession/.

28. Edward Rodrigue and Richard V. Reeves, "Five Bleak Facts on Black Opportunity," *Social Mobility Memos* (blog), Brookings Institution, January 15, 2015, https://www.brookings.edu/blog/social-mobility-memos/2015/01/15/five-bleak-facts-on-black-opportunity/.

29. US Census Bureau, "U.S. Census Bureau QuickFacts Selected: Coahoma County, Mississippi," 2010, https://www.census.gov/quickfacts/fact/table/coahomacountymississippi/RHI725216. Coahoma County is 552 square miles, located in the Yazoo Delta region of Mississippi. The county's population of 26,000 is 76 percent black and 23 percent white; 35 percent of the Coahoma population lives under the poverty line.

30. For a magisterial account of the Great Migration, see Isabel Wilkerson's *The Warmth of Other Suns: The Epic Story of America's Great Migration* (New York: Random House, 2010).

31. Michèle Lamont's *The Dignity of Working Men* (Cambridge, MA: Harvard University Press, 2000) argues that working-class men draw boundaries with their own morality, elevating themselves above professional people and the middle-class morals I describe here. Karyn Lacy's *Blue-Chip Black* argues that a set of moral positions defines middle-class black life, particularly attitudes toward work, as in Lamont's book. For both Lamont's working-class and Lacy's upper-middle-class interviewees, the value of work lies in the independence it brings. For our upwardly mobile black interviewees, like the Gateses, gaining independence was both a value and a virtue, a significance buttressed for the histories of discrimination they bore.

32. On the postwar college boom and the Mississippi legislature's decision, see David G. Sansing, *Making Haste Slowly: The Troubled History of Higher Education in Mississippi* (Jackson: University Press of Mississippi, 1990).

33. See Christopher P. Loss, *Between Citizens and the State: The Politics of American Higher Education in the 20th Century* (Princeton, NJ: Princeton University Press,

2012), 178, and Landry and Marsh, "The Evolution of the New Black Middle Class," *Annual Review of Sociology* 37, no. 1 (2011): 382–83. Education returns were essential to black mobility in the post–civil rights era (Landry and Marsh, 383). But it wasn't until the early 1970s that upward mobility began to work through education for African Americans (Landry and Marsh, quoting Featherman and Hauser, 1976).

34. Black colleges and universities have long relied on a paying student body, even while those students and their families start well behind their white counterparts financially. A federal report in 1942 informed its government readers that, as private funding for black colleges and universities had dried up during the Depression, they raised tuition and fees for their students. African American families' low incomes made paying a challenge, even for the relatively privileged among them (Susan T. Hill, "The Traditionally Black Institutions of Higher Education 1860 to 1982," National Center for Education Statistics, September 26, 1985, xviii).

35. Hill, "Traditionally Black Institutions," xviii. According to Hill's 1985 NCES report, "Historically, the TBI's have operated on small budgets, limited by their students' ability to pay tuition and, for public institutions, by small State appropriations. Most TBI's still operate with a marginal surplus or deficit each year and many have no, or small, endowments to serve as buffers in times of financial hardship" (xvii).

36. The Roebuck and Murty data come from the private historically black colleges, which the United Negro College Fund supports. The "close to half" figure is 42 percent. The "more than three quarters" figure is 80 percent (Julian B. Roebuck and Komanduri S. Murty, *Historically Black Colleges and Universities: Their Place in American Higher Education* (Westport, CT: Praeger, 1993), 6).

37. Radwin et al., "2011–12 National Postsecondary Student Aid Study," National Center for Education Statistics, Department of Education, 2013, https://nces.ed.gov/pubs2013/2013165.pdf.

38. Kim Clark, "How Do I Get a Parent PLUS Loan?: Eight Steps to Getting a Federal Parent Loan," *US News & World Report*, September 27, 2010, https://www.usnews.com/education/best-colleges/paying-for-college/student-loan/articles/2010/09/27/how-do-i-get-a-parent-plus-loan.

39. United Negro College Fund, "The Parent PLUS Loan Crisis: An Urgent Crisis Facing Students at the Nation's HBCUs," 2014, http://www.uncf.org/sites/advocacy/SpecialInitiatives/ParentsPlus/MediaDocuments/UNCF-Report-THE-PARENT-PLUS-LOAN-CRISIS-3.25.14.pdf.

40. Kelly Field, "Advocates for Historically Black Colleges Prepare to Sue over PLUS Loan Changes," *Chronicle of Higher Education*, August 26, 2013, http://www.chronicle.com/article/Historically-Black-Colleges/141257.

41. The bureaucratic appeal as the mechanism of social justice was also at work in the Department of Education's response to college fraud. In the case of Corinthian, a for-profit institution found to have misrepresented the value of its degrees, the

Department of Education decided to extend debt relief to students through a case-by-case review.

42. US Department of Education, "The U.S. Department of Education Strengthens Federal Direct PLUS Loan Program," press release, August 7, 2014, https://www.ed.gov/news/press-releases/us-department-education-strengthens-federal-direct-plus-loan-program.

43. US Department of Education, "Department of Education Strengthens Federal Loan Program."

44. Board of Governors of the Federal Reserve System, "Report to the Congress on Credit Scoring and Its Effects on the Availability and Affordability of Credit," August 2007, http://www.federalreserve.gov/boarddocs/rptcongress/creditscore.

45. Matthew Johnson, Julie Bruch, and Brian Gill, "Changes in Financial Aid and Student Enrollment at Historically Black Colleges and Universities after the Tightening of PLUS Credit Standards," https://files.eric.ed.gov/fulltext/ED555652.pdf.

## Chapter 6. Cultivating Potential

1. Gerald Marwell and Ruth E. Ames, "Economists Free Ride, Does Anyone Else? Experiments on the Provision of Public Goods, IV," *Journal of Public Economics* (1981): 295–310.; John R. Carter and Michael D. Irons, "Are Economists Different, and If So, Why?" *Journal of Economic Perspectives* 5, no. 2 (June 1991): 171–77, https://doi.org/10.1257/jep.5.2.171; Robert H. Frank, Thomas Gilovich, and Dennis T. Regan, "Does Studying Economics Inhibit Cooperation?" *Journal of Economic Perspectives* 7, no. 2 (1993): 159–71, https://doi.org/10.1257/jep.7.2.159; Long Wang, Deepak Malhotra, and J. Keith Murnighan, "Economics Education and Greed," *Academy of Management Learning & Education* 10, no. 4 (December 2011): 643–60.; and Philipp Gerlach, "The Games Economists Play: Why Economics Students Behave More Selfishly Than Other Students," *PLoS ONE* 12, no. 9 (2017), https://doi.org/10.1371/journal.pone.0183814.

2. Bryan Caplan and Stephen C. Miller, "Intelligence Makes People Think Like Economists: Evidence from the General Social Survey," *Intelligence* 38, no. 6 (2010): 636–47. https://doi.org/10.1016/j.intell.2010.09.005.

3. Quoted in "More Anthropologists on Wall Street Please," *Economist*, October 24, 2011, https://www.economist.com/democracy-in-america/2011/10/24/more-anthropologists-on-wall-street-please.

4. David J. Deming, "The Value of Soft Skills in the Labor Market," National Bureau of Economic Research, 2017, https://www.nber.org/reporter/2017number4/deming.html. See also Amy C. Edmondson, Vanessa Hart, and Edgar H. Schein, *Teaming: How Organizations Learn, Innovate, and Compete in the Knowledge Economy* (Grand Haven, MI: Jossey-Bass, 2012).

234 • Notes to Chapter 6

5. John Schmitt and Heather Boushey, "The College Conundrum: Why the Benefits of a College Education May Not Be So Clear, Especially to Men," Center for American Progress, December 2010, https://www.americanprogress.org/wp-content/uploads/issues/2010/12/pdf/college_conundrum.pdf.

6. Louis Hyman, *Temp: How American Work, American Business, and the American Dream Became Temporary* (New York: Viking, 2018).

7. David H. Autor, "Why Are There Still So Many Jobs? The History and Future of Workplace Automation," *Journal of Economic Perspectives* 29, no. 3 (August 2015): 3–30.

8. Will Knight, "Is Technology About to Decimate White-Collar Work?," *MIT Technology Review*, November 6, 2017, https://www.technologyreview.com/s/609337/is-technology-about-to-decimate-white-collar-work/.

9. James Paine, "5 White Collar Jobs That AI Will Soon Take Away," *Inc.*, July 17, 2017, https://www.inc.com/james-paine/5-white-collar-jobs-that-ai-will-soon-take-away.html.

10. Carl Benedikt Frey and Michael A. Osborne, "The Future of Employment: How Susceptible are Jobs to Computerisation?," *Technological Forecasting and Social Change* 114 (January 2017): 254–80, doi.org/10.1016/j.techfore.2016.08.019.

11. These arguments about the danger AI presents to labor characterize technology as a sublime power of transformation that is almost natural in its force. Like venture capitalist Lee, some espouse this view, which gives technology the power to determine the path of economic and social change. Erik Brynjolfsson and Andrew McAfee's *The Second Machine Age: Work, Progress, and Prosperity in a Time of Brilliant Technologies* (New York, London: W. W. Norton, 2016) is a prominent example. Historians, sociologists, and anthropologists disagree with this kind of "technological determinism." In fact, even the cotton gin, which is regularly credited with changing the world and accelerating the second industrial revolution, only had its great effects because of the social system of enslavement and British colonial domination of wide swaths of the globe, as historian Sven Beckert argues in *Empire of Cotton* (New York: Vintage Books, 2015). In other words, the cotton gin only worked within the relations of capitalism and colonial power. Arguments about artificial intelligence should be assessed with the same careful attention to the questions of power and profit that Beckert raises for earlier technologies.

12. Stacy Rapacon, "Best Jobs That Don't Require a College Degree," *Kiplinger*, June 27, 2017, https://www.kiplinger.com/slideshow/business/T012-S001-best-jobs-without-a-college-degree-2017/index.html.

13. According to the National Center for Education Statistics, "The percentage of students enrolling in college in the fall immediately following high school completion was 69.2 percent in 2015" ("Fast Facts: Back to School Statistics," US Department of Education, https://nces.ed.gov/fastfacts/display.asp?id=372.

14. "Career and Technical Education: Learning That Works for Florida," Florida Department of Education, http://www.fldoe.org/core/fileparse.php/5652/urlt/CTE_brochure_online.pdf.

15. Wesleyan University President Michael Roth has revived Dewey's memorable quote in defense of the freedom college education can offer (Roth, "John Dewey's Vision of Learning as Freedom," *New York Times*, September 5, 2012, https://www.nytimes.com/2012/09/06/opinion/john-deweys-vision-of-learning-as-freedom.html).

16. John Dewey, *Human Nature and Conduct: An Introduction to Social Psychology* (New York: Henry Holt, 1922).

17. Joseph E. Aoun, *Robot-Proof: Higher Education in the Age of Artificial Intelligence* (Cambridge, MA: MIT Press, 2017), xiii.

18. Cathy N. Davidson, *The New Education: How to Revolutionize the University and Prepare Students for a World in Flux* (New York: Basic Books, 2017), 8.

19. Christopher Loss, *Between Citizens and the State: The Politics of American Higher Education in the 20th Century* (Princeton, NJ: Princeton University Press, 2011).

20. I discuss the standard program here because it has long been the default option for graduates to repay federal loans, as its name suggests. The Department of Education also offers a number of programs that adjust payments to graduates' income or extend the time of repayment, like the Public Service Loan Forgiveness (PSLF) Program. All of these have been plagued with problems that punish graduates who have tried to use them, as extensive media reporting has shown. In fact, in 2018, the United Federation of Teachers filed a class-action suit against Navient, the largest federal loan servicer, for its mishandling of the PSLF Program.

21. Annette Lareau, *Unequal Childhoods: Class, Race, and Family Life* (Berkeley, CA: University of California Press, 2003).

22. Jeffrey Jensen Arnett, *Emerging Adulthood: The Winding Road from the Late Teens through the Twenties* (Oxford: Oxford University Press, 2004).

23. Richard Fry, "Millennials Aren't Job-Hopping Any Faster Than Generation X Did," Pew Research Center, April 19, 2017, http://www.pewresearch.org/fact-tank/2017/04/19/millennials-arent-job-hopping-any-faster-than-generation-x-did/.

24. Megan Reynolds, "Nostalgia Fact-Check: How Does Felicity Hold Up?," *Vulture*, November 10, 2011, http://www.vulture.com/2011/11/nostalgia-fact-check-how-does-felicity-hold-up.html.

25. Tressie McMillan Cottom, *Lower Ed: The Troubling Rise of For-Profit Colleges in the New Economy* (New York: New Press, 2017), 21.

26. Marceline White and Renee Brown, "Making the Grade? An Analysis of For-Profit and Career Schools in Maryland," Maryland Consumer Rights Division, http://www.marylandconsumers.org/penn_station/folders/about/test_2/For-Profit_School_Report_-_for_website.pdf.

27. Caren A. Arbeit and Laura Horn, "A Profile of the Enrollment Patterns and Demographic Characteristics of Undergraduates at For-Profit Institutions," US Department of Education, National Center for Education Statistics, February 28, 2017, https://nces.ed.gov/pubsearch/pubsinfo.asp?pubid=2017416.

28. Suzanne Mettler, *Degrees of Inequality: How the Politics of Higher Education Sabotaged the American Dream* (New York: Basic Books, 2014), 4.

29. Pew Research Center, "The Rising Cost of Not Going to College," http://assets .pewresearch.org/wp-content/uploads/sites/3/2014/02/SDT-higher-ed-FINAL-02 -11-2014.pdf.

30. Beth Akers and Matthew Chingos, *Game of Loans: The Rhetoric and Reality of Student Debt* (Princeton, NJ: Princeton University Press, 2016), 20.

31. Akers and Chingos, *Game of Loans*, 5.

32. Mark Huelsman, "The Debt Divide: The Racial and Class Bias behind the "New Normal" of Student Borrowing," Demos, May 19, 2015, accessed June 12, 2018, http://www.demos.org/publication/debt-divide-racial-and-class-bias-behind-new -normal-student-borrowing.

33. Rajashri Chakrabarti, Nicole Gorton, and Wilbert van der Klaauw, "Diplomas to Doorsteps: Education, Student Debt, and Homeownership," *Federal Reserve Bank of New York: Liberty Street Economics* (blog), April 3, 2017, http://libertystreete conomics.newyorkfed.org/2017/04/diplomas-to-doorsteps-education-student-debt -and-homeownership.html; and US Department of Education, National Center for Education Statistics, "National Education Longitudinal Study of 1988 (NELS:88)," accessed June 12, 2018, https://nces.ed.gov/surveys/nels88/.

34. Daniel Cooper and Christina Wang, "Student Loan Debt and Economic Outcomes," *Current Policy Perspectives, Federal Reserve Bank of Boston* 14, no. 3 (2014): 11, https://www.bostonfed.org/publications/current-policy-perspectives/2014 /student-loan-debt-and-economic-outcomes.aspx.

35. Robert Hiltonsmith, "At What Cost? How Student Debt Reduces Lifetime Wealth," Demos, August 2013, accessed June 12, 2018, http://www.demos.org/sites /default/files/imce/AtWhatCostFinal.pdf.

## Chapter 7. Conclusion: A Right to the Future

1. A right to the future extends a concept popular with both urban scholars and movements, the "right to the city." For more, see Caitlin Zaloom, "A Right to the Future: Student Debt and the Politics of Crisis," *Cultural Anthropology* 33, no. 4 (2018): 558–569, https://doi.org/10.14506/ca33.4.05.

2. Julie Margetta Morgan and Marshall Steinbaum, "The Student Debt Crisis, Labor Market Credentialization, and Racial Inequality: How the Current Student Debt Debate Gets the Economics Wrong," Roosevelt Institute, 2018,

http://rooseveltinstitute.org/student-debt-crisis-labor-market-credentialization-racial-inequality/.

3. Thomas G. Mortenson, "State Funding: A Race to the Bottom," American Council on Education, 2012, https://www.acenet.edu/the-presidency/columns-and-features/Pages/state-funding-a-race-to-the-bottom.aspx.

4. Michael Mitchell, Michael Leachman, and Kathleen Masterson, "A Lost Decade in Higher Education Funding," Center on Budget and Policy Priorities, 2017, https://www.cbpp.org/research/state-budget-and-tax/a-lost-decade-in-higher-education-funding.

5. "Higher Education Loan Program (HELP) Changes—Sustainability Act," Australian Government Department of Education and Training, September 25, 2018, https://www.education.gov.au/higher-education-loan-program-help-changes-sustainability-act.

6. Economists Matthew Chingos and Susan Dynarski argue for an income-based repayment system and explain that the specific terms of programs make or break their success. Chingos and Dynarski's ideal loan repayment system must be "simple," meaning that it is "based on students' incomes, that spreads loan payments over longer periods and that's able to collect payments automatically through the tax system" (Chingos and Dynarski, "An International Final Four: Which Country Handles Student Debt Best?," *New York Times*, April 4, 2018, sec. Upshot, https://www.nytimes.com/2018/04/02/upshot/an-international-final-four-which-country-handles-student-debt-best.html).

7. Jon Marcus, "How Australia Gets Student Loans Right," *Atlantic*, March 26, 2016. https://www.theatlantic.com/education/archive/2016/03/australia-college-payment-model-exposes-shortcomings-of-new-american-version/473919/.

8. Toni Monkovic, "Why Australian College Graduates Feel Sorry for Their American Counterparts," *New York Times*, May 29, 2018, sec. Upshot, https://www.nytimes.com/2018/05/11/upshot/australia-college-graduates-student-debt-america.html.

9. Marcus provides an excellent description of these politics.

## Methodological Appendix. Family Situations

1. Andrew Cherlin, *The Marriage-Go-Round: The State of Marriage and the Family in America Today* (New York: Vintage Books, 2010).

2. The college students were mostly enrolled at the time of their interview, although a number of them were within five years of graduation.

3. See, for instance, Michèle Lamont and Ann Swidler, "Methodological Pluralism and the Possibility and Limits of Interviewing," *Qualitative Sociology* 37, no. 2 (2014).

# Bibliography

...

Addo, Fenaba R., Jason N. Houle, and Daniel Simon. "Young, Black, and (Still) in the Red: Parental Wealth, Race, and Student Loan Debt." *Race and Social Problems* 8, no. 1 (March 1, 2016): 64–76. https://doi.org/10.1007/s12552-016-9162-0.

Akers, Beth, and Matthew Chingos. *Game of Loans: The Rhetoric and Reality of Student Debt*. Princeton, NJ: Princeton University Press, 2016.

American Academy of Arts and Sciences. "The State of the Humanities 2018: Graduates in the Workforce & Beyond." https://www.amacad.org/content/publications/publication.aspx?d=43025.

Anders, George. *You Can Do Anything: The Surprising Power of a Useless Liberal Arts Education*. New York: Little, Brown, 2017.

Anderson, James D. *The Education of Blacks in the South, 1860–1935*. Chapel Hill: University of North Carolina Press, 1988.

Anderson, Nick. "Tighter Federal Lending Standards Yield Turmoil for Historically Black Colleges." *Washington Post*, June 22, 2013, sec. Education. https://www.washingtonpost.com/local/education/tighter-federal-lending-standards-yield-turmoil-for-historically-black-colleges/2013/06/22/6ade4acc-d9a5-11e2-a9f2-42ee3912aeoe_story.html.

Angeletos, George-Marios, David Laibson, Andrea Repetto, Jeremy Tobacman, and Stephen Weinberg. "The Hyperbolic Consumption Model: Calibration, Simulation, and Empirical Evaluation." *Journal of Economic Perspectives* 15, no. 3 (September 2001): 47–68. https://doi.org/10.1257/jep.15.3.47.

Aoun, Joseph E. *Robot-Proof: Higher Education in the Age of Artificial Intelligence*. Cambridge, MA: MIT Press, 2017.

Appadurai, Arjun. *Banking on Words: The Failure of Language in the Age of Derivative Finance*. Chicago: University of Chicago Press, 2015.

Arbeit, Caren A., and Laura Horn. "A Profile of the Enrollment Patterns and Demographic Characteristics of Undergraduates at For-Profit Institutions." US Department of Education, National Center for Education Statistics, February 28, 2017. https://nces.ed.gov/pubsearch/pubsinfo.asp?pubid=2017416.

Armstrong, Elizabeth, and Laura Hamilton. *Paying for the Party: How College Maintains Inequality.* Cambridge, MA: Harvard University Press, 2015.

Arnett, Jeffrey Jensen. *Emerging Adulthood: The Winding Road from the Late Teens through the Twenties.* Oxford: Oxford University Press, 2006.

Australian Government Department of Education and Training. "Higher Education Loan Program (HELP) Changes—Sustainability Act." September 25, 2018. https://www.education.gov.au/higher-education-loan-program-help-changes -sustainability-act.

Autor, David H. "Why Are There Still So Many Jobs? The History and Future of Workplace Automation." *Journal of Economic Perspectives* 29, no. 3 (August 2015): 3–30. https://doi.org/10.1257/jep.29.3.3.

Baum, Sandy. *Student Debt: Rhetoric and Realities of Higher Education Financing.* New York: Palgrave-Macmillan, 2016.

Beckert, Jens. *Imagined Futures: Fictional Expectations and Capitalist Dynamics.* Cambridge, MA: Harvard University Press, 2016.

Beckert, Sven. *Empire of Cotton: A Global History.* New York: Vintage, 2015.

Beecher, Catharine. *A Treatise on Domestic Economy: For the Use of Young Ladies at Home, and at School.* Boston: T. H. Webb, 1843.

Benner, Aprile D., and Rashmita S. Mistry. "Congruence of Mother and Teacher Educational Expectations and Low-Income Youth's Academic Competence." *Journal of Educational Psychology* 99, no. 1 (February 2007): 140–53.

Bettinger, Eric P., Bridget Terry Long, Philip Oreopoulos, and Lisa Sanbonmatsu. "The Role of Application Assistance and Information in College Decisions: Results from the H&R Block FAFSA Experiment." *Quarterly Journal of Economics* 127, no. 3 (August 1, 2012): 1205–42. https://doi.org/10.1093/qje/qjs017.

———. "The Role of Simplification and Information in College Decisions: Results from the H&R Block FAFSA Experiment." Working Paper. National Bureau of Economic Research, September 2009. https://doi.org/10.3386/w15361.

Brooks, David. "The Cuomo College Fiasco." *New York Times,* January 20, 2018, sec. Opinion. https://www.nytimes.com/2017/04/14/opinion/the-cuomo-college -fiasco.html.

Bryan, Michael, David Radwin, Peter Siegel, and Jennifer Wine. "2011–12 National Postsecondary Student Aid Study (NPSAS:12)—Student Financial Aid Estimates for 2011–12—First Look." *National Center for Education Statistics,* August 2013, 75.

Brynjolfsson, Erik, and Andrew McAfee. *The Second Machine Age: Work, Progress, and Prosperity in a Time of Brilliant Technologies.* First edition. New York, London: W. W. Norton, 2016.

Burd, Stephen. "Undermining Pell: How Colleges Compete for Wealthy Students and Leave the Low-Income Behind." New America Foundation, May 8, 2013. https://s3 .amazonaws.com/new-america-composer/attachments_archive/Merit_Aid%20 Final.pdf.

Camerer, Colin F., George Loewenstein, and Matthew Rabin, eds. *Advances in Behavioral Economics*. Princeton, NJ: Princeton University Press, 2003.

Caplan, Bryan, and Stephen C. Miller. "Intelligence Makes People Think Like Economists: Evidence from the General Social Survey." *Intelligence* 38, no. 6 (2010): 636–47. https://doi.org/10.1016/j.intell.2010.09.005.

Carter, John R., and Michael D. Irons. 1991. "Are Economists Different, and If So, Why?" *Journal of Economic Perspectives* 5, no. 2 (1991): 171–77. https://doi.org/10.1257/jep.5.2.171.

Chakrawbarti, Rajashri, Nicole Gorton, and Wilbert van der Klaauw. "Diplomas to Doorsteps: Education, Student Debt, and Homeownership." Federal Reserve Bank of New York. *Liberty Street Economics* (blog), April 3, 2017. http://libertystreeteconomics.newyorkfed.org/2017/04/diplomas-to-doorsteps-education-student-debt-and-homeownership.html.

"A Chat with Dave Stockman." *Columbia Daily Spectator* 105, no. 1 (October 12, 1981). Financial Aid. http://spectatorarchive.library.columbia.edu/cgi-bin/columbia?a=d&d=cs19811012-01.2.5&srpos=&e=-------en-20--1--txt-txIN.

Cherlin, Andrew J. *Labor's Love Lost: The Rise and Fall of the Working-Class Family in America*. New York: Russell Sage Foundation, 2014.

———. "The Deinstitutionalization of American Marriage." *Journal of Marriage & Family* 66, no. 4 (November 2004): 848–61.

———. *The Marriage-Go-Round: The State of Marriage and the Family in America Today*. New York: Vintage, 2010.

Chetty, Raj, David Grusky, Maximilian Hell, Nathaniel Hendren, Robert Manduca, and Jimmy Narang. "The Fading American Dream: Trends in Absolute Income Mobility since 1940." *Science*, April 24, 2017. https://doi.org/10.1126/science.aal4617.

Chingos, Matthew M. "Who Would Benefit Most from Free College?" *Economic Studies at Brookings*, Evidence Speaks Reports 1, no. 15 (April 21, 2016): 4.

Chingos, Matthew, and Susan Dynarski. "An International Final Four: Which Country Handles Student Debt Best?" *New York Times*, April 4, 2018, sec. Upshot. https://www.nytimes.com/2018/04/02/upshot/an-international-final-four-which-country-handles-student-debt-best.html.

Clark, Kim. "How Do I Get a Parent PLUS Loan?" *US News & World Report*, September 27, 2010. https://www.usnews.com/education/best-colleges/paying-for-college/student-loan/articles/2010/09/27/how-do-i-get-a-parent-plus-loan.

Coates, Ta-Nehisi. "The Case for Reparations." *Atlantic*, June 2014. https://www.theatlantic.com/magazine/archive/2014/06/the-case-for-reparations/361631/.

Cohen, Patricia. "Steady Jobs, with Pay and Hours That Are Anything But." *New York Times*, May 31, 2017, sec. Economy. https://www.nytimes.com/2017/05/31/business/economy/volatile-income-economy-jobs.html.

College Board. "Average Net Price over Time for Full-Time Students, by Sector." Trends in Higher Education Series. Accessed July 6, 2018. https://trends .collegeboard.org/college-pricing/figures-tables/average-net-price-over-time -full-time-students-sector.

———. "Trends in College Pricing 2016: List of Figures and Tables." December 2016. https://trends.collegeboard.org/sites/default/files/2016-trends-college-pricing -source-data_0.xlsx.

———. "Trends in Student Aid 2017." https://trends.collegeboard.org/sites/default /files/2017-trends-student-aid_0.pdf.

———. "Tuition and Fees and Room and Board over Time." Accessed July 6, 2018. https://trends.collegeboard.org/college-pricing/figures-tables/tuition-fees -room-board-over-time.

College Savings Plans Network. "529 Report: An Exclusive Year-End Review of 529 Plan Activity." March 2016. http://www.collegesavings.org/wp-content/up loads/2015/09/FINAL-CSPN-Report-March-15–2016.pdf.

Collier, Stephen, and Andrew Lakoff, "Vital Systems Security: Reflexive Biopolitics and the Government of Emergency." *Theory, Culture and Society* 32, no. 2 (March 2015): 19–51. https://doi.org/10.1177/0263276413510050.

Coontz, Stephanie. *The Way We Never Were: American Families and the Nostalgia Trap.* New York: Basic Books, 1992.

Cooper, Daniel, and Christina Wang. "Student Loan Debt and Economic Outcomes." Current Policy Perspectives. Federal Reserve Bank of Boston, October 2014. https://www.bostonfed.org/publications/current-policy-perspectives/2014 /student-loan-debt-and-economic-outcomes.aspx.

Cooper, Marianne. "Why Financial Literacy Will Not Save America's Finances." *At-lantic*, May 2, 2016. https://www.theatlantic.com/business/archive/2016/05 /financial-literacy/480807/.

Cooper, Melinda. *Family Values: Between Neoliberalism and the New Social Conserva-tism.* New York: Zone Books, 2017.

Cott, Nancy F. *Public Vows: A History of Marriage and the Nation.* Cambridge, MA: Harvard University Press, 2000.

Cottom, Tressie McMillan. *Lower Ed: The Troubling Rise of For-Profit Colleges in the New Economy.* New York: New Press, 2017.

Cowley, Stacy. "Teachers Sue Navient, Claiming Student Loan Forgiveness Failures." *New York Times*, October 3, 2018, sec. Business. https://www.nytimes.com/2018 /10/03/business/student-loan-forgiveness-lawsuit.html.

———. "28,000 Public Servants Sought Student Loan Forgiveness. 96 Got It." *New York Times*, September 27, 2018, sec. Business. https://www.nytimes.com/2018 /09/27/business/student-loan-forgiveness.html.

Coyle, Diane. *GDP: A Brief but Affectionate History.* Revised and expanded edition. Princeton, NJ: Princeton University Press, 2015.

Davidson, Cathy N. *The New Education: How to Revolutionize the University to Prepare Students for a World in Flux*. First edition. New York: Basic Books, 2017.

Deming, David J. "The Value of Soft Skills in the Labor Market." National Bureau of Economic Research, 2017. https://www.nber.org/reporter/2017number4/deming.html.

Dettling, Lisa J., Joanne W. Hsu, Lindsay Jacobs, Kevin B. Moore, and Jeffrey P. Thompson. "Recent Trends in Wealth-Holding by Race and Ethnicity: Evidence from the Survey of Consumer Finances." *FEDS Notes* (blog), September 27, 2017. https://www.federalreserve.gov/econres/notes/feds-notes/recent-trends-in-wealth-holding-by-race-and-ethnicity-evidence-from-the-survey-of-consumer-finances-20170927.htm.

Dewey, John. *Human Nature and Conduct*. New York: Henry Holt, 1922. http://archive.org/details/humannatureandco011182mbp.

Douglas, Mary. "No Free Gift." In *The Gift*. New York: Routledge, 1990.

———. *Purity and Danger: An Analysis of Concepts of Pollution and Taboo*. New York: Routledge, [1965] 2002.

Dynarski, Susan M. "An Economist's Perspective on Student Loans in the United States." Brookings, November 30, 2001. https://www.brookings.edu/research/an-economists-perspective-on-student-loans-in-the-united-states/.

Edin, Kathryn, and Laura Lein. *Making Ends Meet: How Single Mothers Survive Welfare and Low-Wage Work*. New York: Russell Sage Foundation, 1997.

Edmondson, Amy. *Teaming: How Organizations Learn, Innovate, and Compete in the Knowledge Economy*. San Francisco: Jossey-Bass, 2012.

Ehrenreich, Barbara. *Fear of Falling: The Inner Life of the Middle Class*. New York: HarperCollins, 1990.

Fass, Paula. *The End of American Childhood: A History of Parenting from Life on the Frontier to the Managed Child*. Princeton, NJ: Princeton University Press, 2016.

Federal Reserve Board. "Report to the Congress on Credit Scoring and Its Effects on the Availability and Affordability of Credit." August 2007. https://www.federalreserve.gov/boarddocs/rptcongress/creditscore/.

Field, Kelly. "Advocates for Historically Black Colleges Prepare to Sue over PLUS Loan Changes." *Chronicle of Higher Education*, August 26, 2013. https://www.chronicle.com/article/Historically-Black-Colleges/141257.

Fiscal Federalism Initiative. "How Governments Support Higher Education through the Tax Code." Accessed March 12, 2018. http://pew.org/2mj7CgJ.

Fisher, Robert. "Failure to Launch Syndrome." *Psychology Today*, January 20, 2015. https://www.psychologytoday.com/us/blog/failure-launch/201501/failure-launch-syndrome.

Fishman, Rachel. "The Wealth Gap PLUS Debt: Introduction." New America, May 15, 2018. https://www.newamerica.org.

Fligstein, Neil, and Adam Goldstein. "The Emergence of a Finance Culture in American Households, 1989–2007." *Socio-Economic Review* 13, no. 3 (2015): 575–601.

Florida Department of Education. "Career and Technical Education: Learning That
Works for Florida." Accessed June 12, 2018. http://www.fldoe.org/core/fileparse
.php/5652/urlt/CTE_brochure_online.pdf.

Florida Prepaid College Foundation. "Busting the Top 7 Myths about Prepaid Plans."
Accessed March 12, 2018. http://www.myfloridaprepaid.com/collegedefinitely
/busting-top-7-myths-prepaid-plans/.

Foner, Eric. *Reconstruction: America's Unfinished Revolution, 1863–1877*. New York:
Harper & Row, 1988.

Frank, Robert H. *Success and Luck: Good Fortune and the Myth of Meritocracy.*
Princeton, NJ: Princeton University Press, 2016.

Frank, Robert H., Thomas Gilovich, and Dennis T. Regan. "Does Studying Economics Inhibit Cooperation?" *Journal of Economic Perspectives* 7, no. 2 (1993): 159–71.
https://doi.org/10.1257/jep.7.2.159.

Fraser, Nancy. "Contradictions of Capital and Care." *New Left Review* II, no. 100
(2016): 99–117.

Fraser, Nancy, and Linda Gordon. " 'Dependency' Demystified: Inscriptions of
Power in a Keyword of the Welfare State." *Social Politics: International Studies in
Gender, State & Society* 1, no. 1 (March 1, 1993): 4–31. https://doi.org/10.1093/sp
/1.1.4.

Freund, David M. P. *Colored Property: State Policy and White Racial Politics in Suburban
America.* Chicago: University of Chicago Press, 2010.

Frey, Carl Benedikt, and Michael A. Osborne. "The Future of Employment: How Susceptible Are Jobs to Computerisation?" *Technological Forecasting and Social
Change* 114 (January 2017): 254–80. https://doi.org/10.1016/j.techfore.2016.08.019.

Friedersdorf, Conor. "Universal Free College Would Be a Regressive Scandal." *Atlantic*, July 30, 2013. https://www.theatlantic.com/politics/archive/2013/07
/universal-free-college-would-be-a-regressive-scandal/278201/.

Fry, Richard. "Millennials Aren't Job-Hopping Any Faster Than Generation X Did."
Pew Research Center. *Fact Tank—Our Lives in Numbers* (blog), April 19, 2017.
http://www.pewresearch.org/fact-tank/2017/04/19/millennials-arent-job
-hopping-any-faster-than-generation-x-did/.

Fuller, Matthew. "A History of Financial Aid to Students." *Journal of Student Financial Aid* 44, no. 1 (July 25, 2014). https://publications.nasfaa.org/jsfa/vol44
/iss1/4.

Gal, Susan, and Gail Kligman. *The Politics of Gender after Socialism: A Comparative-
Historical Essay.* Princeton, NJ: Princeton University Press, 2000.

Geiger, Roger. *The History of American Higher Education: Learning and Culture from the
Founding to World War II.* Princeton, NJ: Princeton University Press, 2016.

Gerlach, Philipp. "The Games Economists Play: Why Economics Students Behave More Selfishly Than Other Students." *PLoS ONE* 12, no. 9 (2017). https://doi.org /10.1371/journal.pone.0183814.

Ghilarducci, Teresa. *When I'm Sixty-Four: The Plot against Pensions and the Plan to Save Them.* Princeton, NJ: Princeton University Press, 2008.

Gitleman, Lisa. *Paper Knowledge: Toward a Media History of Documents.* Durham, NC: Duke University Press, 2014.

Goldrick-Rab, Sara. *Paying the Price: College Costs, Financial Aid, and the Betrayal of the American Dream.* Chicago: University of Chicago Press, 2016.

Gordon, Linda. *Pitied but Not Entitled: Single Mothers and the History of Welfare.* New York: Free Press, 1994.

Graeber, David. *Debt: The First 5000 Years.* New York: Melville House, 2011.

Great Speculations. "A Look at the Loan Portfolios of the Largest U.S. Banks." *Forbes,* June 24, 2014. https://www.forbes.com/sites/greatspeculations/2014/06/24/a -look-at-the-loan-portfolios-of-the-largest-u-s-banks/#109371d5c397.

Guyer, Jane I. *Marginal Gains: Monetary Transactions in Atlantic Africa.* Chicago: University of Chicago Press, 2004.

Hamilton, Laura. *Parenting to a Degree: How Family Matters for College Women's Success.* Chicago: University of Chicago Press, 2016.

Heiman, Rachel. *Driving after Class: Anxious Times in an American Suburb.* Berkeley: University of California Press, 2015.

Hill, Susan T. "The Traditionally Black Institutions of Higher Education 1860 to 1982." National Center for Education Statistics, September 26, 1985. https://nces.ed.gov /pubsearch/pubsinfo.asp?pubid=84308.

Hiltonsmith, Robert. "At What Cost? How Student Debt Reduces Lifetime Wealth." Demos, August 2013. http://www.demos.org/sites/default/files/imce/AtWhat CostFinal.pdf.

Holmes, Douglas R. *Economy of Words: Communicative Imperatives in Central Banks.* Chicago: University of Chicago Press, 2013.

Hoschschild, Jennifer. *Facing Up to the American Dream, Race, Class, and the Soul of the Nation.* Princeton, NJ: Princeton University Press, 1995.

Huelsman, Mark. "The Debt Divide: The Racial and Class Bias Behind the 'New Normal' of Student Borrowing." Demos, May 19, 2015. http://www.demos.org/publication /debt-divide-racial-and-class-bias-behind-new-normal-student-borrowing.

Hull, Matthew S. *Government of Paper: The Materiality of Bureaucracy in Urban Pakistan.* Berkeley: University of California Press, 2012.

Hyman, Louis. *Temp: How American Work, American Business, and the American Dream Became Temporary.* New York: Viking, 2018.

———. *Debtor Nation: The History of America in Red Ink.* Princeton, NJ: Princeton University Press, 2012.

Jackson, Kenneth T. *Crabgrass Frontier: The Suburbanization of the United States*. New York: Oxford University Press, 1987.

Jacob, Brian A. "What We Know about Career and Technical Education in High School." Brookings, October 5, 2017. https://www.brookings.edu/research/what -we-know-about-career-and-technical-education-in-high-school/.

Johnson, Lyndon. "Remarks on Signing the Higher Education Act of 1965: Common Experience 2008–2009: Texas State University." November 8, 1965. http://www .txstate.edu/commonexperience/pastsitearchives/2008–2009/lbjresources /higheredact.html.

Johnson, Matthew, Julie Bruch, and Brian Gill. "Changes in Financial Aid and Student Enrollment at Historically Black Colleges and Universities after the Tightening of PLUS Credit Standards." US Department of Education, Institute of Education Sciences, April 2015.

Johnstone, D. Bruce, and Pamela N. Marcucci. *Financing Education Worldwide*. Baltimore: Johns Hopkins University Press, 2010.

"J. P. Morgan, Wells Fargo and Citi Report First-Quarter Earnings." *Wall Street Journal*, April 13, 2017. https://www.wsj.com/livecoverage/jpmorgan-wells-fargo -and-citi-report-first-quarter-earnings.

Kafka, Ben. *The Demon of Writing: Powers and Failures of Paperwork*. New York: Zone Books, 2012.

Kantrowitz, Mark, and David Levy. *Filing the FAFSA: The Edvisors Guide to Completing the Free Application for Federal Student Aid*. Las Vegas: Edvisors Network, Inc., 2013.

Keynes, John Maynard. "The Problem of Unemployment II." *Listener* (January 14, 1931): 46–47. http://www.hetwebsite.net/het/texts/keynes/keynes1931saving spending.htm.

Kirk, Chris Michael, Rhonda K. Lewis-Moss, Corinne Nilsen, and Deltha Q. Colvin. "The Role of Parent Expectations on Adolescent Educational Aspirations." *Educational Studies* 37, no. 1 (February 1, 2011): 89–99. https://doi.org/10.1080 /03055691003728965.

Knight, Will. "Is Technology About to Decimate White-Collar Work?" *MIT Technology Review*, November 6, 2017. https://www.technologyreview.com/s/609337/is -technology-about-to-decimate-white-collar-work/.

Kochhar, Rakesh, and Richard Fry. "Wealth Inequality Has Widened along Racial, Ethnic Lines since End of Great Recession." Pew Research Center. *Fact Tank—Our Lives in Numbers* (blog), December 12, 2014. http://www.pewresearch.org/fact -tank/2014/12/12/racial-wealth-gaps-great-recession/.

Lacy, Karyn. *Blue-Chip Black: Race, Class, and Status in the New Black Middle Class*. Berkeley: University of California Press, 2007.

Lakoff, Andrew. *Unprepared: Global Health in a Time of Emergency*. Berkeley: University of California Press, 2017.

Lamont, Michèle. *Money, Morals, and Manners: The Culture of the French and the American Upper-Middle Class*. Chicago: University of Chicago Press, 1994.

———. *The Dignity of Working Men: Morality and the Boundaries of Race, Class, and Immigration*. Cambridge, MA: Harvard University Press, 2002.

Lamont, Michèle, and Ann Swidler. "Methodological Pluralism and the Possibilities and Limits of Interviewing." *Qualitative Sociology* 37, no. 2 (June 1, 2014): 153–71. https://doi.org/10.1007/s11133-014-9274-z.

Landry, Bart. *The New Black Middle Class*. Berkeley: University of California Press, 1987.

Landry, Bart, and Kris Marsh. "The Evolution of the New Black Middle Class." *Annual Review of Sociology* 37, no. 1 (2011): 373–94. https://doi.org/10.1146/annurev-soc-081309-150047.

Lareau, Annette. *Unequal Childhoods: Class, Race, and Family Life*. Berkeley: University of California Press, 2003.

Lawrence, Mishel, Elise Gould, and Josh Bivens. "Wage Stagnation in Nine Charts." January 6, 2015. http://www.epi.org/publication/charting-wage-stagnation/.

Lee, Elizabeth. *Class and Campus Life: Managing and Experiencing Inequality at an Elite College*. Ithaca, NY: Cornell University Press, 2016.

Leins, Stefan. *Stories of Capitalism: Inside the Role of Financial Analysts*. First edition. Chicago: University of Chicago Press, 2018.

Lewis, Jamie M., and Rose M. Kreider. "Remarriage in the United States." US Census Bureau, March 2015. https://www.census.gov/content/dam/Census/library/publications/2015/acs/acs-30.pdf.

Liebenthal, Ryann. "The Incredible, Rage-Inducing Inside Story of America's Student Debt Machine." *Mother Jones*, September/October 2018.

Long, Heather. "School Lunch Shaming: Inside America's Hidden Debt Crisis." *CNN Money*, May 10, 2017. http://money.cnn.com/2017/05/09/news/economy/school-lunch-shaming-debt-crisis/.

Loss, Christopher P. *Between Citizens and the State: The Politics of American Higher Education in the 20th Century*. Princeton, NJ: Princeton University Press, 2011. https://www.amazon.com/Between-Citizens-State-Education-Twentieth-Century/dp/0691148279.

Lusardi, Annamaria, and Olivia S. Mitchell. "The Economic Importance of Financial Literacy: Theory and Evidence." Working Paper. National Bureau of Economic Research, April 2013. https://doi.org/10.3386/w18952.

Lusardi, Annamaria, Olivia S. Mitchell, and Vilsa Curto. "Financial Literacy among the Young." *Journal of Consumer Affairs* 44, no. 2 (June 1, 2010): 358–80. https://doi.org/10.1111/j.1745-6606.2010.01173.x.

Ma, Jennifer, and Sandy Baum. "Trends in Tuition and Fees, Enrollment, and State Appropriations for Higher Education by State." College Board Advocacy & Policy Center Analysis Brief. Trends in Higher Education Series. College Board, July 2012. https://trends.collegeboard.org/sites/default/files/analysis-brief-trends-by -state-july-2012.pdf.

Ma, Jennifer, Matea Pender, and Meredith Welch. "Education Pays 2016: The Benefits of Higher Education for Individuals and Society." Trends in Higher Education Series. College Board, 2016. https://eric.ed.gov/?id=ED572548.

Malinowski, Bronislaw. *Argonauts of the Western Pacific.* New York: George Routledge & Sons, 1932. http://archive.org/details/argonautsoftheweo32976mbp.

Marcus, Jon. "How Australia Gets Student Loans Right." *Atlantic,* March 16, 2016. https://www.theatlantic.com/education/archive/2016/03/australia-college -payment-model-exposes-shortcomings-of-new-american-version/473919/.

———. "Why It's Almost Impossible to Default on Student Debt in Australia." *Atlantic,* March 16, 2016. https://www.theatlantic.com/education/archive/2016/03 /australia-college-payment-model-exposes-shortcomings-of-new-american -version/473919/.

Margo, Robert A. *Race and Schooling in the South, 1880–1950: An Economic History.* Chicago: University of Chicago Press, 1990.

Marwell, Gerald, and Ruth E. Ames. "Economists Free Ride, Does Anyone Else? Experiments on the Provision of Public Goods, IV." *Journal of Public Economics* (1981): 295–310.

Mauss, Marcel. *The Gift: The Form and Reason for Exchange in Archaic Societies.* New York: W. W. Norton, 2000.

McCloskey, Deirdre N. *The Rhetoric of Economics.* Madison: University of Wisconsin Press, 1998.

Mettler, Suzanne. *Degrees of Inequality: How the Politics of Higher Education Sabotaged the American Dream.* New York: Basic Books, 2014.

———. *The Submerged State: How Invisible Government Policies Undermine American Democracy.* Chicago: University of Chicago Press, 2011.

Mills, C. Wright. *White Collar: The American Middle Classes.* Fiftieth anniversary edition. New York: Oxford University Press, 2002.

Mintz, Steven, and Susan Kellogg. *Domestic Revolutions: A Social History of American Family Life.* New York: Free Press, 1988.

Mistry, Rashmita S., Elizabeth S. White, Aprile D. Benner, and Virginia W. Huynh. "A Longitudinal Study of the Simultaneous Influence of Mothers' and Teachers' Educational Expectations on Low-Income Youth's Academic Achievement." *Journal of Youth and Adolescence* 38, no. 6 (July 1, 2009): 826–38. https://doi.org/10 .1007/s10964-008-9300-0.

Mitchell, Michael, Michael Leachman, and Kathleen Masterson. "A Lost Decade in Higher Education Funding." Center on Budget and Policy Priorities, August 23, 2017. https://www.cbpp.org/research/state-budget-and-tax/a-lost-decade-in-higher-education-funding.

Monkovic, Toni. "Why Australian College Graduates Feel Sorry for Their American Counterparts." *New York Times*, May 29, 2018, sec. Upshot. https://www.nytimes.com/2018/05/11/upshot/australia-college-graduates-student-debt-america.html.

Morduch, Jonathan, and Rachel Schneider. *The Financial Diaries: How American Families Cope in a World of Uncertainty*. Princeton, NJ: Princeton University Press, 2017.

Morgan, Julie, and Marshall Steinbaum. "The Student Debt Crisis, Labor Market Credentialization, and Racial Inequality: How the Current Student Debt Debate Gets the Economics Wrong." Roosevelt Institute, 2018. http://rooseveltinstitute.org/student-debt-crisis-labor-market-credentialization-racial-inequality/.

Mortenson, Thomas G. "State Funding: A Race to the Bottom." *American Council on Education*, 2012. https://www.acenet.edu/the-presidency/columns-and-features/Pages/state-funding-a-race-to-the-bottom.aspx.

Moynihan, Daniel P. "The Negro Family: The Case for National Action." US Department of Labor, March 1965. https://web.stanford.edu/~mrosenfe/Moynihan's%20The%20Negro%20Family.pdf.

Munnell, Alicia H., Anthony Webb, and Francesca N. Golub-Sass. "Is There Really a Retirement Savings Crisis? An NRRI Analysis." Center for Retirement Research at Boston College, August 2007. http://crr.bc.edu/briefs/is-there-really-a-retirement-savings-crisis-an-nrri-analysis/.

Murty, Komandur, and Julian Roebuck. *Historically Black Colleges and Universities: Their Place in American Higher Education*. Westport, CT: Praeger, 1993.

National Center for Education Statistics. "Fast Facts: Back to School Statistics." Accessed June 12, 2018. https://nces.ed.gov/fastfacts/display.asp?id=372.

"National Education Longitudinal Study of 1988 (NELS:88)—Overview." Accessed June 13, 2018. https://nces.ed.gov/surveys/nels88/.

Nelson, Margaret K. *Parenting Out of Control: Anxious Parents in Uncertain Times*. New York: NYU Press, 2012.

Newman, Katherine S. *The Accordion Family: Boomerang Kids, Anxious Parents, and the Private Toll of Global Competition*. Boston: Beacon Press, 2013.

———. *Falling from Grace: Downward Mobility in the Age of Affluence*. First edition. Berkeley: University of California Press, 1999.

Nocera, Joe. *A Piece of the Action: How the Middle Class Joined the Money Class*. Simon & Schuster, 2013.

Ochs, Elinor. *Fast-Forward Family: Home, Work, and Relationships in Middle-Class America*. Berkeley: University of California Press, 2013.

Olen, Helaine. *Pound Foolish: Exposing the Dark Side of the Personal Finance Industry*. New York: Penguin Books, 2013.

Ortner, Sherry B. *New Jersey Dreaming: Capital, Culture, and the Class of '58*. Durham, NC: Duke University Press Books, 2005.

Paine, James. "5 White Collar Jobs That AI Will Soon Take Away." *Inc.*, July 17, 2017. https://www.inc.com/james-paine/5-white-collar-jobs-that-ai-will-soon-take -away.html.

Palm, Michael. *Technologies of Consumer Labor: A History of Self-Service*. New York: Routledge, 2017.

Patten, Eileen. "Racial, Gender Wage Gaps Persist in U.S. Despite Some Progress." Pew Research Center. *Fact Tank—Our Lives in Numbers* (blog), July 1, 2016. http:// www.pewresearch.org/fact-tank/2016/07/01/racial-gender-wage-gaps-persist-in -u-s-despite-some-progress/.

Pattillo, Mary. 2008. *Black on the Block: The Politics of Race and Class in the City*. Chicago: University of Chicago Press, 2008.

———. *Black Picket Fences: Privilege and Peril among the Black Middle Class*. Chicago: University of Chicago Press, 2000.

Penn Graduate School of Education, Institute for Research on Higher Education. "College Affordability Diagnosis." Accessed March 12, 2018. https://irhe.gse.upenn .edu/affordability-diagnosis.

Perin, Constance. *Everything in Its Place: Social Order and Land Use in America*. Princeton, NJ: Princeton University Press, 1977.

Pew Research Center. "The Rising Cost of Not Going to College." Pew Research Center, February 11, 2014.

Phillips, Matt. "College in Sweden Is Free but Students Still Have a Ton of Debt. How Can That Be?" Quartz. *Debt* (blog), May 31, 2013. https://qz.com/85017/college -in-sweden-is-free-but-students-still-have-a-ton-of-debt-how-can-that-be/.

Poovey, Mary. *Genres of the Credit Economy: Mediating Value in Eighteenth- and Nineteenth-Century Britain*. Chicago: University of Chicago Press, 2008.

———. *A History of the Modern Fact: Problems of Knowledge in the Sciences of Wealth and Society*. Chicago: University of Chicago Press, 1998.

Porter Katherine, ed. *Broke: How Debt Bankrupts the Middle Class*. Stanford, CA: Stanford University Press, 2012.

Pugh, Allison. *Longing and Belonging: Parents, Children, and Consumer Culture*. Berkeley: University of California Press, 2009.

———. *The Tumbleweed Society: Working and Caring in an Age of Insecurity*. New York: Oxford University Press, 2015.

Quart, Alissa. *Squeezed: Why Our Families Can't Afford America*. New York: Ecco, 2018.

Rapacon, Stacy. "Best Jobs That Don't Require a College Degree." *Kiplinger*, June 27, 2017. http://www.kiplinger.com/slideshow/business/T012-S001-best-jobs-without-a-college-degree-2017/index.html.

Reeves, Richard V. *Dream Hoarders: How the American Upper Middle Class Is Leaving Everyone Else in the Dust, Why That Is a Problem, and What to Do about It.* Washington, DC: Brookings Institution Press, 2017.

Regeringskansliet. "Financial Aid for Studies." April 22, 2015. https://www.government.se/government-policy/education-and-research/the-swedish-financial-aid-system-for-studies/.

Reynolds, Megan. "Nostalgia Fact-Check: How Does Felicity Hold Up?" *Vulture*, November 10, 2011. http://www.vulture.com/2011/11/nostalgia-fact-check-how-does-felicity-hold-up.html.

Roberts, Elizabeth F. S. "Assisted Existence: An Ethnography of Being in Ecuador." *Journal of the Royal Anthropological Institute* 19, no. 3 (2013): 562–80. https://doi.org/10.1111/1467-9655.12050.

Rodrigue, Edward, and Richard V. Reeves. "Five Bleak Facts on Black Opportunity." Brookings. *Social Mobility Memos* (blog), January 15, 2015. https://www.brookings.edu/blog/social-mobility-memos/2015/01/15/five-bleak-facts-on-black-opportunity/.

Roth, Michael S. "John Dewey's Vision of Learning as Freedom." *New York Times*, September 5, 2012, sec. Opinion. https://www.nytimes.com/2012/09/06/opinion/john-deweys-vision-of-learning-as-freedom.html.

Ryan, Mary P. *Cradle of the Middle Class: The Family in Oneida County, New York, 1790–1865.* Cambridge: Cambridge University Press, 1983.

Sallie Mae Bank. "How America Pays for College 2016: Sallie Mae's National Study of College Students and Parents." http://news.salliemae.com/files/doc_library/file/HowAmericaPaysforCollege2016FNL.pdf.

Sansing, David G. *Making Haste Slowly: The Troubled History of Higher Education in Mississippi.* Jackson: University Press of Mississippi, 1990.

Saunders, Katherine M., Krystal L. Williams, and Cheryl L. Smith. "Fewer Resources, More Debt: Loan Debt Burdens Students at Historically Black Colleges and Universities." UNCF Frederick D. Patterson Research Institute, 2016. http://images.uncf.org/production/reports/FINAL_HBCU_Loan_Debt_Burden_Report.pdf.

Schmitt, John, and Heather Boushey. "The College Conundrum: Why the Benefits of a College Education May Not Be So Clear, Especially to Men." Center for American Progress, December 2010.

Schor, Elana. "Senate Kills Rule Limiting Drug Testing for Unemployment Benefits." *Politico*, March 14, 2017. http://www.politico.com/story/2017/03/drug-testing-unemployment-senate-236049.

Schüll, Natasha. *Addiction by Design: Machine Gambling in Las Vegas.* Princeton, NJ: Princeton University Press, 2012.

Scott, James C. *Seeing Like a State: How Certain Schemes to Improve the Human Condition Have Failed.* New Haven, CT: Yale University Press, 1998.

Servon, Lisa. *The Unbanking of America: How the New Middle Class Survives.* New York: Mariner Books, 2017.

Shapiro, Thomas M., and Melvin L. Oliver. *Black Wealth/White Wealth: A New Perspective on Racial Inequality.* New York: Routledge, 1995.

Sherman, Rachel. *Uneasy Street: The Anxieties of Affluence.* Princeton, NJ: Princeton University Press, 2017.

Siegel, Bettina Elias. "Shaming Children So Parents Will Pay the School Lunch Bill." *New York Times,* April 30, 2017. https://www.nytimes.com/2017/04/30/well/family/lunch-shaming-children-parents-school-bills.html.

Skocpol, Theda. *The Missing Middle: Working Families and the Future of American Social Policy.* New York: W. W. Norton, 2000.

———. *Protecting Soldiers and Mothers: The Political Origins of Social Policy in the United States.* Cambridge, MA: Harvard University Press, 1992.

Stack, Carol B. *All Our Kin: Strategies for Survival in a Black Community.* New York: Basic Books, 1983.

Stevens, Mitchell. *Creating a Class: College Admissions and the Education of Elites.* Cambridge, MA: Harvard University Press, 2009.

Stivers, Abby, and Elizabeth Popp Berman. "Student Loans as a Pressure on U.S. Higher Education." Special issue: "The University under Pressure," *Research in the Sociology of Organizations* 46 (2016): 129–60. https://doi.org/10.1108/S0733-558X20160000046005.

Sullivan, Teresa A., Elizabeth Warren, and Jay Lawrence Westbrook. *The Fragile Middle Class: Americans in Debt.* New Haven, CT: Yale University Press, 2000.

Taylor, Joanna, and Tatjana Meschede. "Inherited Prospects: The Importance of Financial Transfers for White and Black College-Educated Households' Wealth Trajectories." *American Journal of Economics and Sociology* 77, no. 3–4 (2018): 1049–76. https://doi.org/10.1111/ajes.12227.

Thaler, Richard H., and Cass R. Sunstein. *Nudge: Improving Decisions about Health, Wealth, and Happiness.* New Haven, CT: Yale University Press, 2008.

United Negro College Fund. "The Parent PLUS Loan Crisis: An Urgent Crisis Facing Students at the Nation's HBCUs." 2014. http://www.uncf.org/sites/advocacy/SpecialInitiatives/ParentsPlus/MediaDocuments/UNCF-Report-THE-PARENT-PLUS-LOAN-CRISIS-3.25.14.pdf.

Urban Institute. "Nine Charts about Wealth Inequality in America (Updated)." February 2015. http://urbn.is/wealthcharts.

US Bureau of Economic Analysis. "Personal Saving Rate." FRED, Federal Reserve Bank of St. Louis. Accessed March 12, 2018. https://fred.stlouisfed.org/series/PSAVERT.

US Census Bureau. "Income in the Past 12 Months." 2005–2015 American Community Survey 1-Year Estimates. Accessed May 29, 2017. https://factfinder.census.gov/faces/tableservices/jsf/pages/productview.xhtml?pid=ACS_15_1YR_S1901&prodType=table.

———. "Median Household Income in the Past 12 Months (in 2015 Inflation-Adjusted Dollars)." 2015 American Community Survey 1-Year Supplemental Estimates with a Population Threshold of 20,000 or More. Accessed May 29, 2017. https://factfinder.census.gov/faces/tableservices/jsf/pages/productview.xhtml?pid=ACS_15_SPL_K201902&prodType=table.

———. "QuickFacts: Coahoma County, Mississippi." Accessed July 9, 2018. https://www.census.gov/quickfacts/fact/table/coahomacountymississippi/RHI725217.

US Department of Education. "Education Department Announces Changes to FAFSA Form to More Accurately and Fairly Assess Students' Need for Aid." April 29, 2013. https://www.ed.gov/news/press-releases/education-department-announces-changes-fafsa-form-more-accurately-and-fairly.

———. "The EFC Formula, 2017–2018." Federal Student Aid. Accessed July 8, 2018. https://studentaid.ed.gov/sa/sites/default/files/2017–18-efc-formula.pdf.

———. "Federal Student Loan Portfolio." Federal Student Aid. Accessed July 5, 2018. https://studentaid.ed.gov/about/data-center/student/portfolio.

———. "The U.S. Department of Education Strengthens Federal Direct PLUS Loan Program." August 7, 2014. https://www.ed.gov/news/press-releases/us-department-education-strengthens-federal-direct-plus-loan-program.

US Department of Education, National Center for Education Statistics. "Integrated Postsecondary Education Data System (IPEDS), 'Fall Enrollment' and 'Institutional Characteristics' Surveys." August 2001. https://nces.ed.gov/programs/digest/d01/dt317.asp.

US Department of Housing and Urban Development. "Risk or Race: An Assessment of Subprime Lending Patterns in Nine Metropolitan Areas." August 2009.

US Government Accountability Office. "Higher Education: Small Percentage of Families Save in 529 Plans." December 2012. https://www.gao.gov/assets/660/650759.pdf.

US Inflation Calculator. "Inflation Calculator." Accessed May 15, 2017. http://www.usinflationcalculator.com/.

US Selective Service System. "Official Legislation by States, Territories, and the District of Columbia." Accessed July 6, 2018. https://www.sss.gov/Registration/State-Commonwealth-Legislation/Other-Legislations.

Usher, Alex. "Global Debt Patterns: An International Comparison of Student Loan Burdens and Repayment Conditions." Educational Policy Institute, September 2005. http://educationalpolicy.org/pdf/global_debt_patterns.pdf.

Vaisey, Stephen. "What People Want: Rethinking Poverty, Culture, and Educational Attainment." *Annals of the American Academy of Political and Social Science* 629, no. 1 (May 1, 2010): 75–101. https://doi.org/10.1177/0002716209357146.

Veblen, Thorstein. *The Theory of the Leisure Class*, edited by Martha Banta. Reissue edition. Oxford: Oxford University Press, 2009.

Venkatesh, Sudhir. *Off the Books: The Underground Economy of the Urban Poor*. Cambridge, MA: Harvard University Press, 2009.

Wang, Long, Deepak Malhotra, and J. Keith Murnighan. "Economics Education and Greed." *Academy of Management Learning & Education* 10, no. 4 (2011): 643–60.

Wang, Marian, Becky Supiano, and Andrea Fuller. "The Parent Loan Trap." *Chronicle of Higher Education*, October 4, 2012. https://www.chronicle.com/article/The-Parent-Loan-Trap/134844/.

Weisman, Jonathan. "Obama Relents on Proposal to End '529' College Savings Plans." *New York Times*, January 27, 2015, sec. Politics. https://www.nytimes.com/2015/01/28/us/politics/obama-will-drop-proposal-to-end-529-college-savings-plans.html.

Wexler, Ellen. "Student Loans Lessons from Abroad." Inside Higher Ed (website), June 14, 2016. https://www.insidehighered.com/news/2016/06/14/what-other-countries-can-teach-us-about-student-loans.

White, Deborah Gray. *Too Heavy a Load: Black Women in Defense of Themselves, 1894–1994*. New York: W. W. Norton, 1999.

White, Marceline, and Renee Brown. "Making the Grade? An Analysis of For-Profit and Career Schools in Maryland." Maryland Consumer Rights Division, n.d. http://www.marylandconsumers.org/penn_station/folders/about/test_2/For-Profit_School_Report_-_for_website.pdf.

Whyte, William H. *The Organization Man*. Garden City, NY: Doubleday, 1956.

Wightman, Patrick, Megan Patrick, Robert Schoeni, and John Schulenberg. "Historical Trends in Parental Financial Support of Young Adults." *Population Studies Center*, Report 13–801 (September 2013): 35.

Wilkerson, Isabel. *The Warmth of Other Suns: The Epic Story of America's Great Migration*. New York: Vintage, 2011.

Wilkinson, Rupert. *Aiding Students, Buying Students: Financial Aid in America*. Nashville, TN: Vanderbilt University Press, 2005.

Yanagisako, Sylvia. *Producing Culture and Capital: Family Firms in Italy*. Princeton, NJ: Princeton University Press, 2002.

Zaloom, Caitlin. "How to Read the Future: The Yield Curve, Affect, and Financial Prediction." *Public Culture* 21, no. 2 (May 1, 2009): 245–68. https://doi.org/10.1215/08992363-2008-028.

———. *Out of the Pits: Traders and Technology from Chicago to London*. Chicago: University of Chicago Press, 2006.

———. "A Right to the Future: Student Debt and the Politics of Crisis." *Cultural Anthropology* 33, no. 4 (2018): 558–69. https://doi.org/10.14506/ca33.4.05.

————. "What Does 'Middle Class' Really Mean?" *Atlantic*, November 4, 2018. https://www.theatlantic.com/ideas/archive/2018/11/what-does-middle-class-really-mean/574534/.

Zelizer, Viviana A. *Pricing the Priceless Child: The Changing Social Value of Children.* Princeton, NJ: Princeton University Press, 1994.

# Index

**. . .**

Page numbers followed by *f* indicate a figure.

United Negro College Fund, 127, 150, 152

upward mobility, 122–27, 132–45; African American activism for, 135–37; African American reality in, 137–45, 231n33; case studies of, 141–45, 148–50, 154–55; cultivation of children's potential in, 173–80; debt as mechanism of, 171–72; historically black colleges and universities and, 123–27; as moral imperative, 123–24, 132–37, 229n16, 231n31; overall declines in, 139–40

Vaisey, Stephen, 44
Veblen, Thorstein, 65
Venkatesh, Sudhir, 57

Veterans Administration, 138
vocational training, 167–69

Warren, Elizabeth, 83
welfare, 55–56, 220–21nn26–27
Westbrook, Jay, 83
White, Deborah Gray, 135
*White Collar: The American Middle Classes* (Mills), 10
Whyte, William H., 10, 215nn4–5
Wilberforce University, 125
Wilkinson, Rupert, 226n7
women's suffrage movement, 135–36

Yanagisako, Sylvia, 217–18n19

Zelizer, Viviana, 25